KORE
YAMAZAKI

FRAU
FAUST

3

STORY

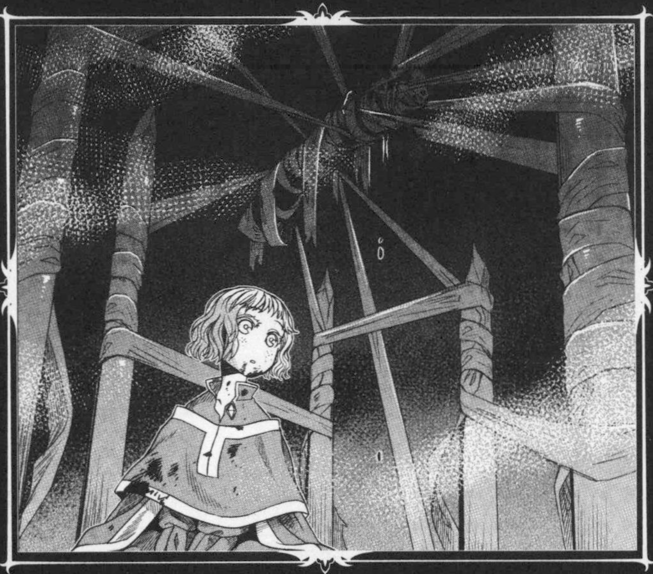

This is the story of a reunion a hundred years in the making…

Johanna Faust is on a journey to find the body of the demon Mephistopheles, whose scattered parts have been sealed away in several locations. With the help of a curious boy named Marion, she retrieved Mephisto's right arm. Following the ordeal, she traveled to a safehouse run by her homunculus daughter, Nico, in order to heal. While there, however, she was attacked by Lorenzo, an inquisitor who seeks to prevent her from summoning her demon. The stress and fatigue of the ensuing battle caused Johanna to pass out.

The curse of immortality placed upon her healed her wounds, but Johanna's body became smaller as a result. She left Marion with Nico and headed to a new town harboring another of Mephisto's lost parts. Meanwhile, Lorenzo and his partner Vito visited the same town to claim and transport the limb. Noticing their presence in the town, Johanna confirmed that the town's church contains Mephisto's right leg. Later, Marion and Nico followed Johanna into the town. They were soon attacked, as was Vito, while snooping around in the church. In order to save their companions, Johanna and Lorenzo must temporarily help each other. Deep in the church is a girl named Lea who ought to be dead, but a diet of Mephisto's blood has transformed her into something else…

CHARACTERS

Johanna Faust

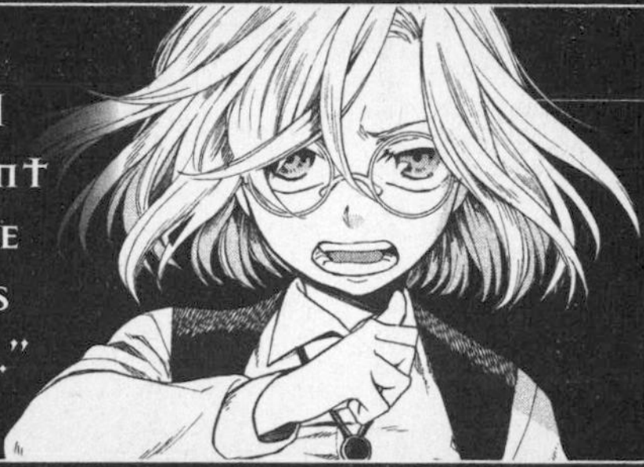

"Until I die, I want you to be my arms and legs."

Dr. Faust, who supposedly died a century ago. She travels seeking the scattered parts of her demon, Mephistopheles, so that she may make him whole again. She is under a curse of immortality that shrinks her body each time she suffers an injury.

Mephistopheles

A legendary demon. He was quartered for the crime of providing immortality to the dead without good reason. His head, left arm, and right leg are still missing.

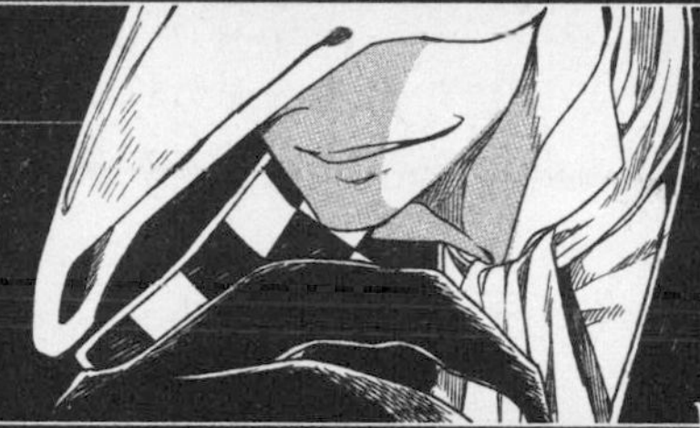

"Do. Not. Touch. This one... belongs to me."

Nico Bernstein

Johanna's daughter. Or rather, Johanna's creation—a homunculus.

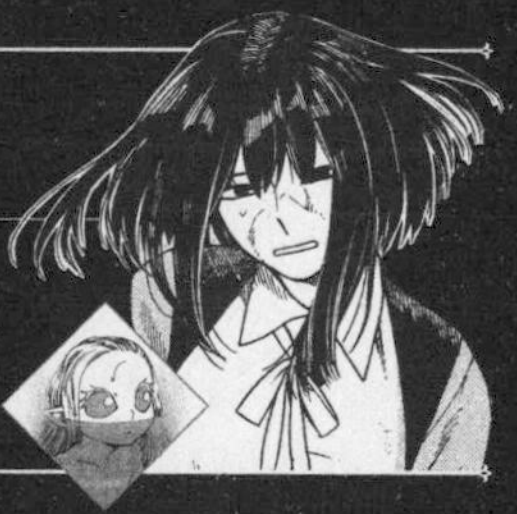

Marion

A pure-hearted, kind, and curious youth. His thirst for knowledge drives him to accompany Faust on her journey.

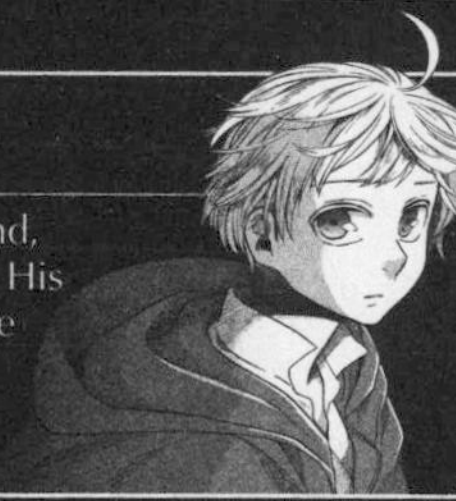

The Church

Vito

Lorenzo's partner. Undertaking his own research into Mephistopheles.

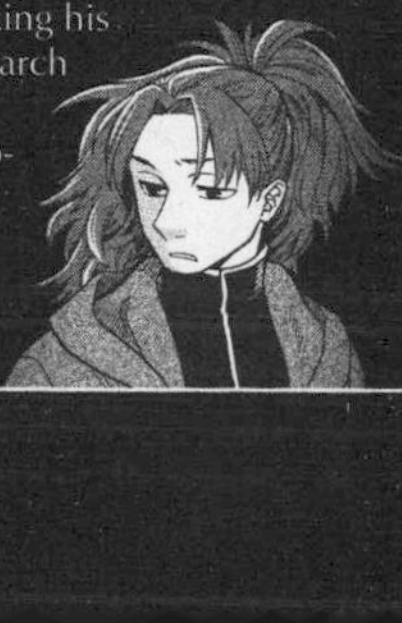

Lorenzo

An inquisitor pursuing Johanna to prevent her from reviving her demon.

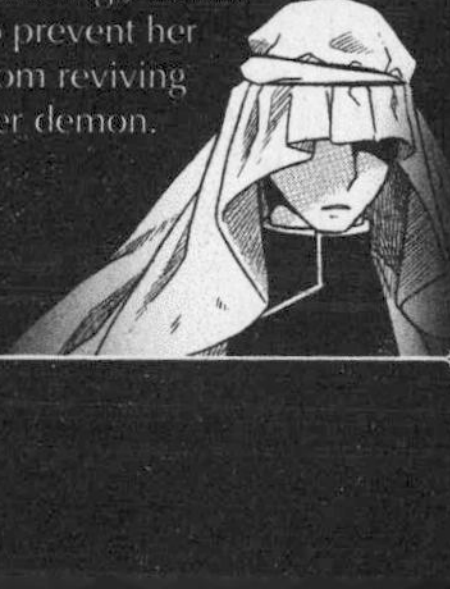

Wagner

A demonologist assisting Johanna. Great-grandson of the man who created Nico.

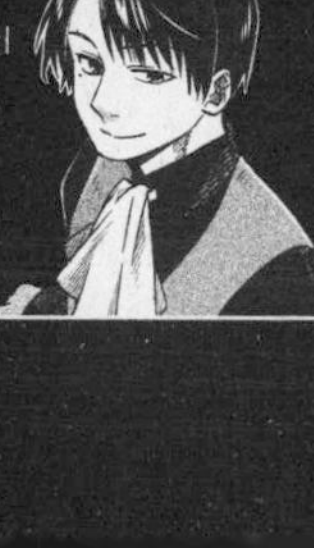

contents

FRAU FAUST

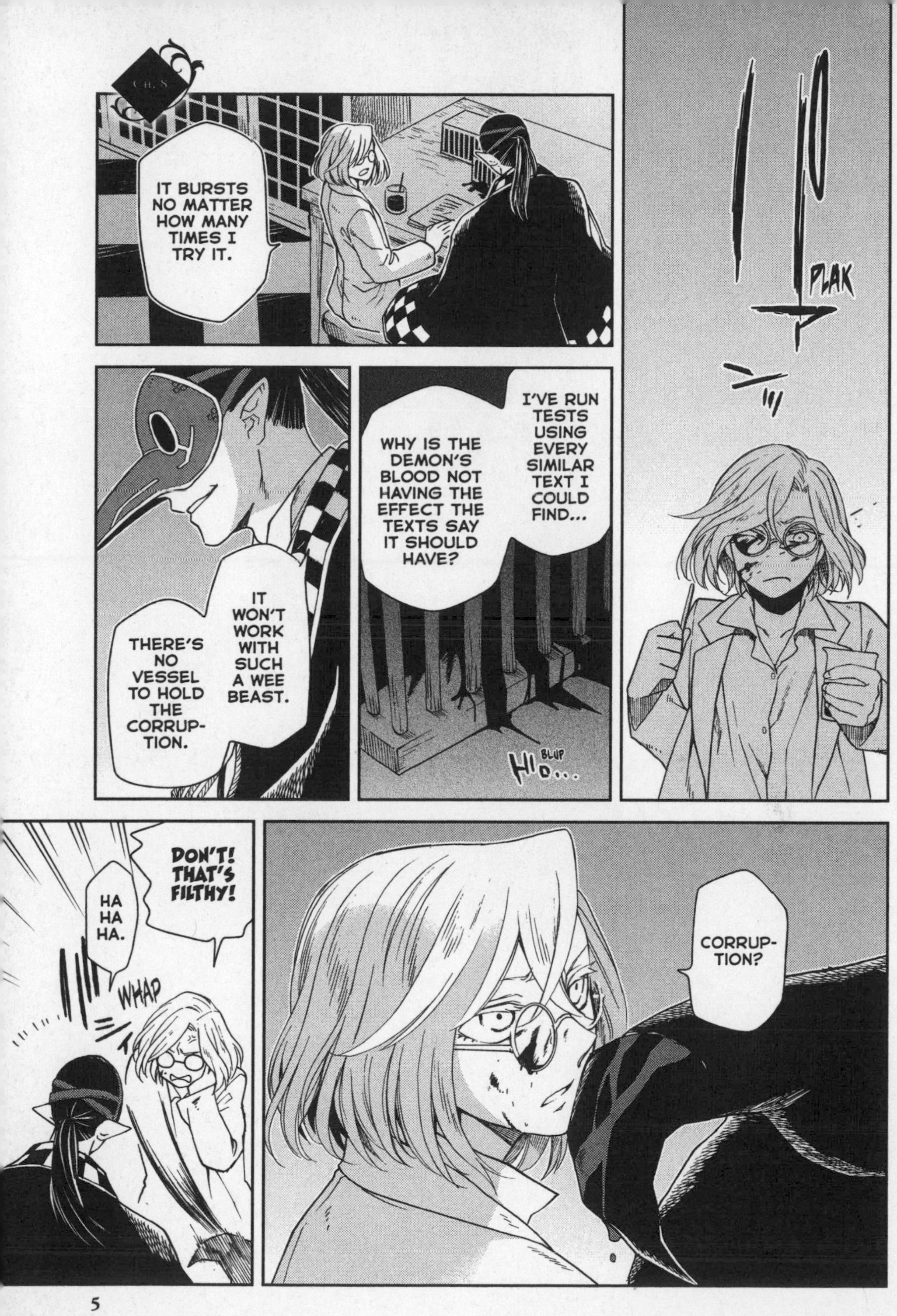
PLAK
IT BURSTS NO MATTER HOW MANY TIMES I TRY IT.
I'VE RUN TESTS USING EVERY SIMILAR TEXT I COULD FIND...
WHY IS THE DEMON'S BLOOD NOT HAVING THE EFFECT THE TEXTS SAY IT SHOULD HAVE?
BLUP
IT WON'T WORK WITH SUCH A WEE BEAST.
THERE'S NO VESSEL TO HOLD THE CORRUPTION.
CORRUPTION?
DON'T! THAT'S FILTHY!
HA HA HA.
WHAP

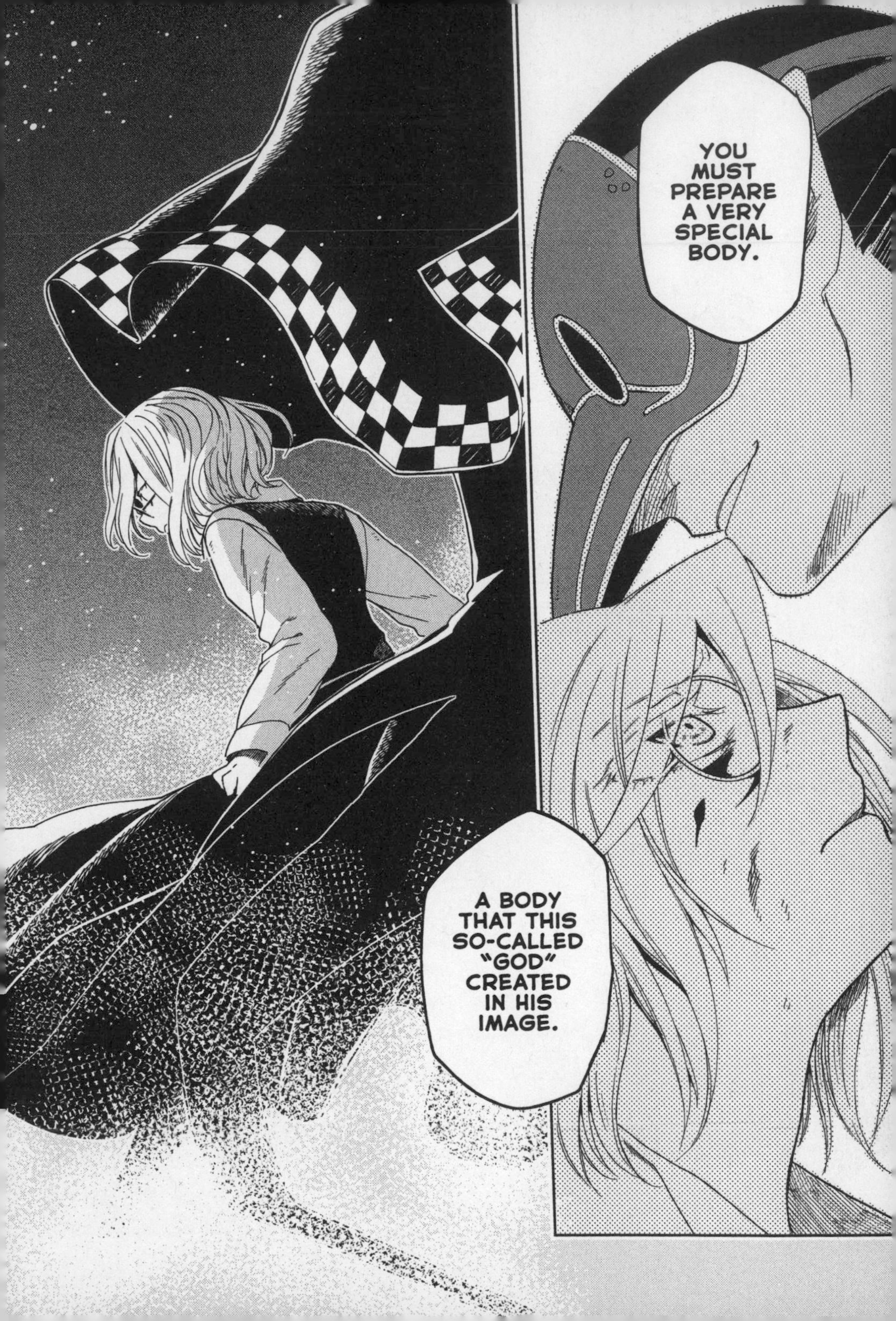
YOU MUST PREPARE A VERY SPECIAL BODY.
A BODY THAT THIS SO-CALLED "GOD" CREATED IN HIS IMAGE.

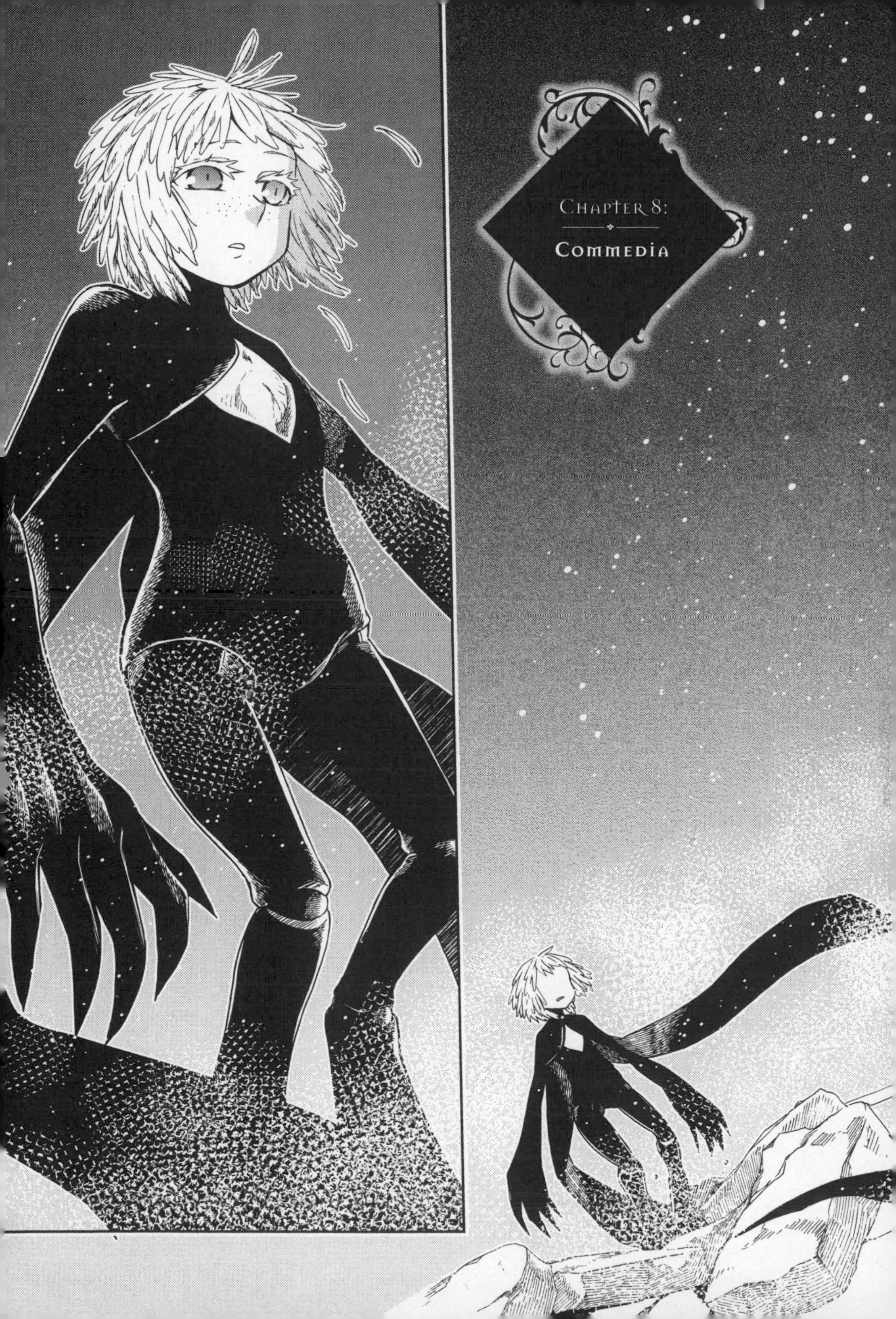
Chapter 8:
Commedia

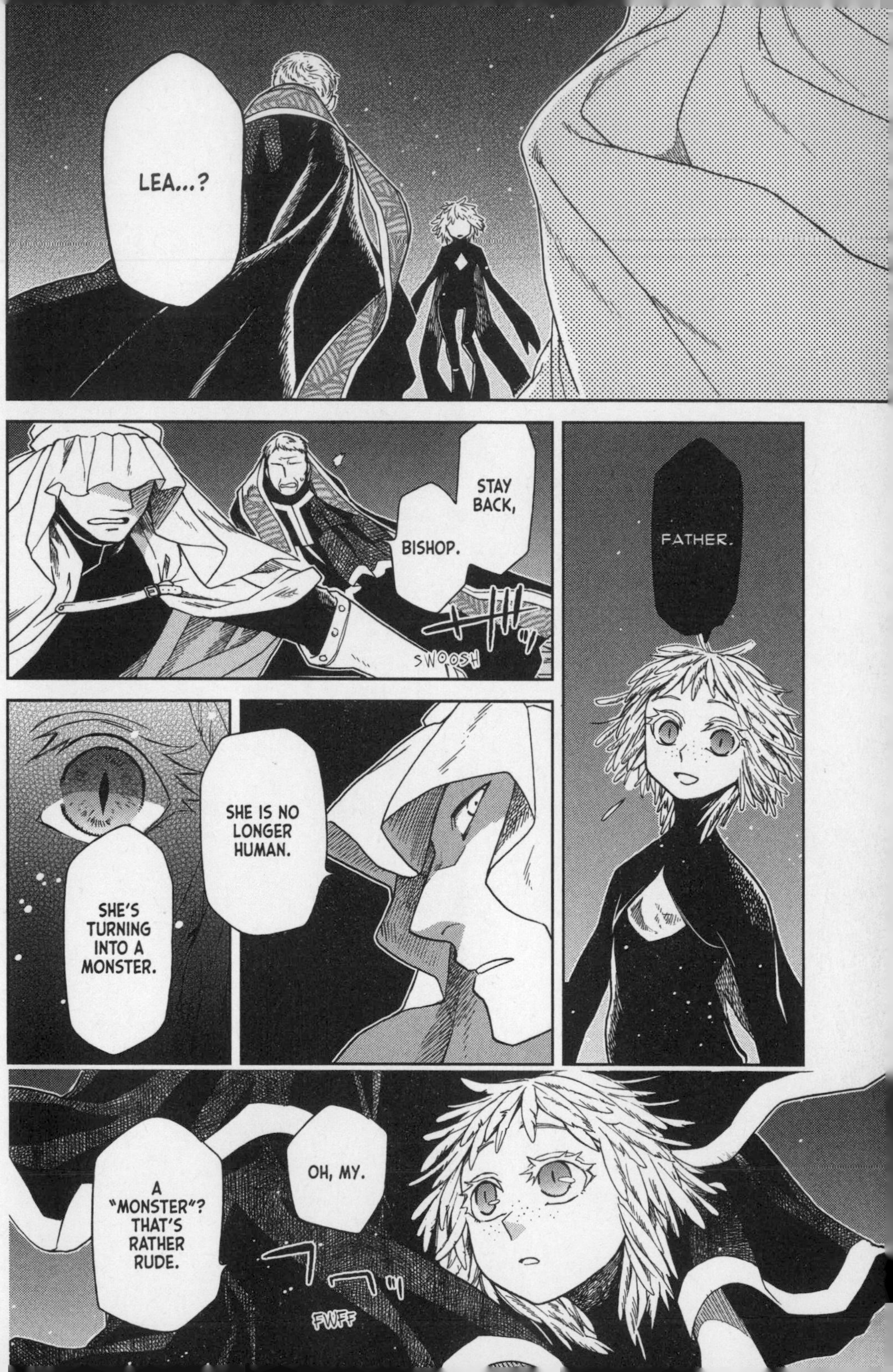
LEA...?
FATHER.
STAY BACK,
BISHOP.
SWOOSH
SHE IS NO LONGER HUMAN.
SHE'S TURNING INTO A MONSTER.
OH, MY.
A "MONSTER"? THAT'S RATHER RUDE.
FWFF

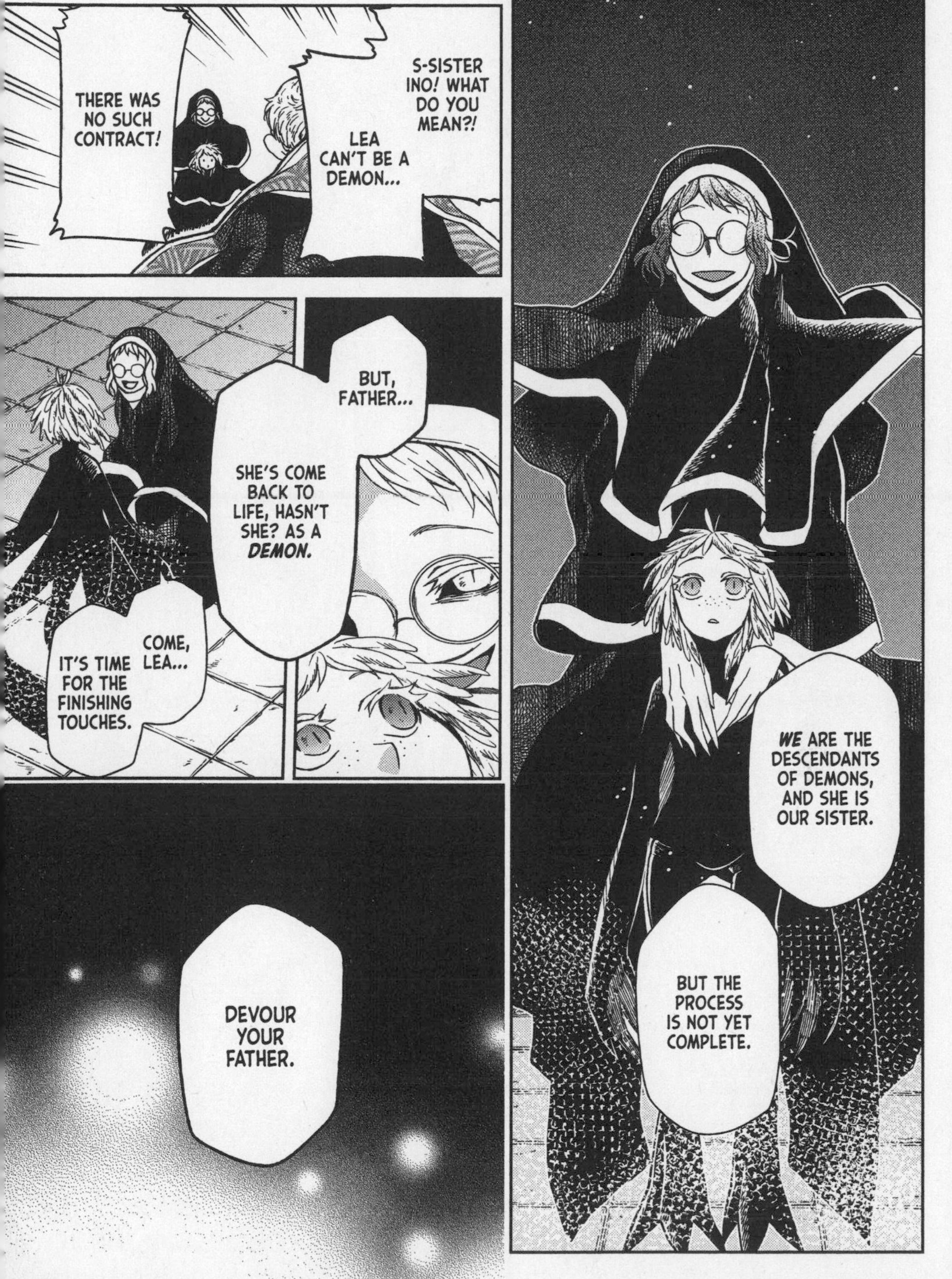
WE ARE THE DESCENDANTS OF DEMONS, AND SHE IS OUR SISTER.
BUT THE PROCESS IS NOT YET COMPLETE.
S-SISTER INO! WHAT DO YOU MEAN?!
LEA CAN'T BE A DEMON...
THERE WAS NO SUCH CONTRACT!
BUT, FATHER...
SHE'S COME BACK TO LIFE, HASN'T SHE? AS A DEMON.
COME, LEA...
IT'S TIME FOR THE FINISHING TOUCHES.
DEVOUR YOUR FATHER.

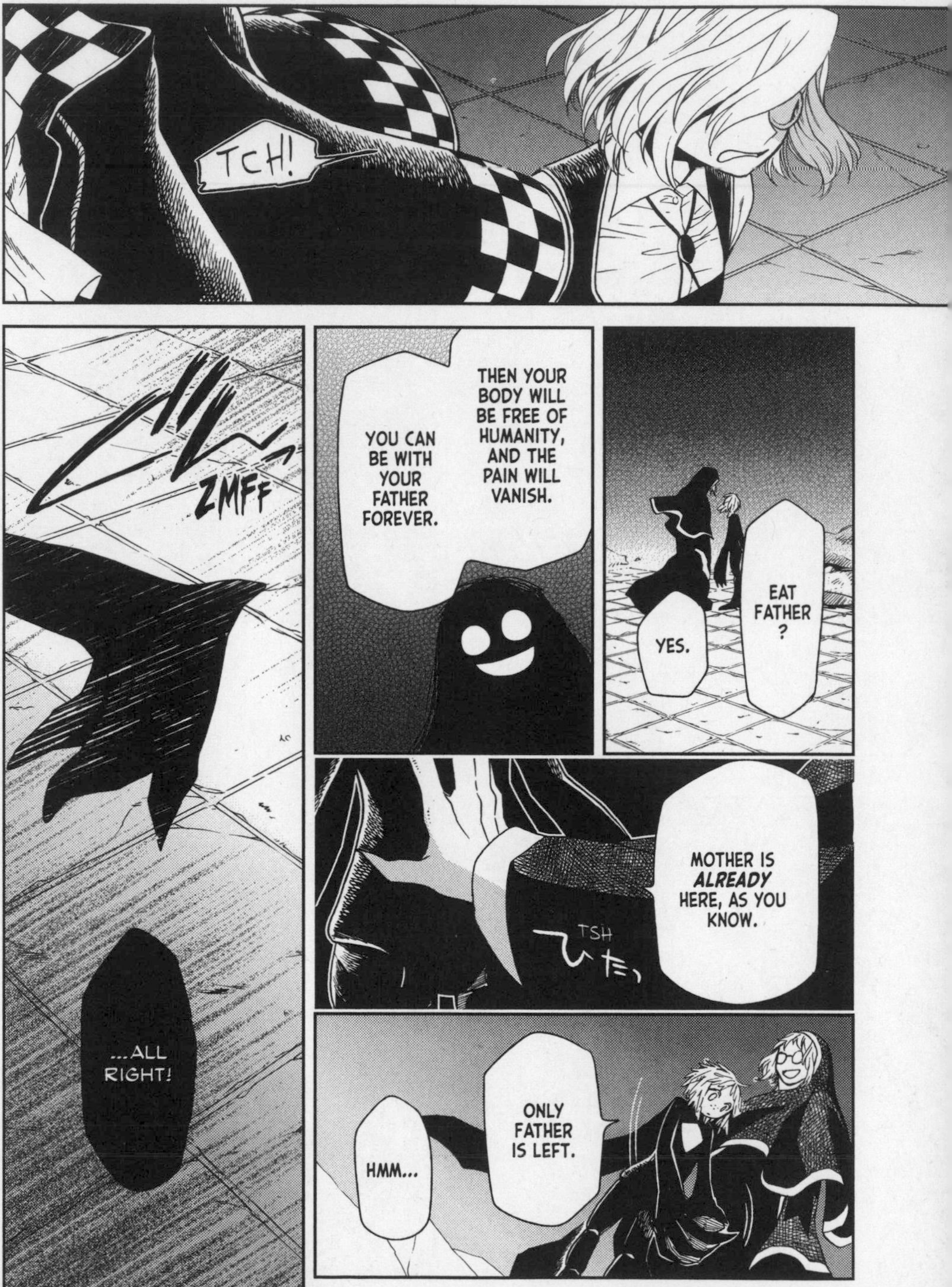
TCH!
EAT FATHER?
YES.
THEN YOUR BODY WILL BE FREE OF HUMANITY, AND THE PAIN WILL VANISH.
YOU CAN BE WITH YOUR FATHER FOREVER.
MOTHER IS *ALREADY* HERE, AS YOU KNOW.
TSH
ONLY FATHER IS LEFT.
HMM...
ZMFF
...ALL RIGHT!

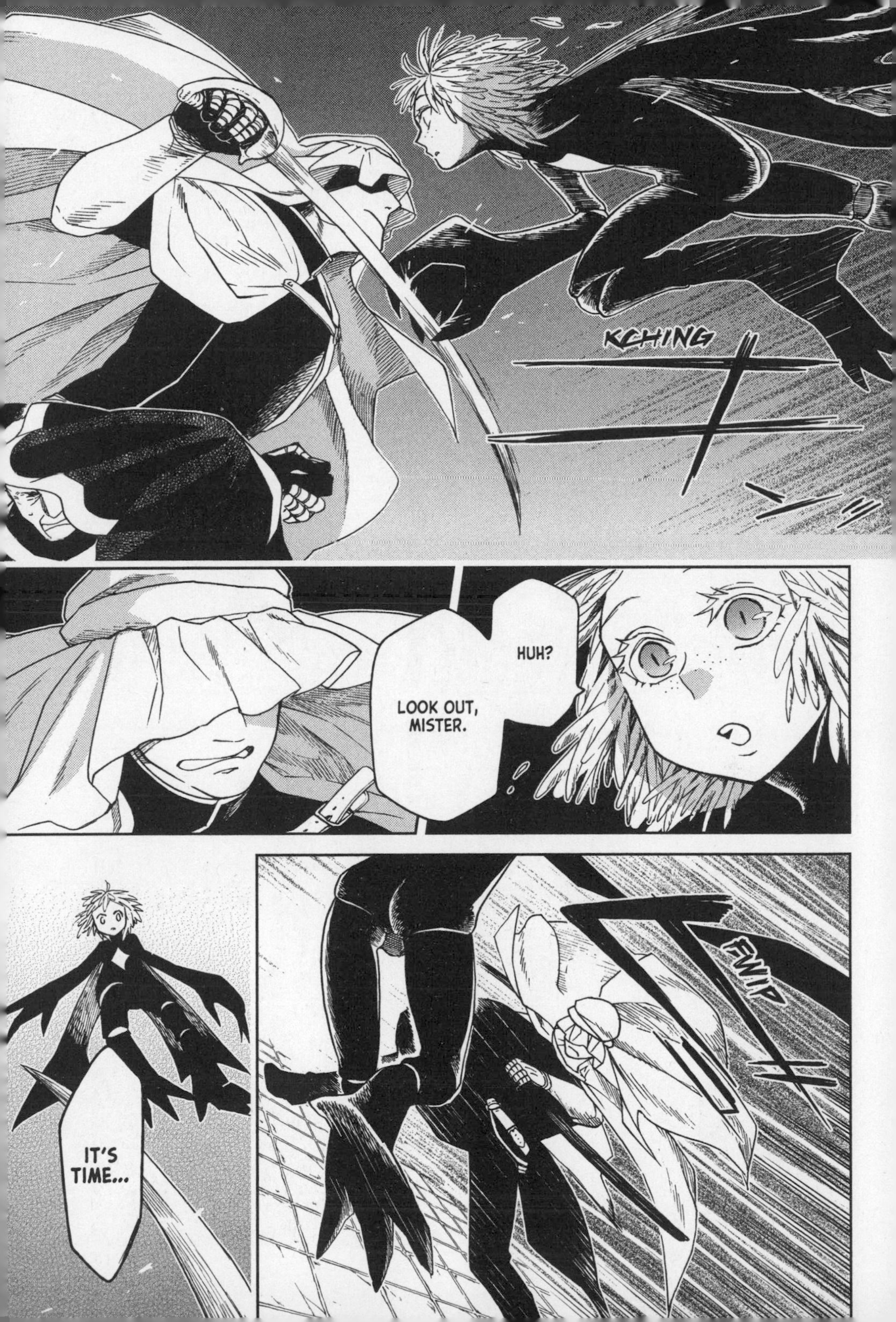
KCHING
HUH?
LOOK OUT, MISTER.
FWIP
IT'S TIME...

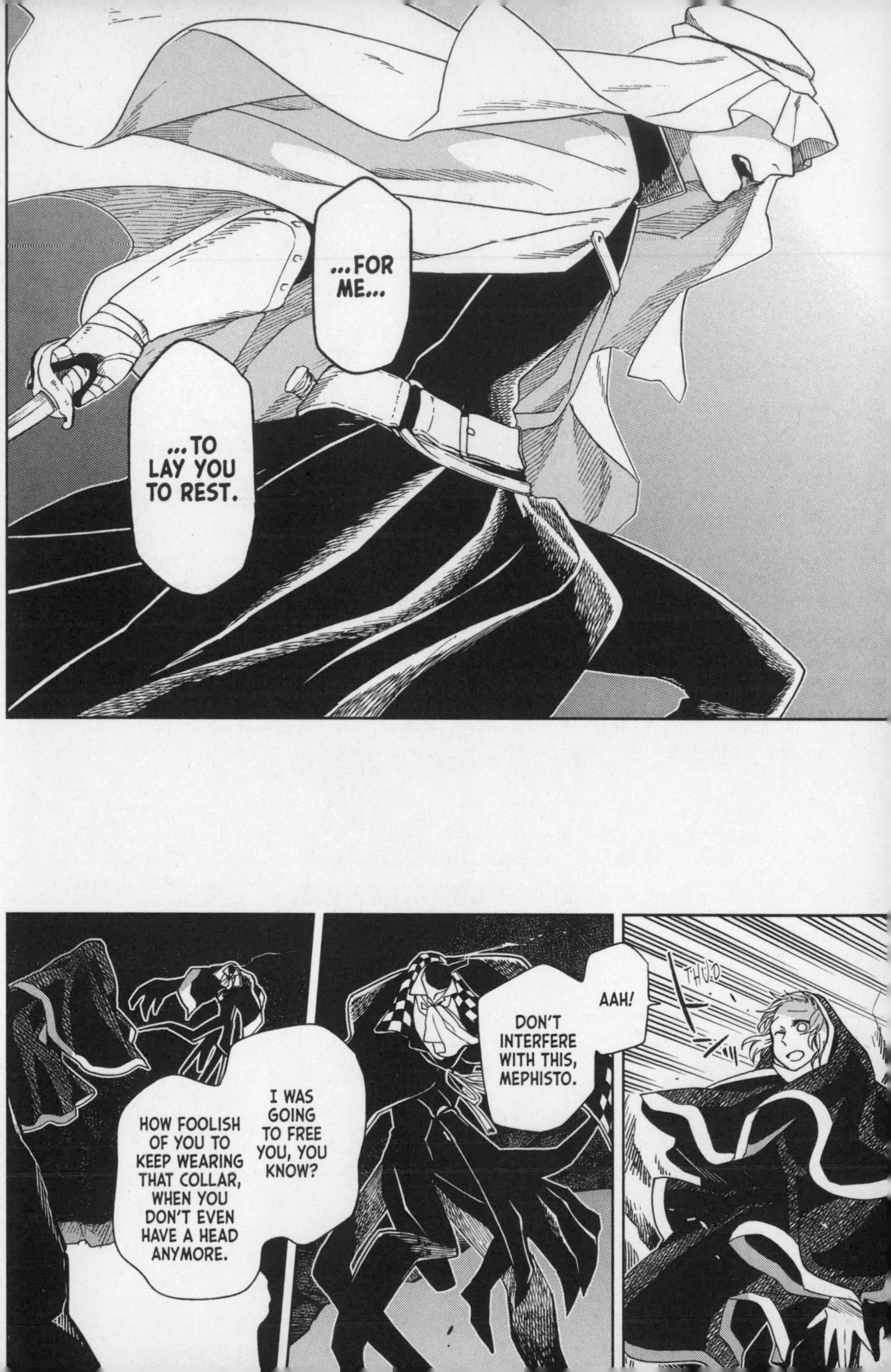
...FOR ME...
...TO LAY YOU TO REST.
THUD
AAH!
DON'T INTERFERE WITH THIS, MEPHISTO.
I WAS GOING TO FREE YOU, YOU KNOW?
HOW FOOLISH OF YOU TO KEEP WEARING THAT COLLAR, WHEN YOU DON'T EVEN HAVE A HEAD ANYMORE.

LEA
...

WHY
...?

ALL I
WANTED
...

TUG

KEEP HIM
UNDER
CONTROL,
MARION.

OKAY.

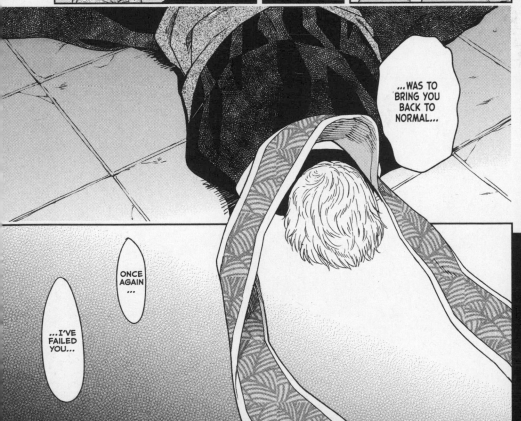

...WAS TO
BRING YOU
BACK TO
NORMAL...

ONCE
AGAIN
...

...I'VE
FAILED
YOU...

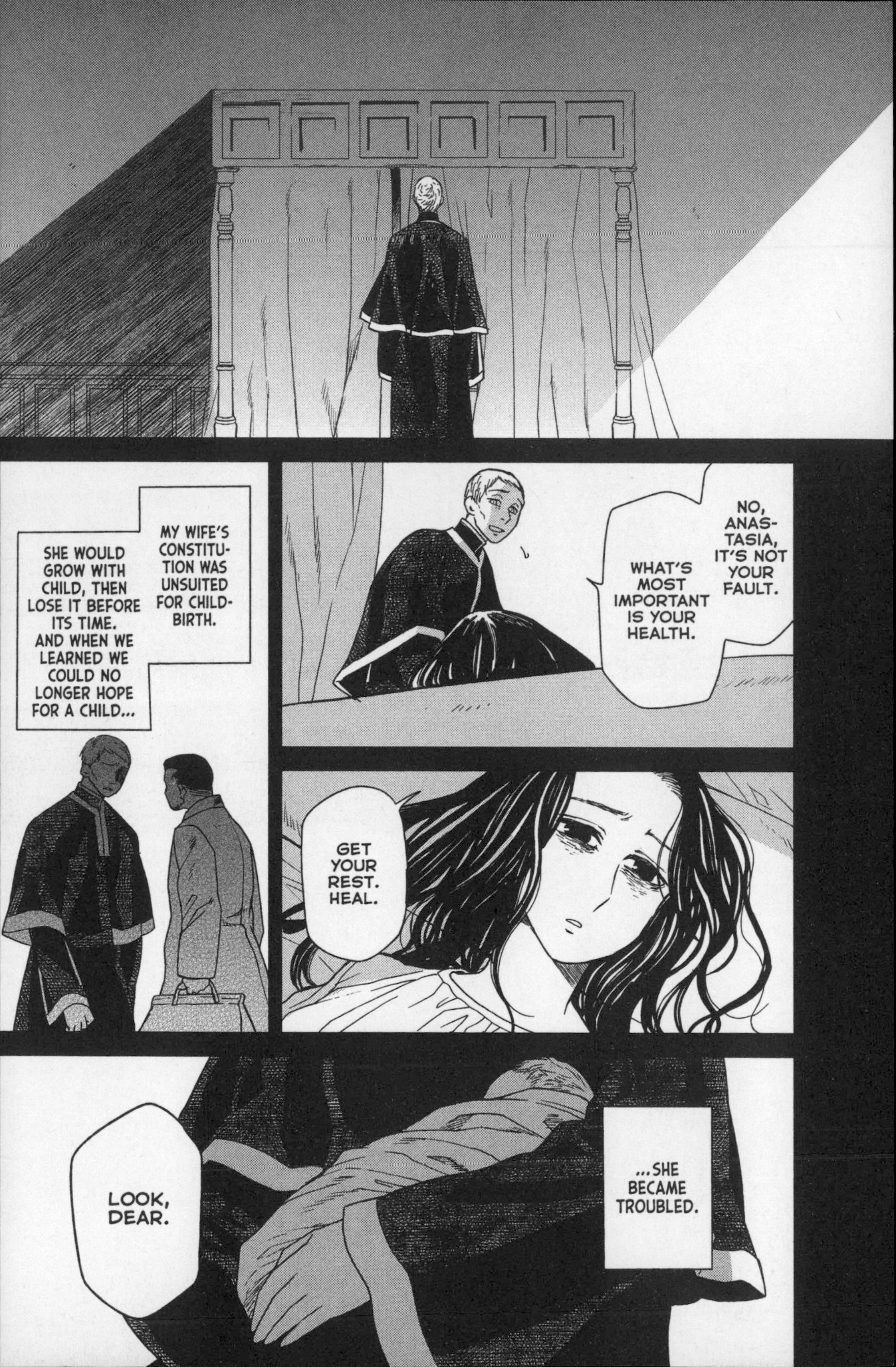
NO, ANASTASIA, IT'S NOT YOUR FAULT.
WHAT'S MOST IMPORTANT IS YOUR HEALTH.
GET YOUR REST. HEAL.
MY WIFE'S CONSTITUTION WAS UNSUITED FOR CHILDBIRTH.
SHE WOULD GROW WITH CHILD, THEN LOSE IT BEFORE ITS TIME. AND WHEN WE LEARNED WE COULD NO LONGER HOPE FOR A CHILD...
...SHE BECAME TROUBLED.
LOOK, DEAR.

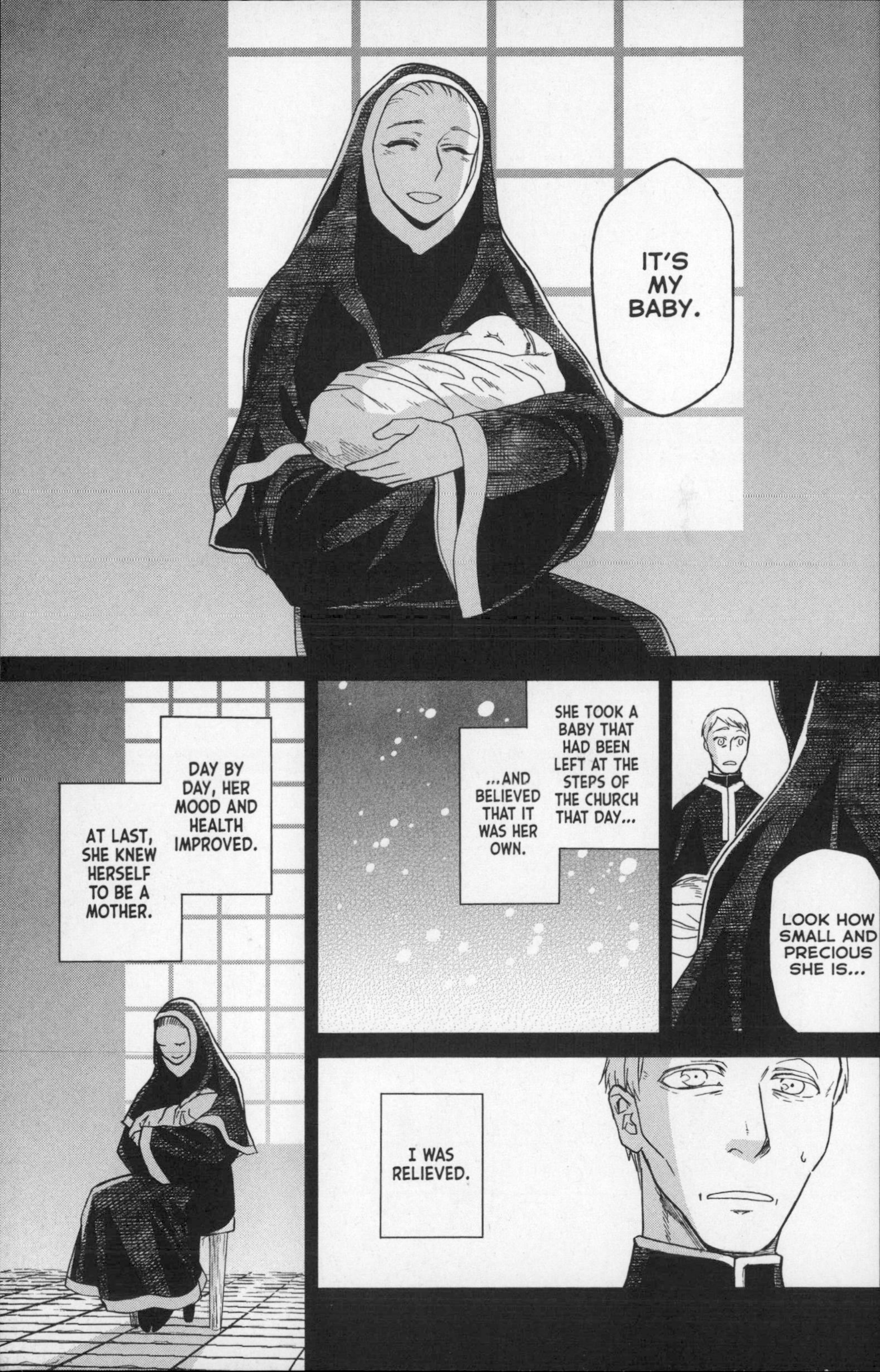
IT'S MY BABY.
LOOK HOW SMALL AND PRECIOUS SHE IS...
SHE TOOK A BABY THAT HAD BEEN LEFT AT THE STEPS OF THE CHURCH THAT DAY...
...AND BELIEVED THAT IT WAS HER OWN.
I WAS RELIEVED.
DAY BY DAY, HER MOOD AND HEALTH IMPROVED.
AT LAST, SHE KNEW HERSELF TO BE A MOTHER.

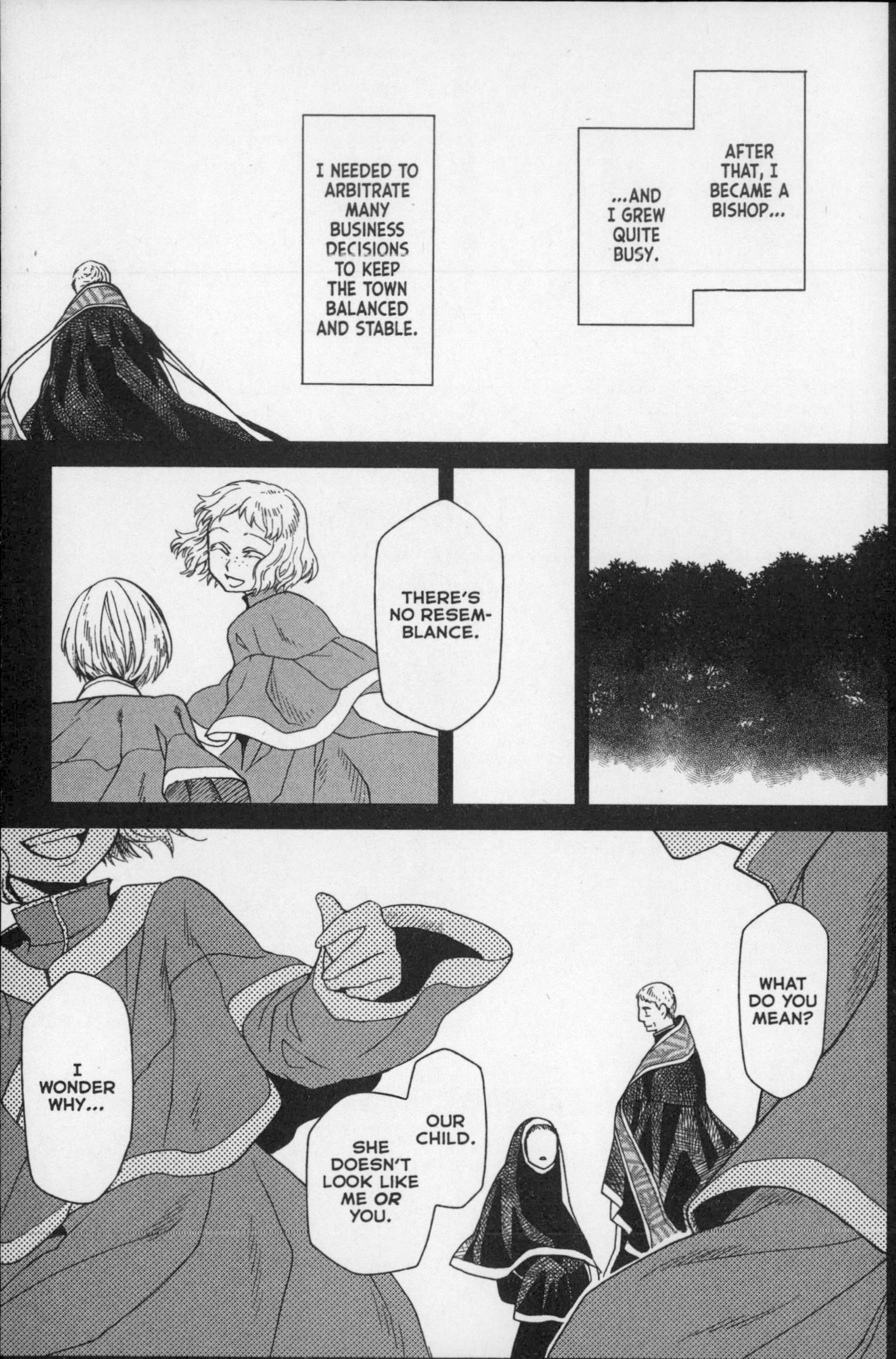
AFTER THAT, I BECAME A BISHOP...
...AND I GREW QUITE BUSY.
I NEEDED TO ARBITRATE MANY BUSINESS DECISIONS TO KEEP THE TOWN BALANCED AND STABLE.
THERE'S NO RESEMBLANCE.
WHAT DO YOU MEAN?
OUR CHILD.
SHE DOESN'T LOOK LIKE ME *OR* YOU.
I WONDER WHY...

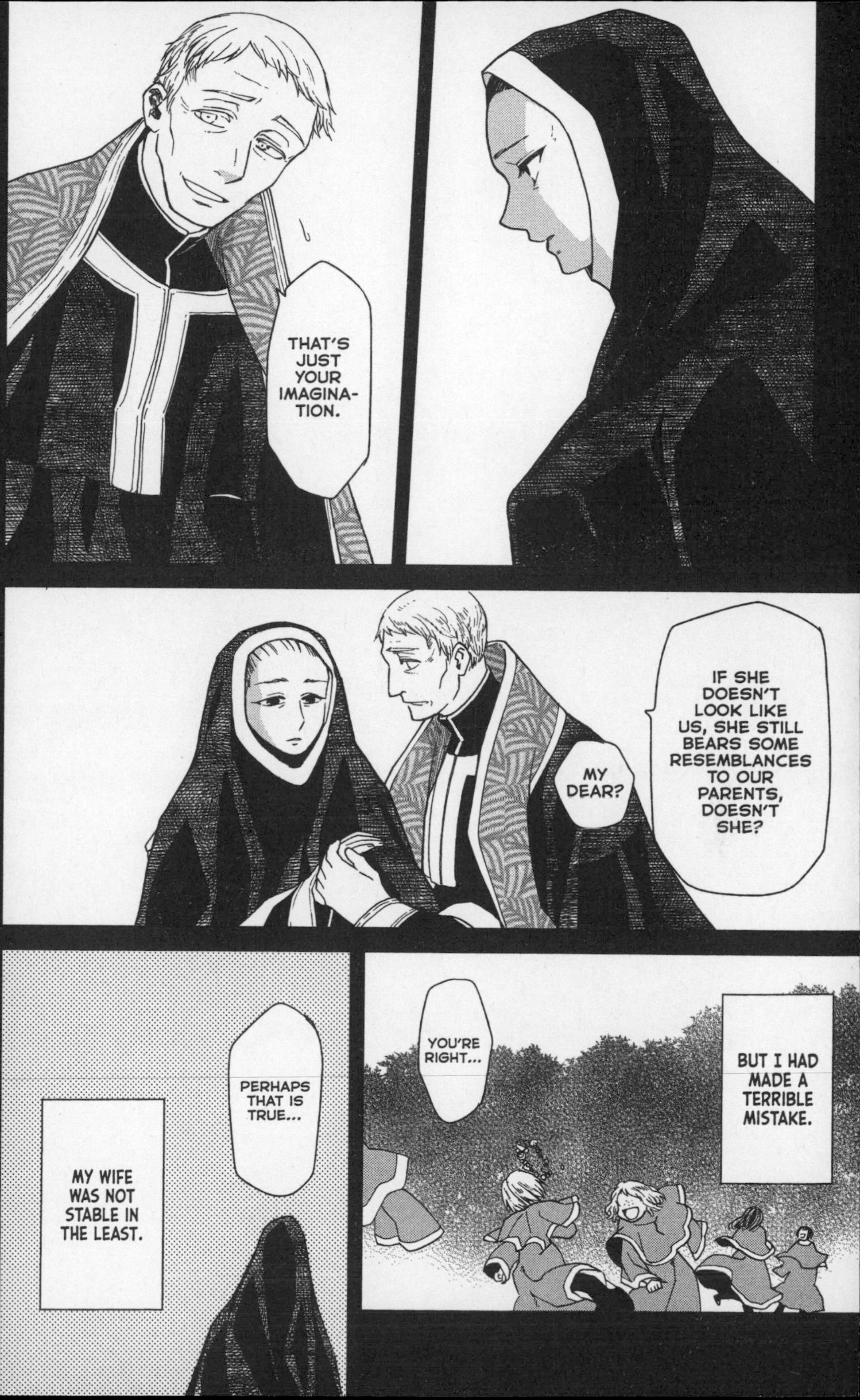
THAT'S JUST YOUR IMAGINATION.
IF SHE DOESN'T LOOK LIKE US, SHE STILL BEARS SOME RESEMBLANCES TO OUR PARENTS, DOESN'T SHE?
MY DEAR?
YOU'RE RIGHT...
BUT I HAD MADE A TERRIBLE MISTAKE.
PERHAPS THAT IS TRUE...
MY WIFE WAS NOT STABLE IN THE LEAST.

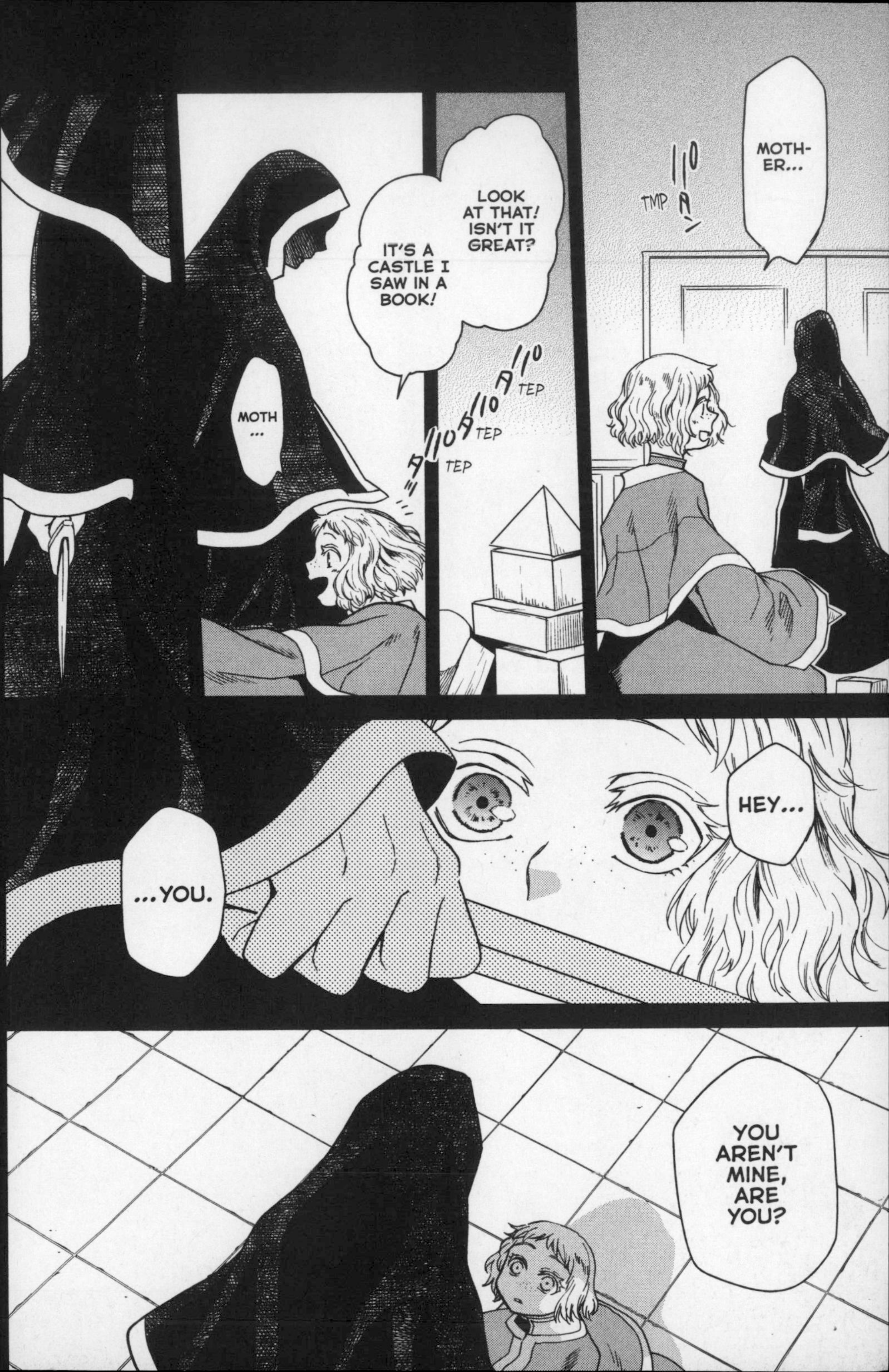
MOTH-ER...
TMP
LOOK AT THAT! ISN'T IT GREAT?
IT'S A CASTLE I SAW IN A BOOK!
TEP
TEP
TEP
MOTH ...
HEY...
...YOU.
YOU AREN'T MINE, ARE YOU?

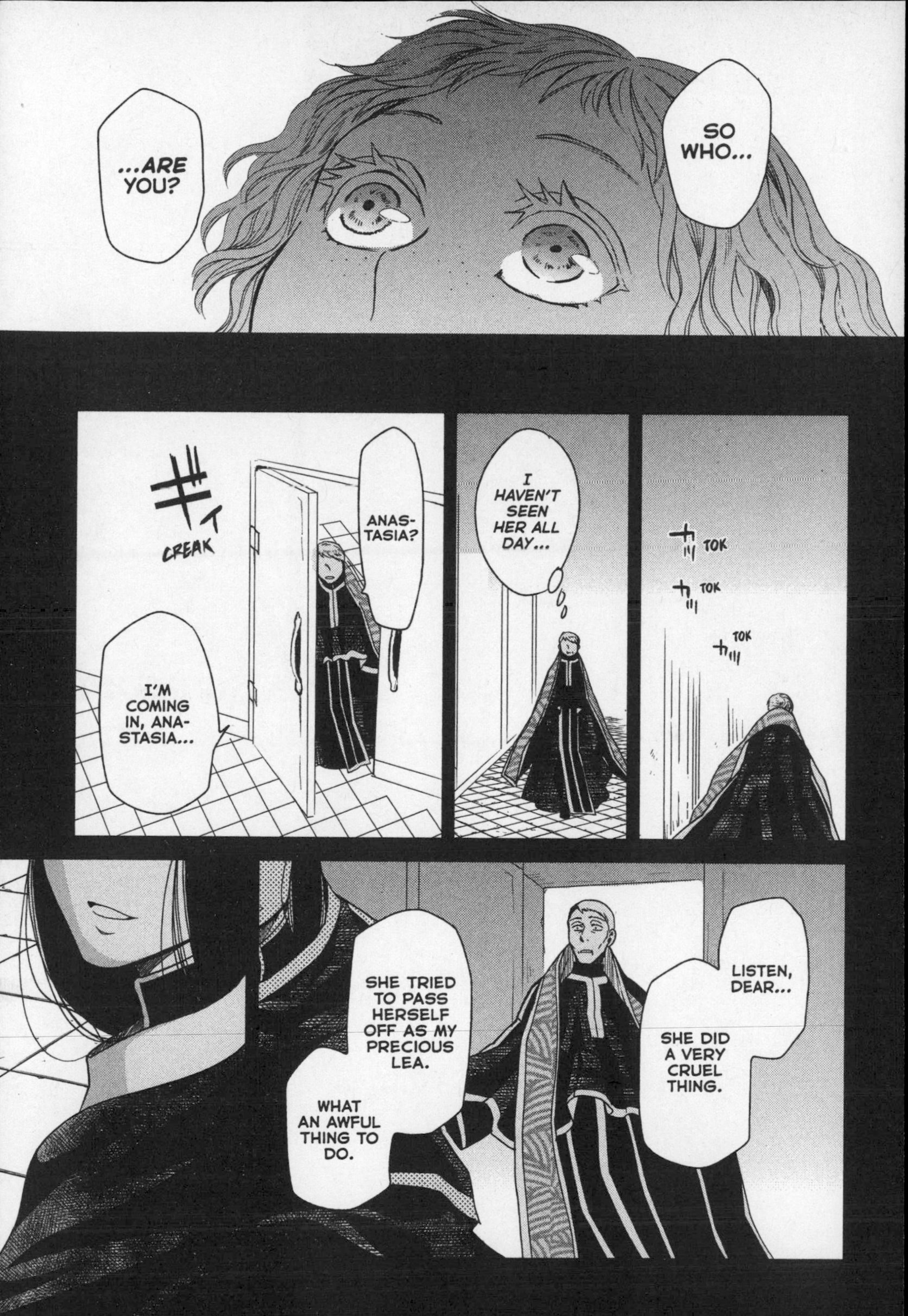
SO WHO...
...ARE YOU?
TOK
TOK
TOK
I HAVEN'T SEEN HER ALL DAY...
ANASTASIA?
CREAK
I'M COMING IN, ANASTASIA...
LISTEN, DEAR...
SHE DID A VERY CRUEL THING.
SHE TRIED TO PASS HERSELF OFF AS MY PRECIOUS LEA.
WHAT AN AWFUL THING TO DO.

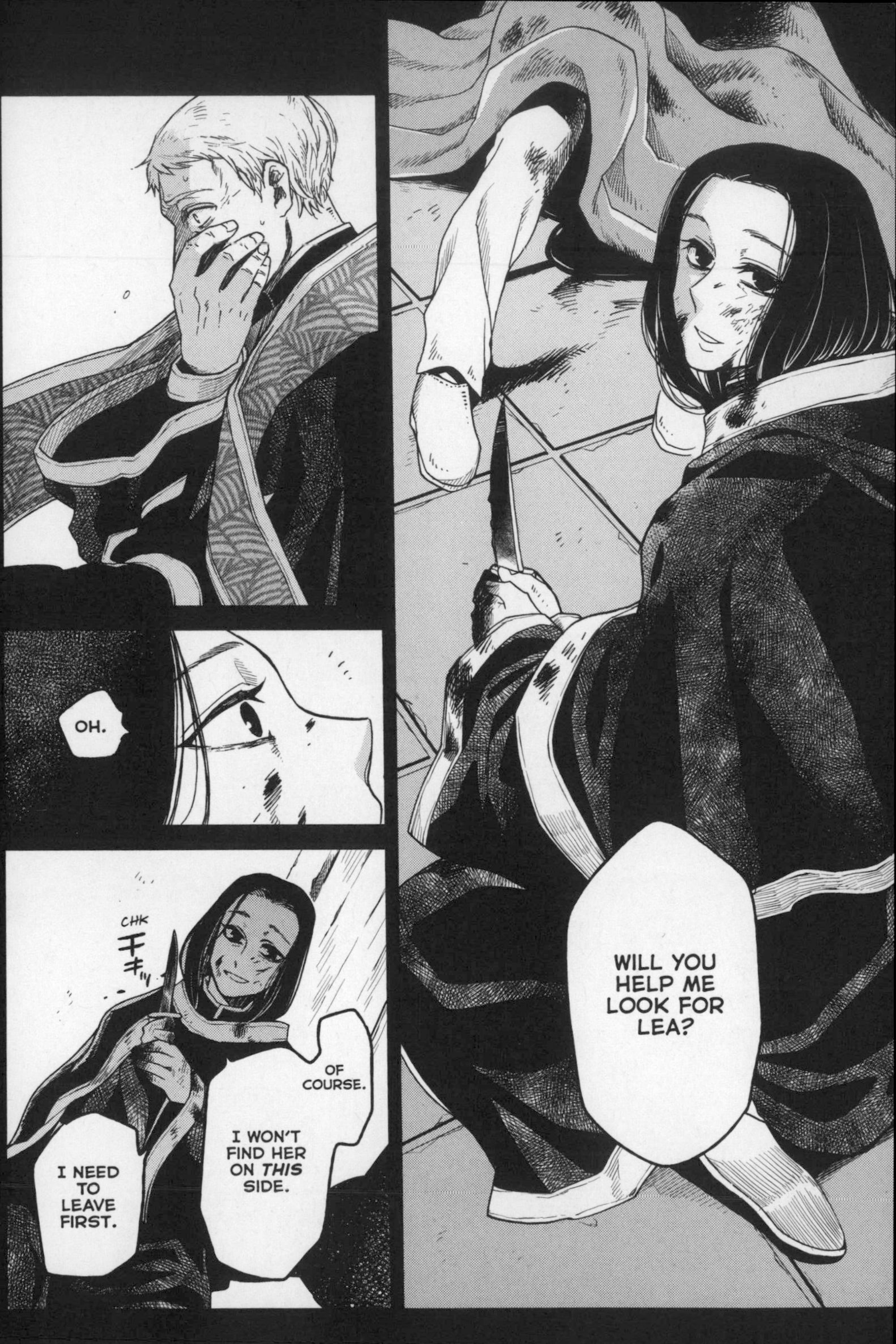
WILL YOU HELP ME LOOK FOR LEA?
OH.
CHK
チキッ
OF COURSE.
I WON'T FIND HER ON *THIS* SIDE.
I NEED TO LEAVE FIRST.

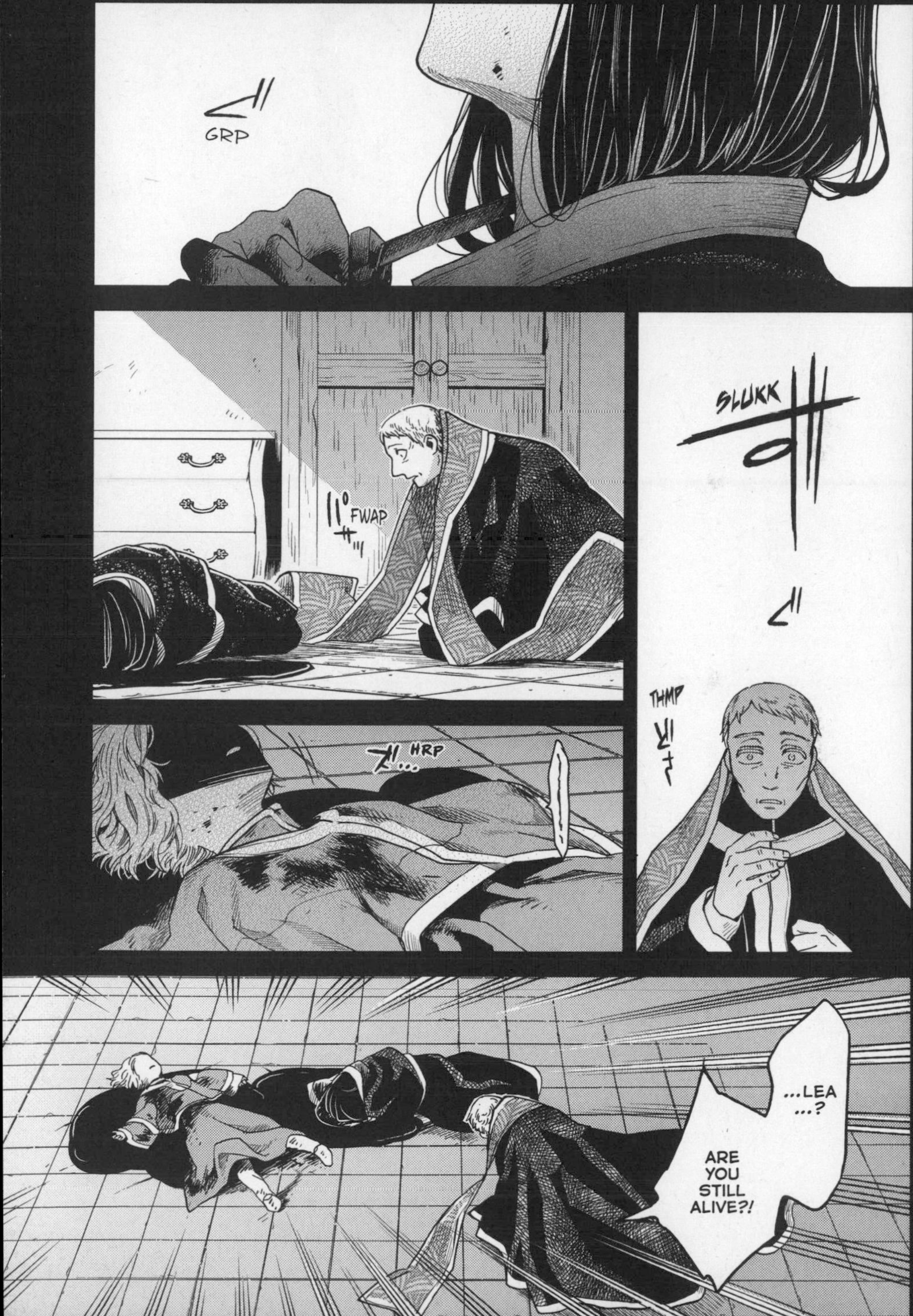
GRP
SLUKK
THMP
FWAP
HRP
...
...LEA ...?
ARE YOU STILL ALIVE?!

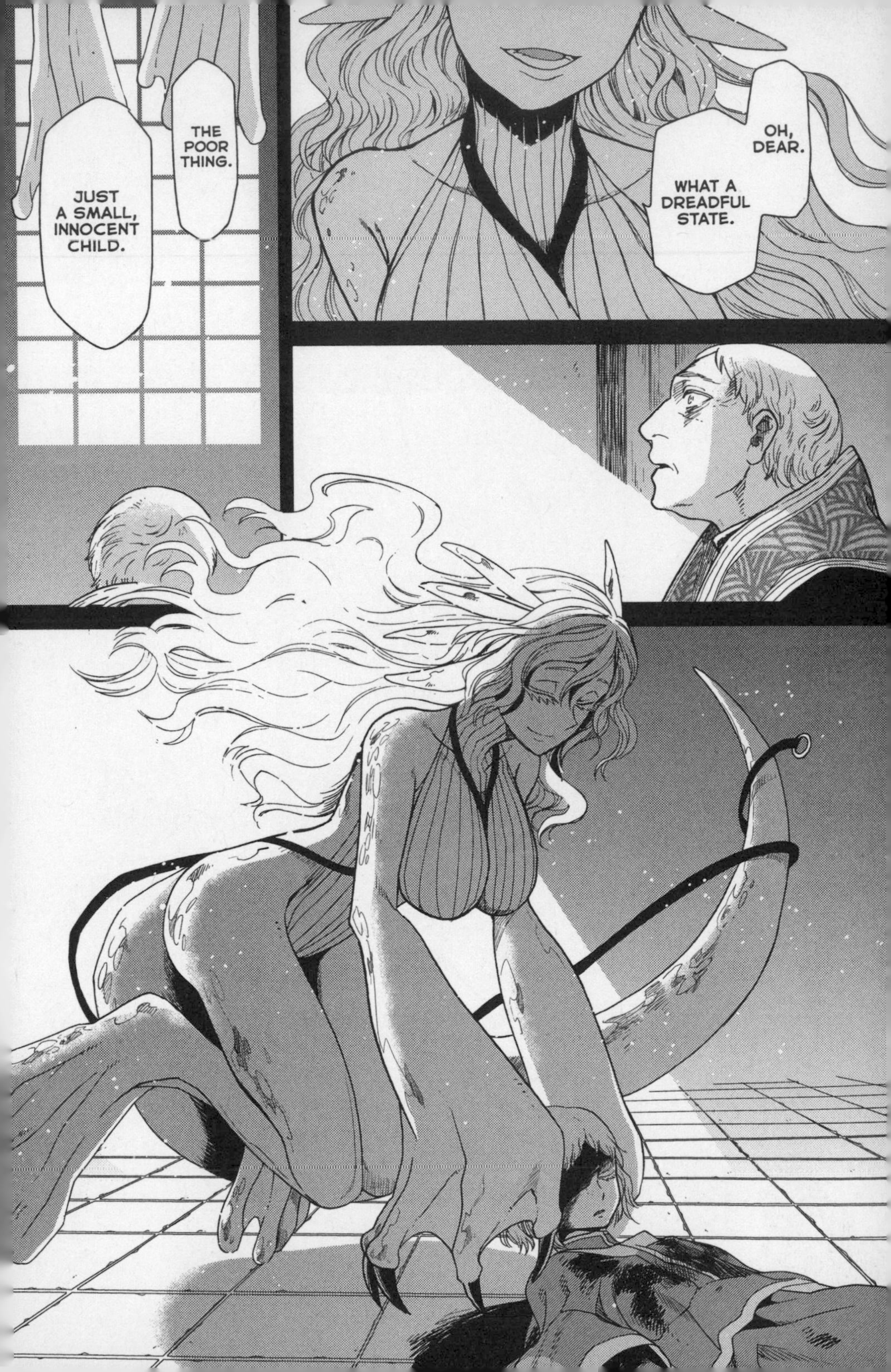
OH, DEAR.
WHAT A DREADFUL STATE.
THE POOR THING.
JUST A SMALL, INNOCENT CHILD.

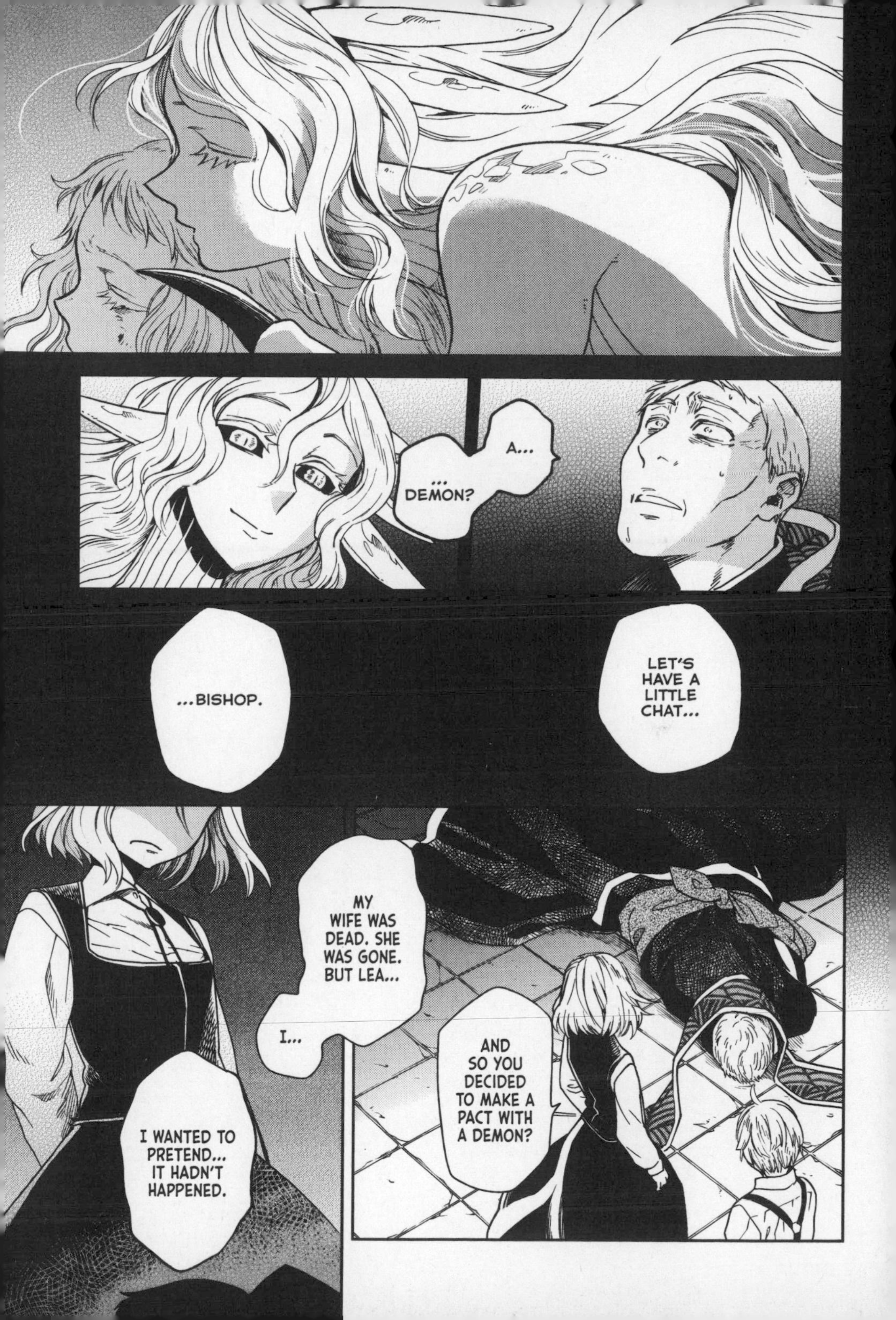
A... ...DEMON?
LET'S HAVE A LITTLE CHAT...
...BISHOP.
AND SO YOU DECIDED TO MAKE A PACT WITH A DEMON?
MY WIFE WAS DEAD. SHE WAS GONE. BUT LEA...
I...
I WANTED TO PRETEND... IT HADN'T HAPPENED.

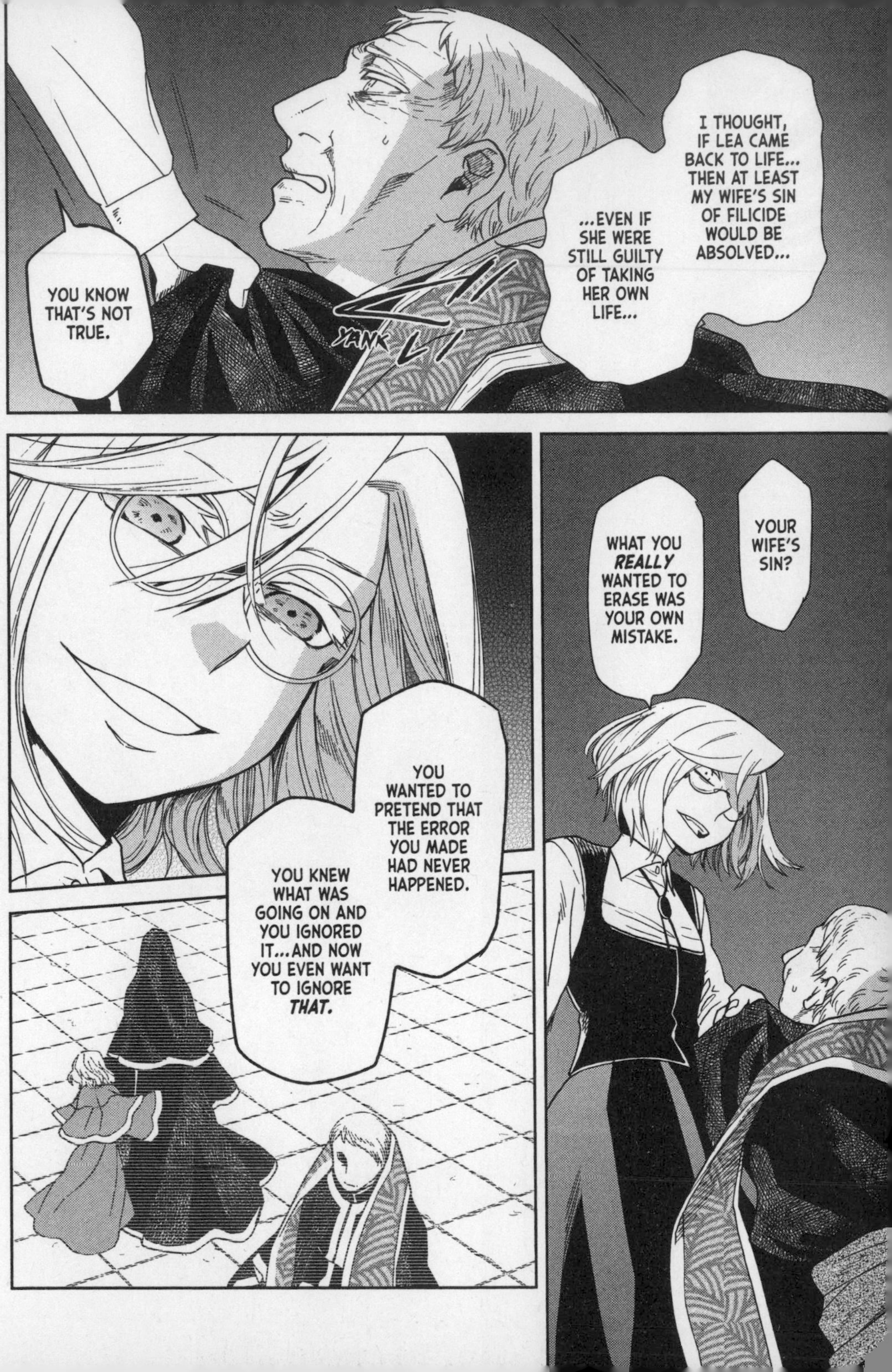
I THOUGHT, IF LEA CAME BACK TO LIFE... THEN AT LEAST MY WIFE'S SIN OF FILICIDE WOULD BE ABSOLVED...
...EVEN IF SHE WERE STILL GUILTY OF TAKING HER OWN LIFE...
YANK
YOU KNOW THAT'S NOT TRUE.
YOUR WIFE'S SIN?
WHAT YOU *REALLY* WANTED TO ERASE WAS YOUR OWN MISTAKE.
YOU WANTED TO PRETEND THAT THE ERROR YOU MADE HAD NEVER HAPPENED.
YOU KNEW WHAT WAS GOING ON AND YOU IGNORED IT...AND NOW YOU EVEN WANT TO IGNORE *THAT.*

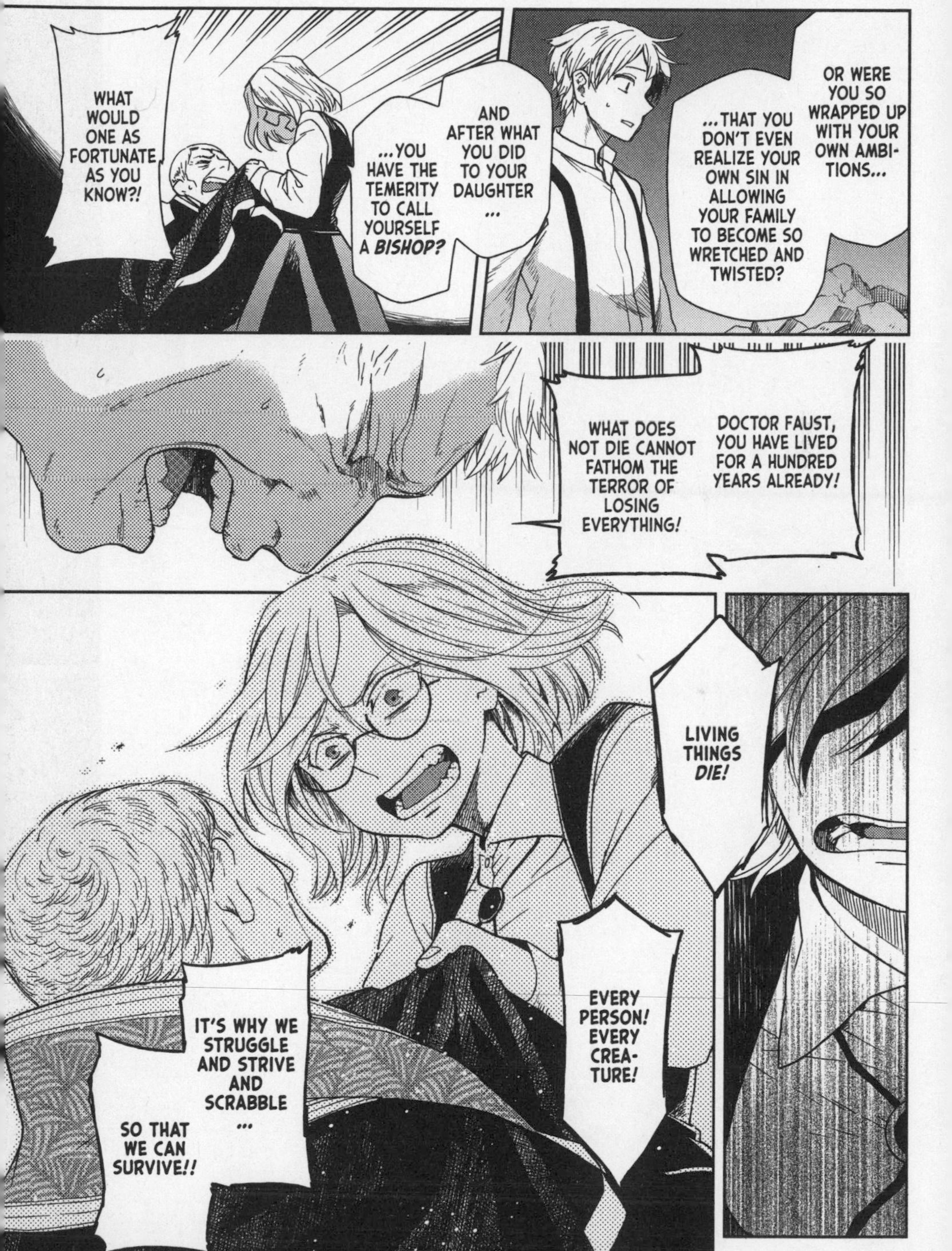
OR WERE YOU SO WRAPPED UP WITH YOUR OWN AMBITIONS...
...THAT YOU DON'T EVEN REALIZE YOUR OWN SIN IN ALLOWING YOUR FAMILY TO BECOME SO WRETCHED AND TWISTED?
AND AFTER WHAT YOU DID TO YOUR DAUGHTER ...
...YOU HAVE THE TEMERITY TO CALL YOURSELF A *BISHOP?*
WHAT WOULD ONE AS FORTUNATE AS YOU KNOW?!
DOCTOR FAUST, YOU HAVE LIVED FOR A HUNDRED YEARS ALREADY!
WHAT DOES NOT DIE CANNOT FATHOM THE TERROR OF LOSING EVERYTHING!
LIVING THINGS *DIE!*
EVERY PERSON! EVERY CREATURE!
IT'S WHY WE STRUGGLE AND STRIVE AND SCRABBLE ...
SO THAT WE CAN SURVIVE!!

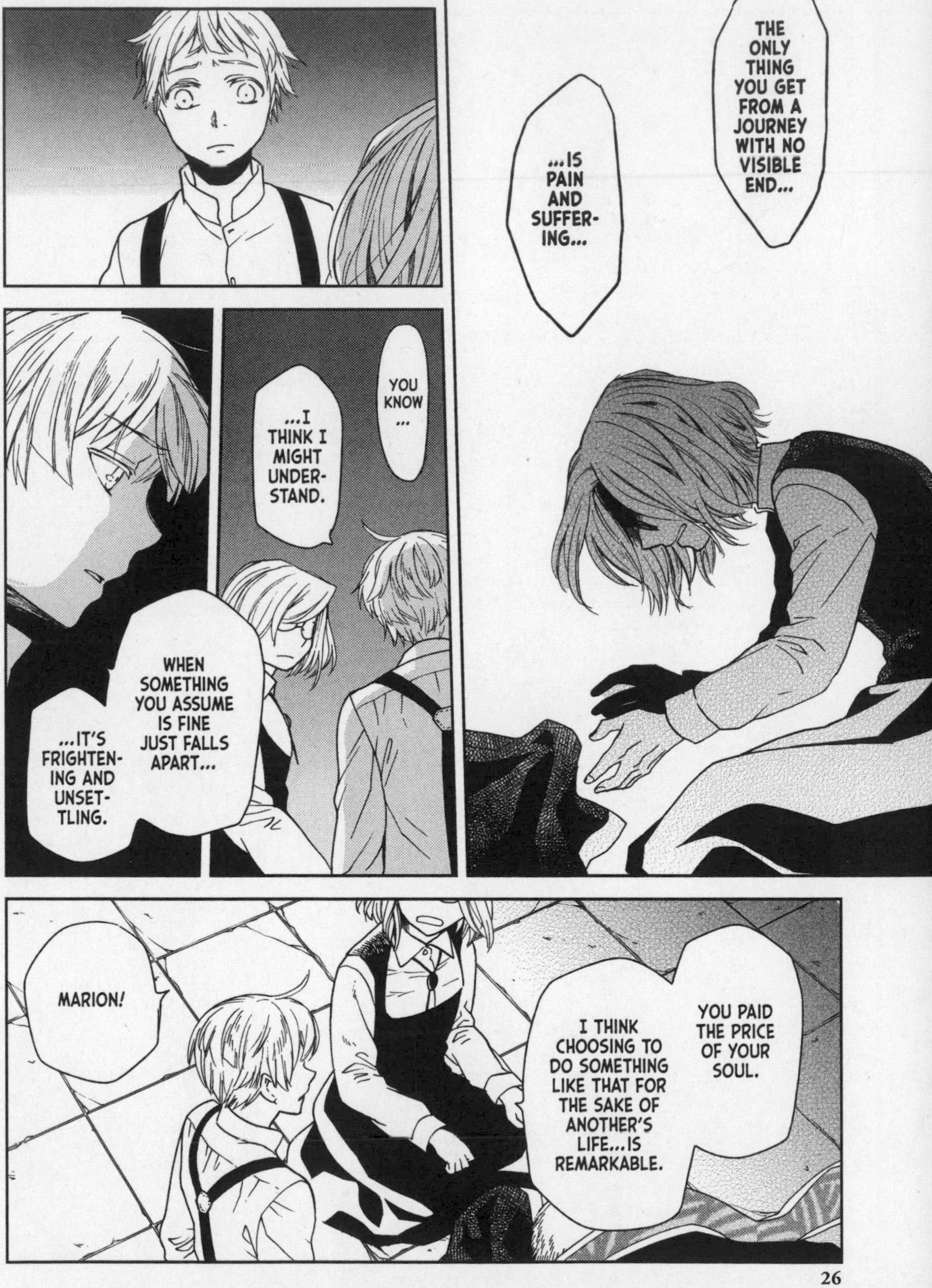
THE ONLY THING YOU GET FROM A JOURNEY WITH NO VISIBLE END...
...IS PAIN AND SUFFER-ING...
YOU KNOW...
...I THINK I MIGHT UNDER-STAND.
WHEN SOMETHING YOU ASSUME IS FINE JUST FALLS APART...
...IT'S FRIGHTEN-ING AND UNSET-TLING.
YOU PAID THE PRICE OF YOUR SOUL.
I THINK CHOOSING TO DO SOMETHING LIKE THAT FOR THE SAKE OF ANOTHER'S LIFE...IS REMARKABLE.
MARION!

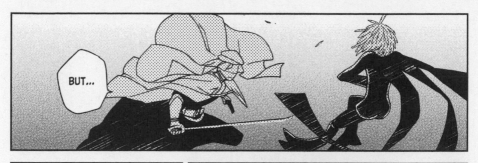

BUT...
...TO ALLOW YOUR OWN CHILD, RELATED BY BLOOD OR NOT...
...TO EAT OTHER HUMAN BEINGS...
...IS BEYOND THE PALE.
I MIGHT NOT KNOW MUCH... ABOUT GOOD AND EVIL...
BUT NO MATTER HOW PITIFUL SHE MIGHT BE...
...THERE ARE STILL THINGS YOU SHOULDN'T DO...OR FORCE HER TO DO... TO MAKE UP FOR IT.
!
I COULDN'T BEAR TO SEE...
...SOME-THING LIKE THAT...

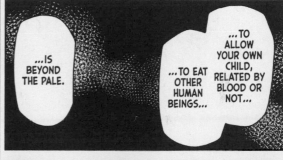

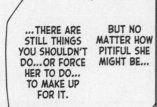

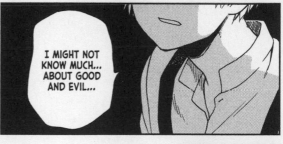

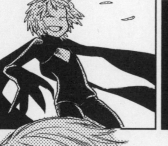

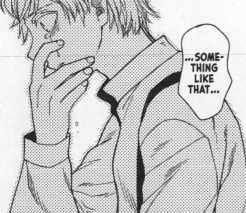

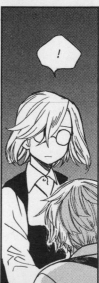

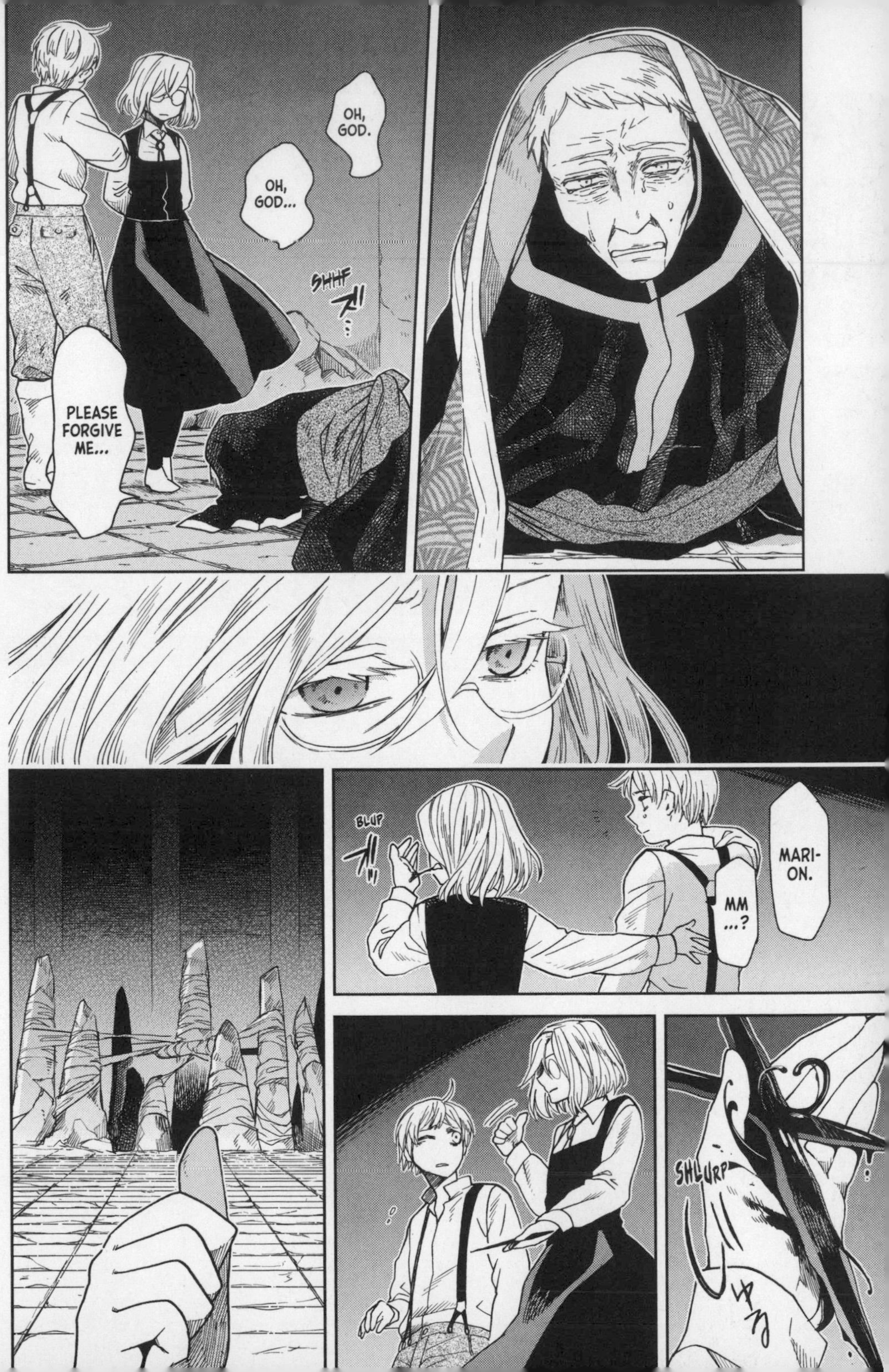
OH, GOD.
OH, GOD...
SHHF
PLEASE FORGIVE ME...
MARI-ON.
MM ...?
BLUP
SHLURP

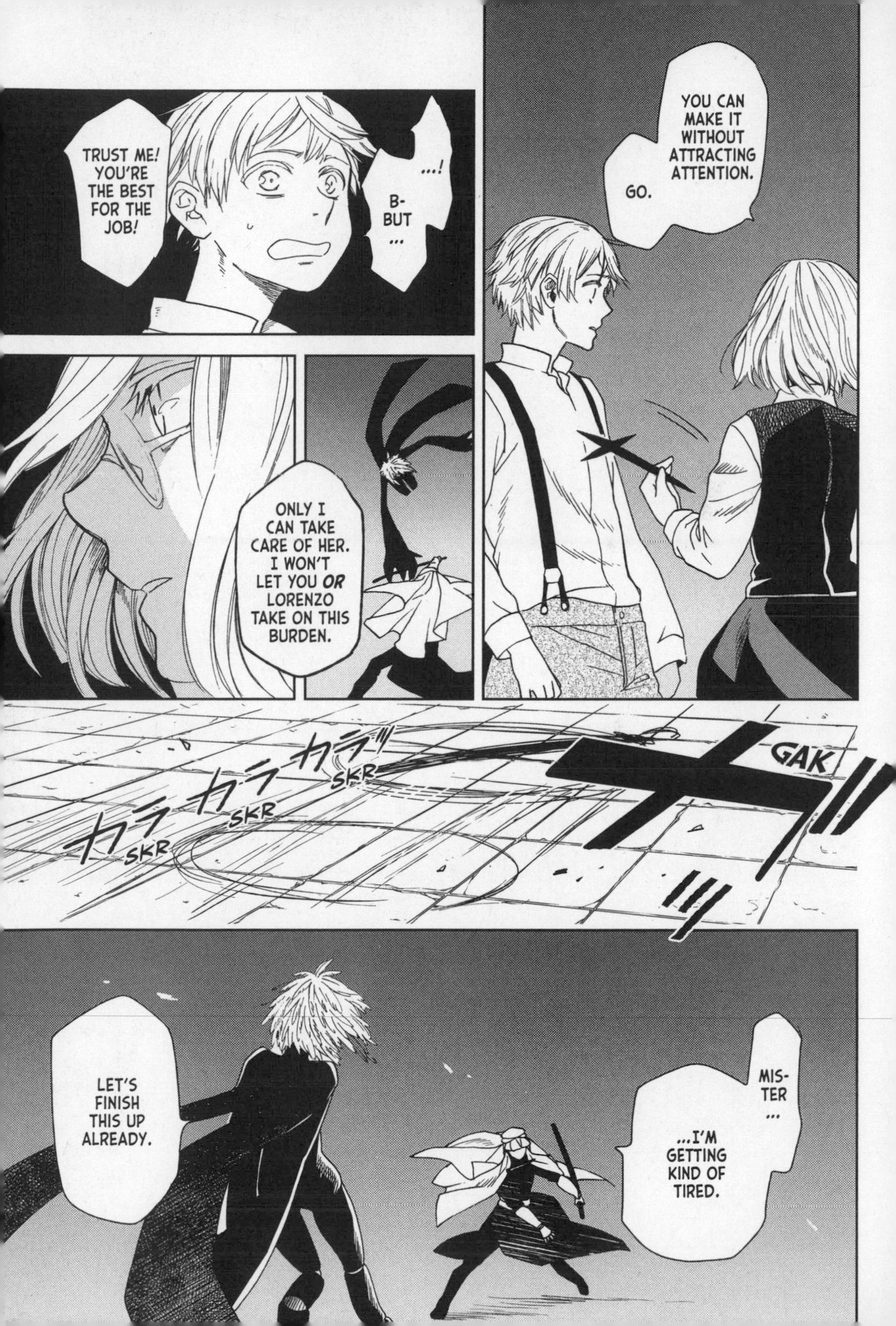
YOU CAN MAKE IT WITHOUT ATTRACTING ATTENTION.
GO.
...!
B-BUT...
TRUST ME! YOU'RE THE BEST FOR THE JOB!
ONLY I CAN TAKE CARE OF HER. I WON'T LET YOU *OR* LORENZO TAKE ON THIS BURDEN.
GAK
カラ
SKR
カラ
SKR
カラ
SKR
MIS-TER...
...I'M GETTING KIND OF TIRED.
LET'S FINISH THIS UP ALREADY.

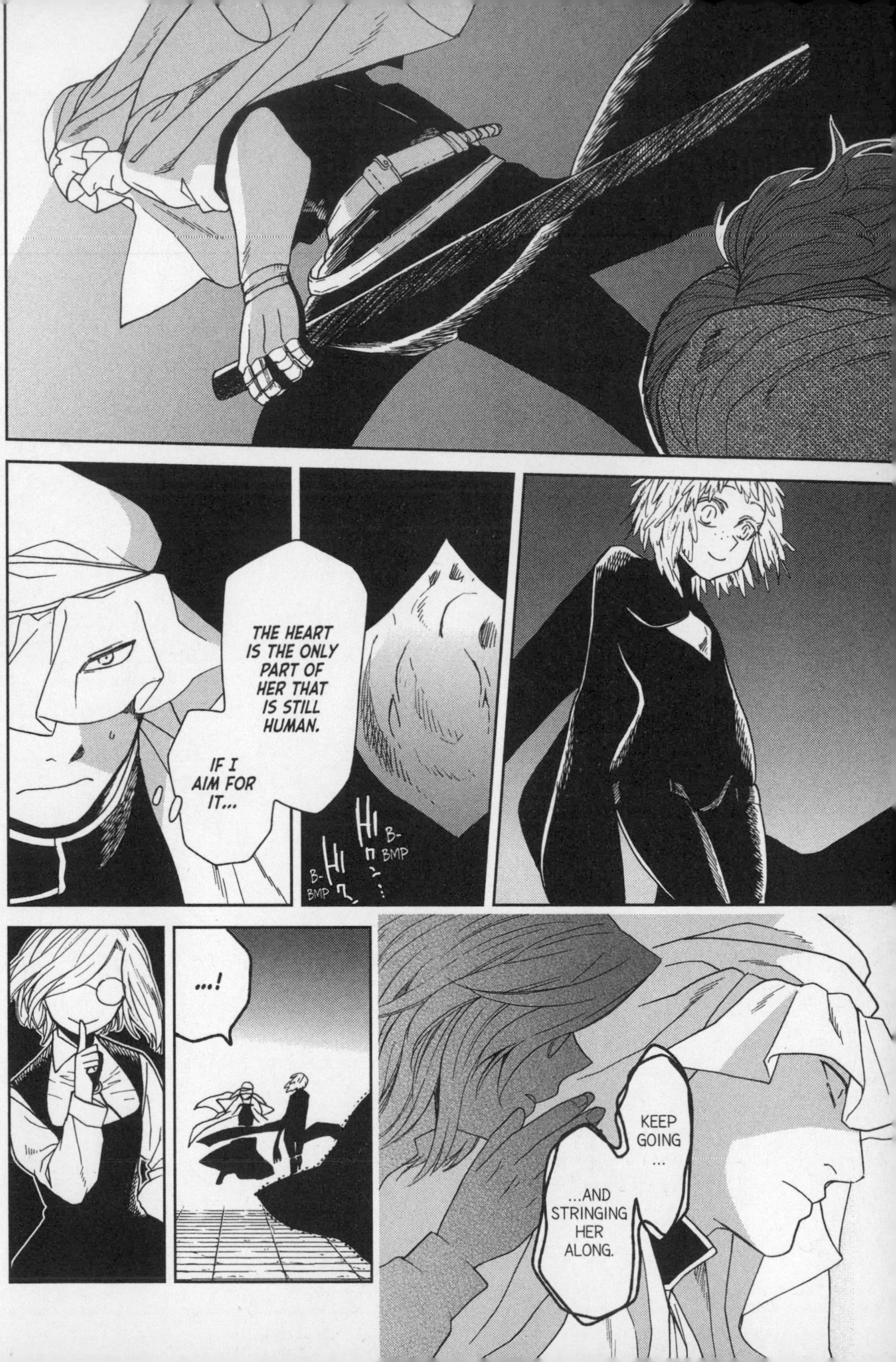
B-BMP
B-BMP
THE HEART IS THE ONLY PART OF HER THAT IS STILL HUMAN.
IF I AIM FOR IT...
KEEP GOING...
...AND STRINGING HER ALONG.
...!

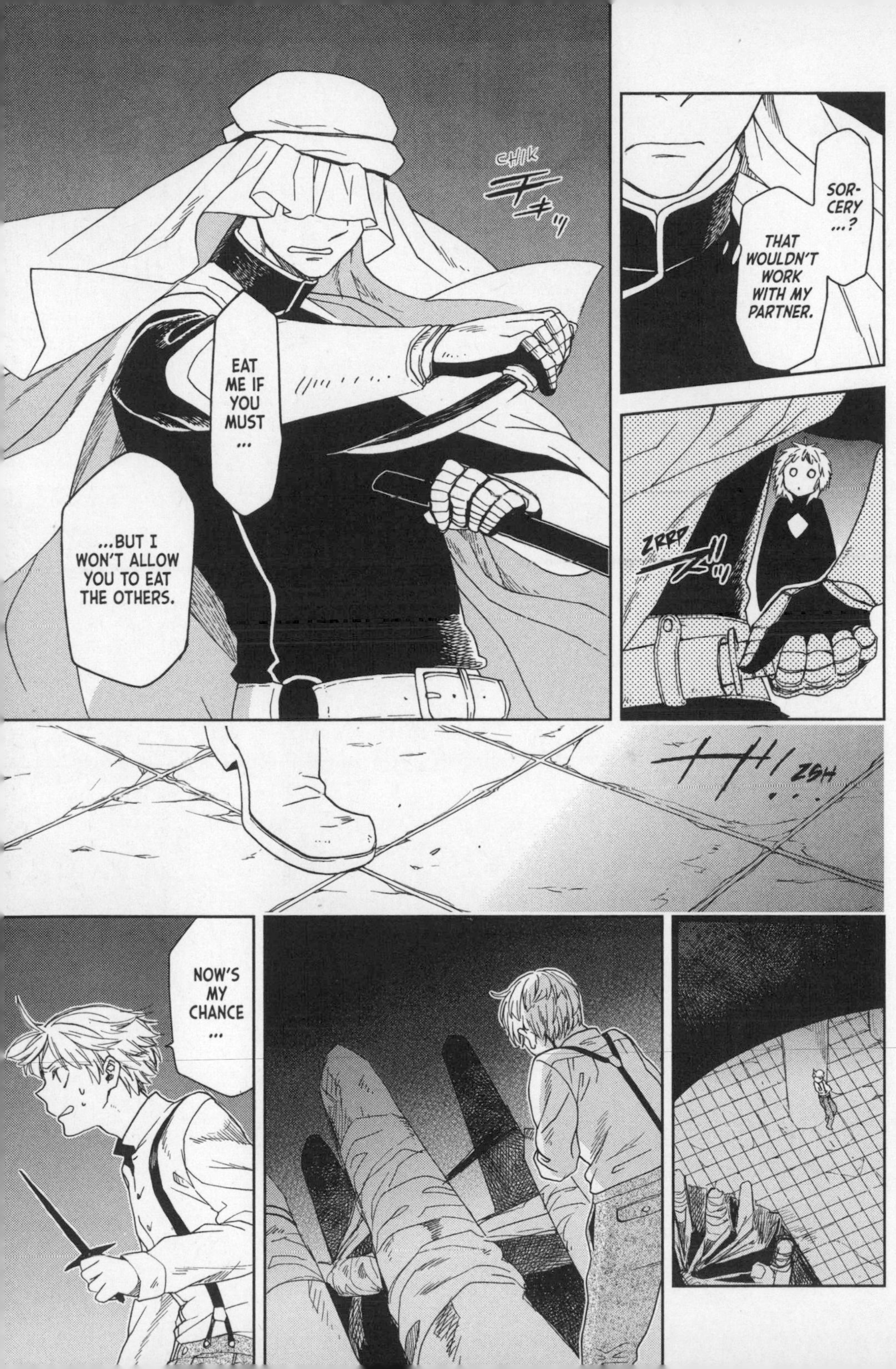
SOR-CERY ...?
THAT WOULDN'T WORK WITH MY PARTNER.
ZRRP
CHIK
EAT ME IF YOU MUST ...
...BUT I WON'T ALLOW YOU TO EAT THE OTHERS.
ZSH
NOW'S MY CHANCE ...

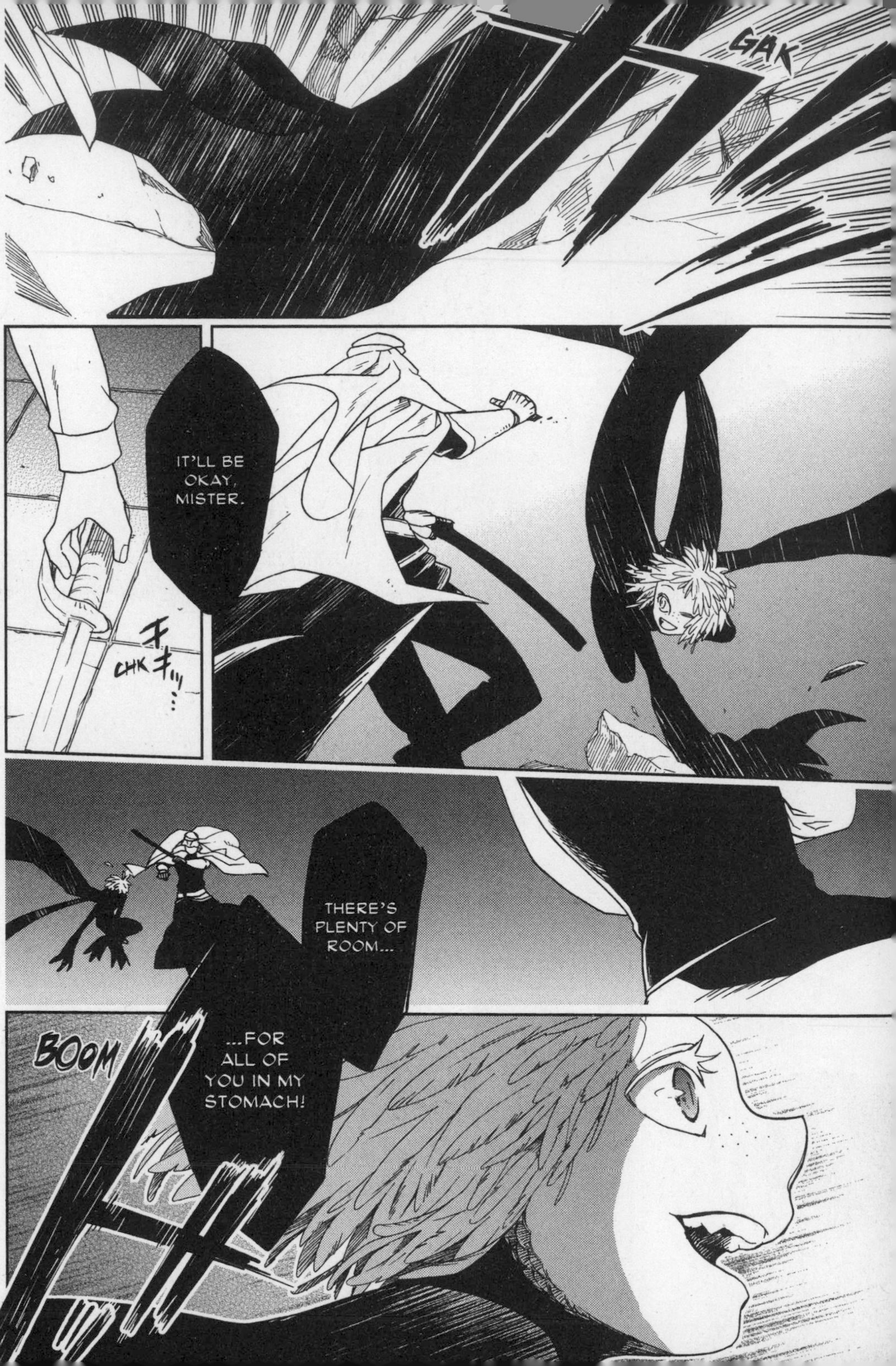
GAK
IT'LL BE OKAY, MISTER.
CHK
THERE'S PLENTY OF ROOM...
...FOR ALL OF YOU IN MY STOMACH!
BOOM

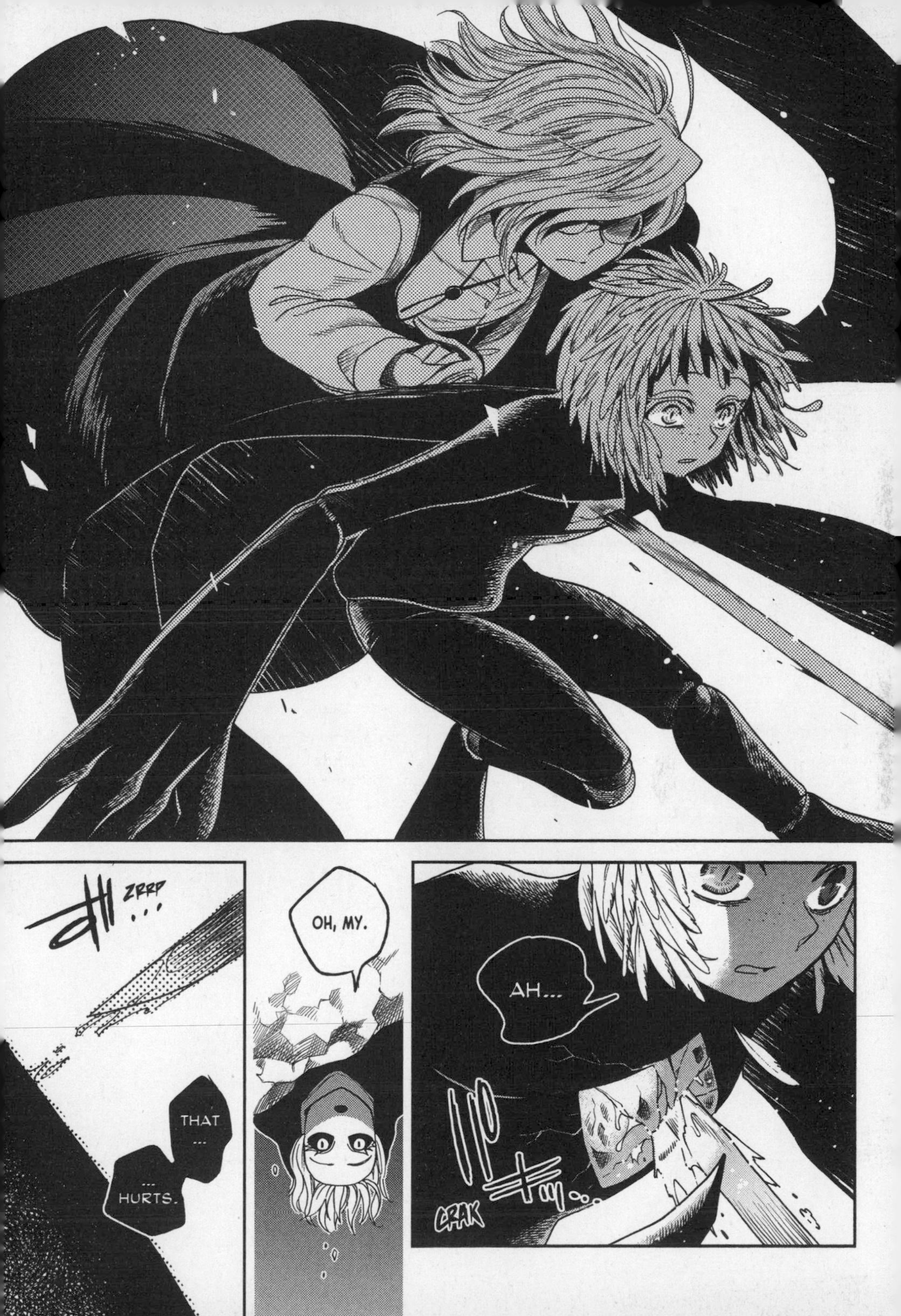
AH...
CRAK
OH, MY.
ZRRP...
THAT ...
... HURTS.

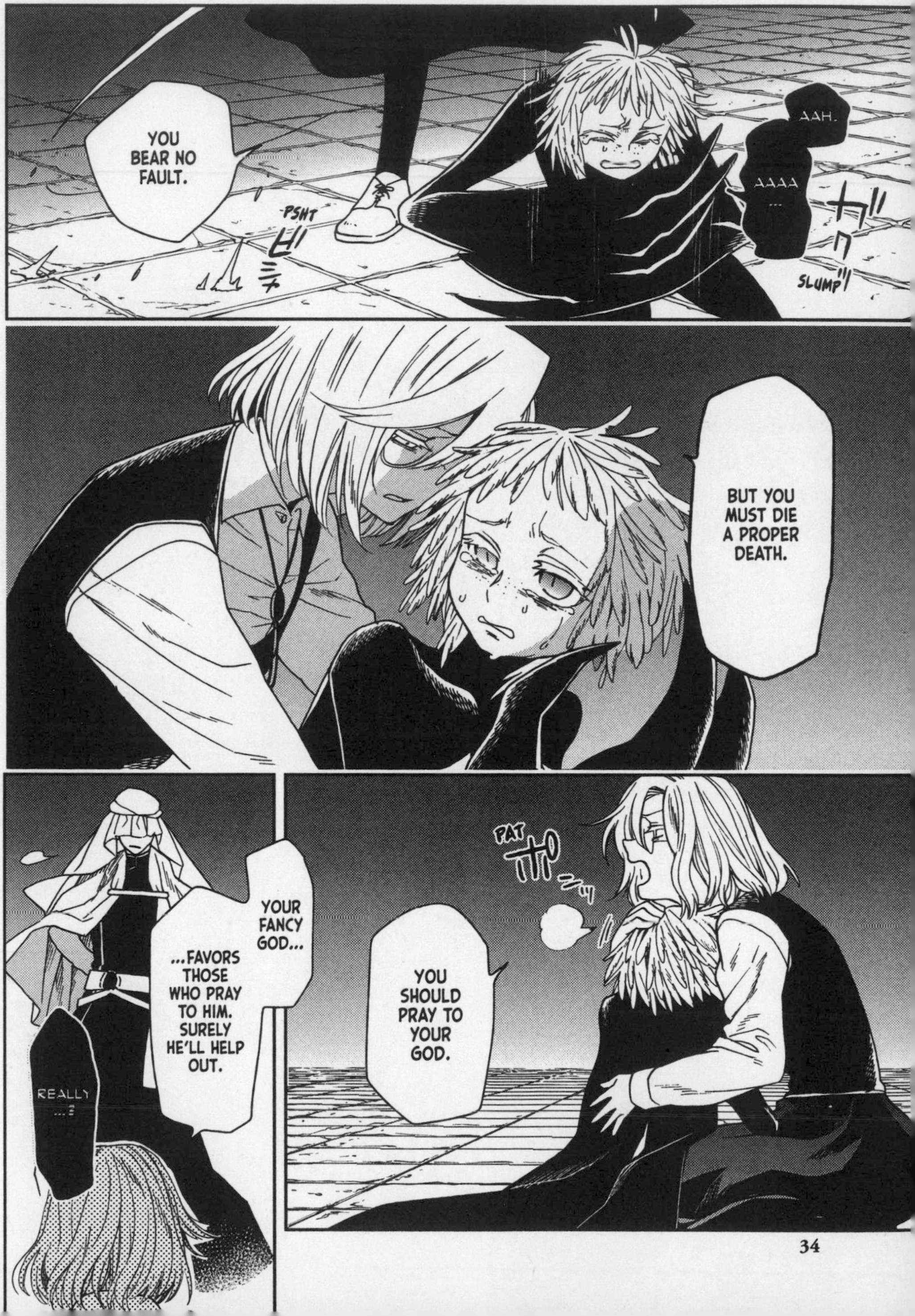
AAH.
AAAA...
SLUMP
YOU BEAR NO FAULT.
PSHT
BUT YOU MUST DIE A PROPER DEATH.
PAT
YOU SHOULD PRAY TO YOUR GOD.
YOUR FANCY GOD...
...FAVORS THOSE WHO PRAY TO HIM. SURELY HE'LL HELP OUT.
REALLY...?

KSHUNK

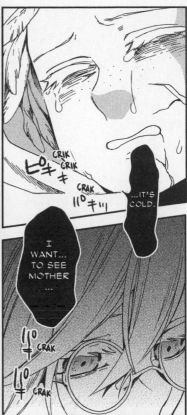

CRIK CRIK

CRAK

...IT'S COLD.

I WANT... TO SEE MOTHER...

CRAK

CRAK

OH, MY.

SO IT DIDN'T WORK OUT.

I SUPPOSE I WAS OUT-NUMBERED.

CLINK

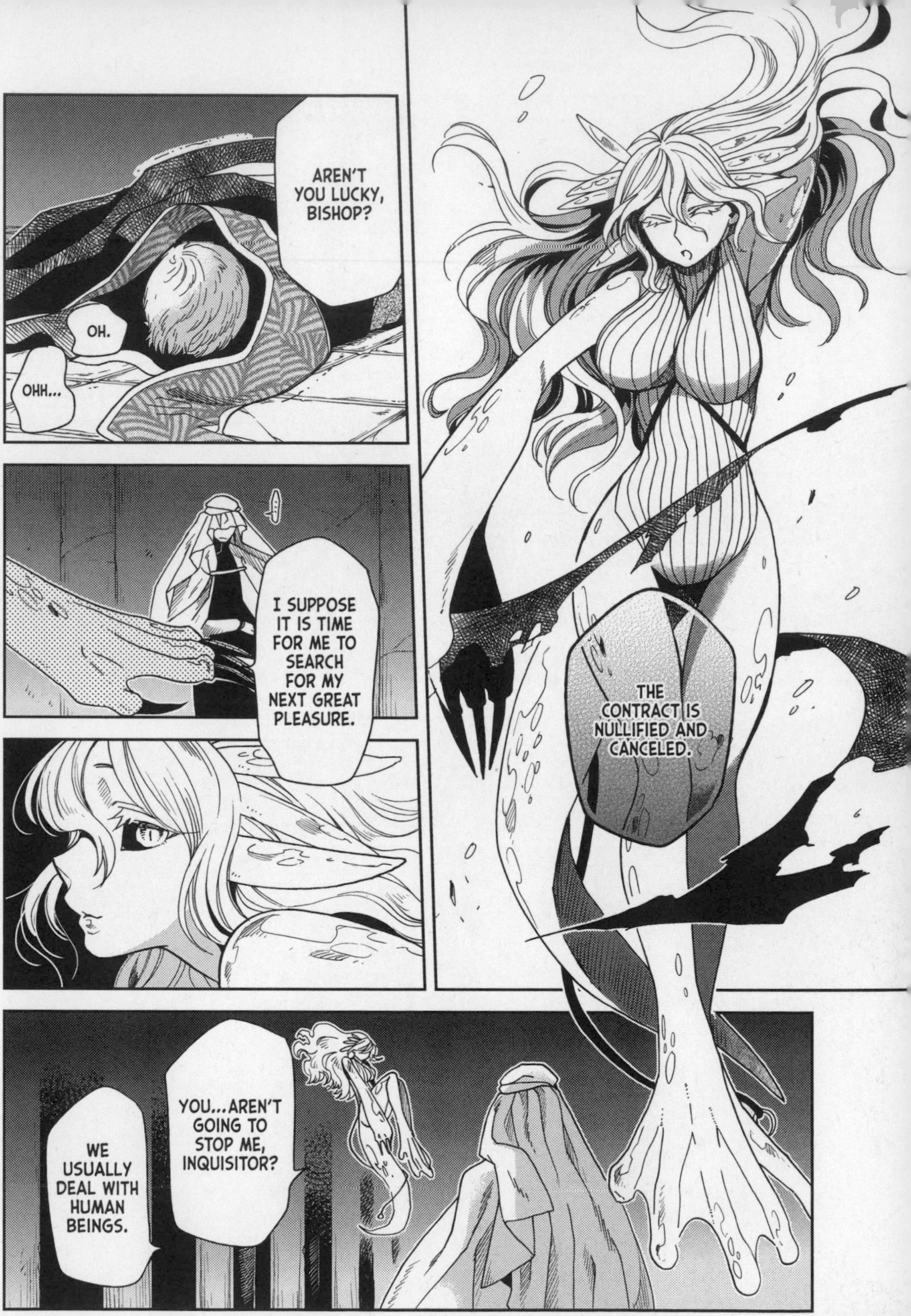
THE CONTRACT IS NULLIFIED AND CANCELED.
AREN'T YOU LUCKY, BISHOP?
OH.
OHH...
I SUPPOSE IT IS TIME FOR ME TO SEARCH FOR MY NEXT GREAT PLEASURE.
YOU...AREN'T GOING TO STOP ME, INQUISITOR?
WE USUALLY DEAL WITH HUMAN BEINGS.

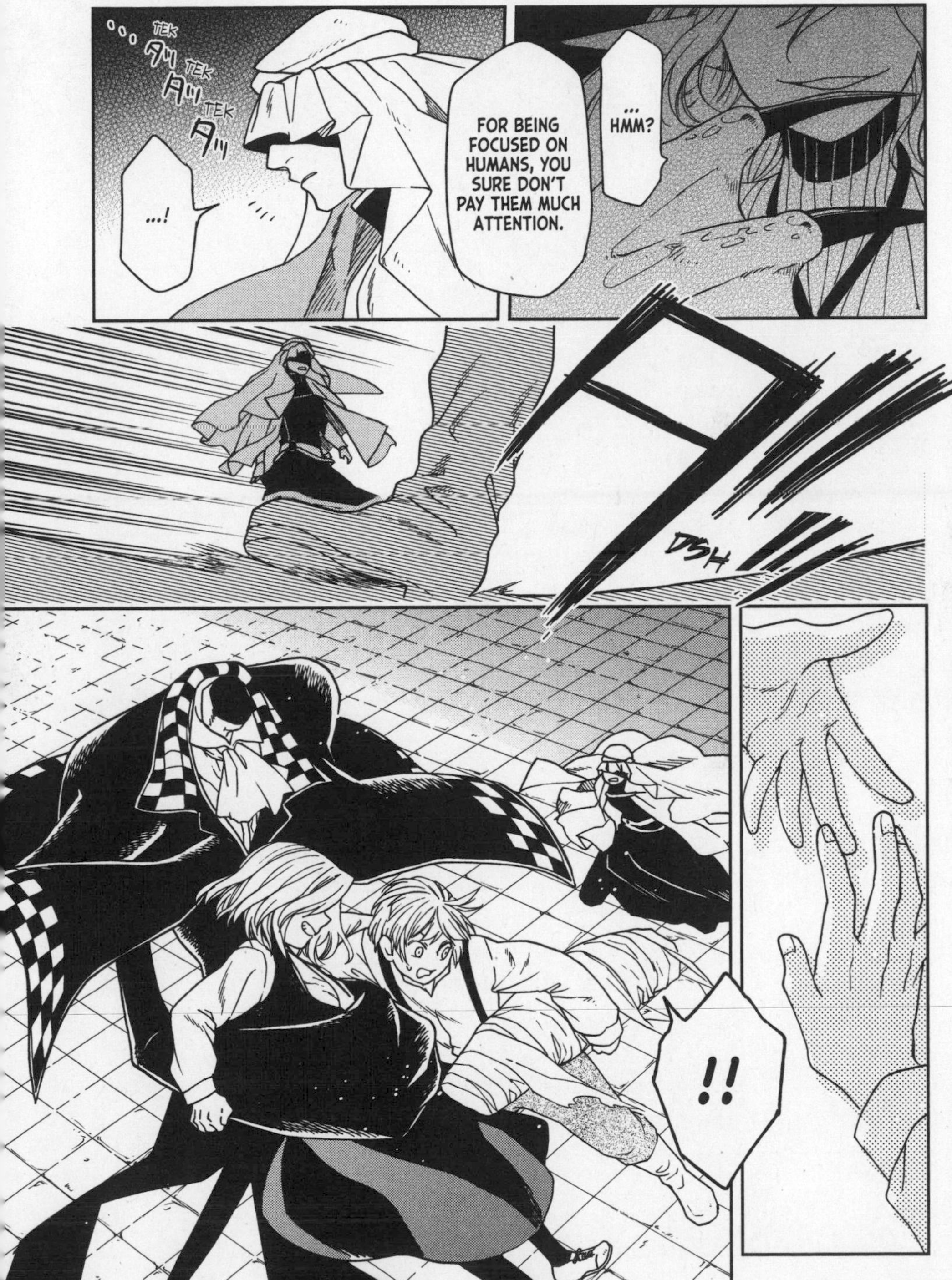
...HMM?
FOR BEING FOCUSED ON HUMANS, YOU SURE DON'T PAY THEM MUCH ATTENTION.
TEK タッ TEK タッ TEK タッ
...!
DASH
!!

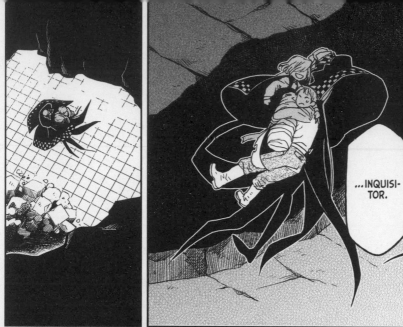

WELL DONE...

...INQUISI-TOR.

VWOOSH

FWUH

POP

TEE-HEE.

GET LOST!

UNTIL WE MEET AGAIN, DOCTOR.

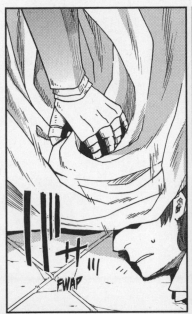

SIGH...

...WHEN I'M ALONE.

IT'S SO MUCH EASIER...

YOU DID WELL, MARION.

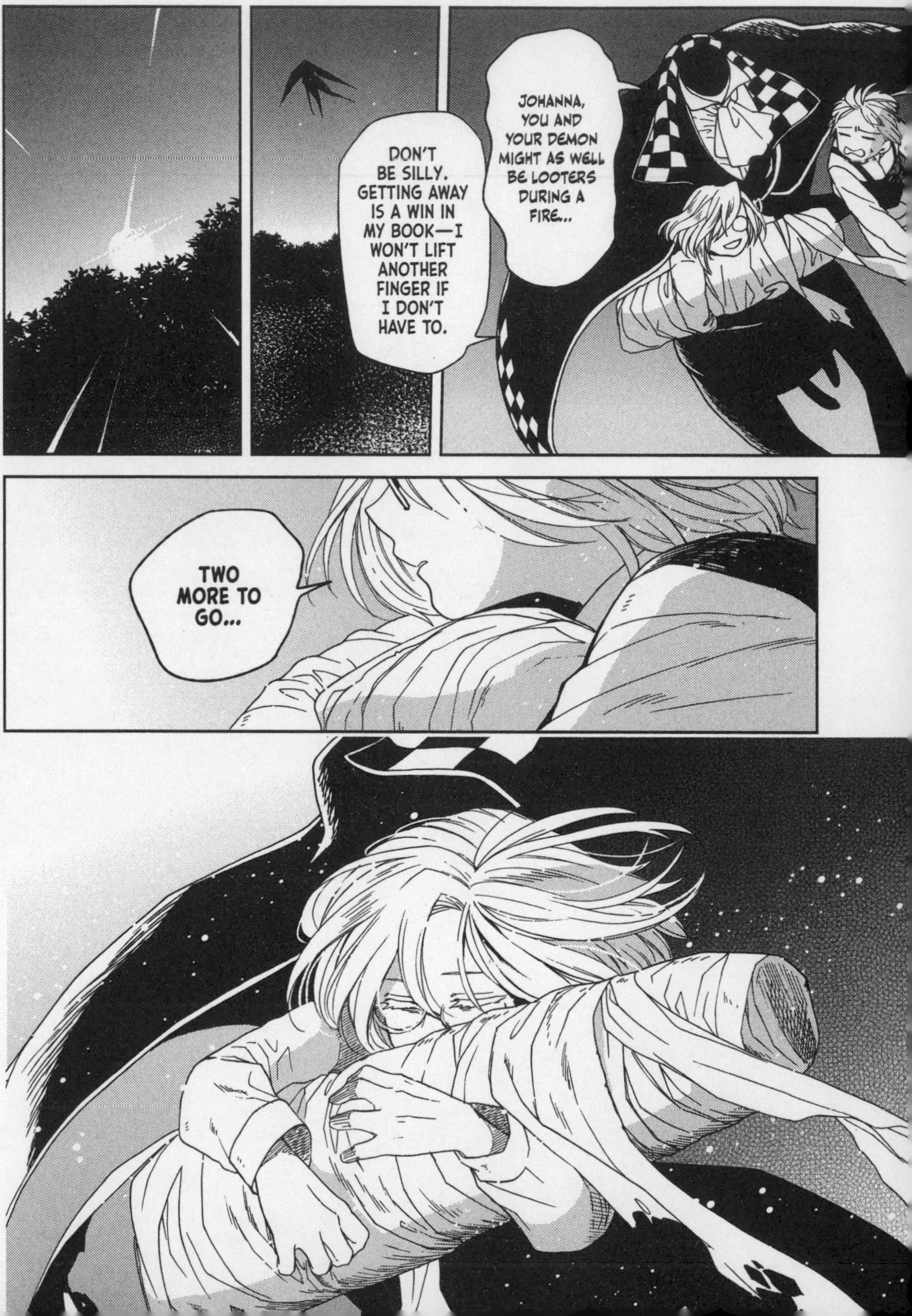
JOHANNA, YOU AND YOUR DEMON MIGHT AS WELL BE LOOTERS DURING A FIRE...
DON'T BE SILLY.
GETTING AWAY IS A WIN IN MY BOOK—I WON'T LIFT ANOTHER FINGER IF I DON'T HAVE TO.
TWO MORE TO GO...

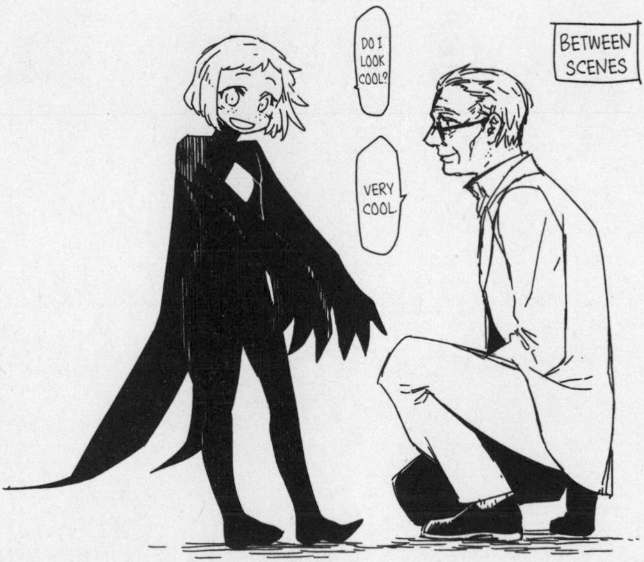
BETWEEN SCENES
DO I LOOK COOL?
VERY COOL.

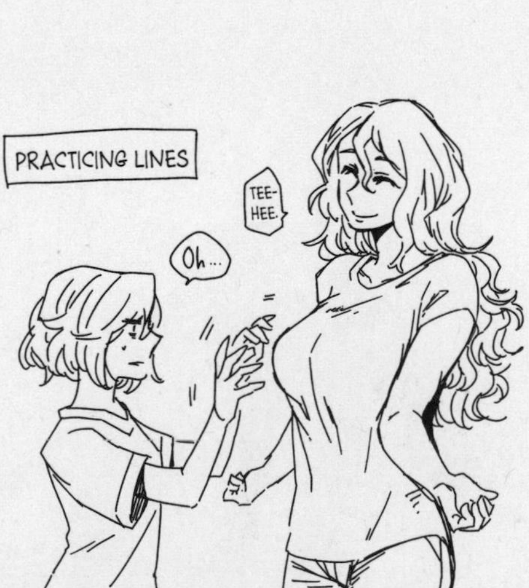
PRACTICING LINES
TEE-
HEE.
Oh...

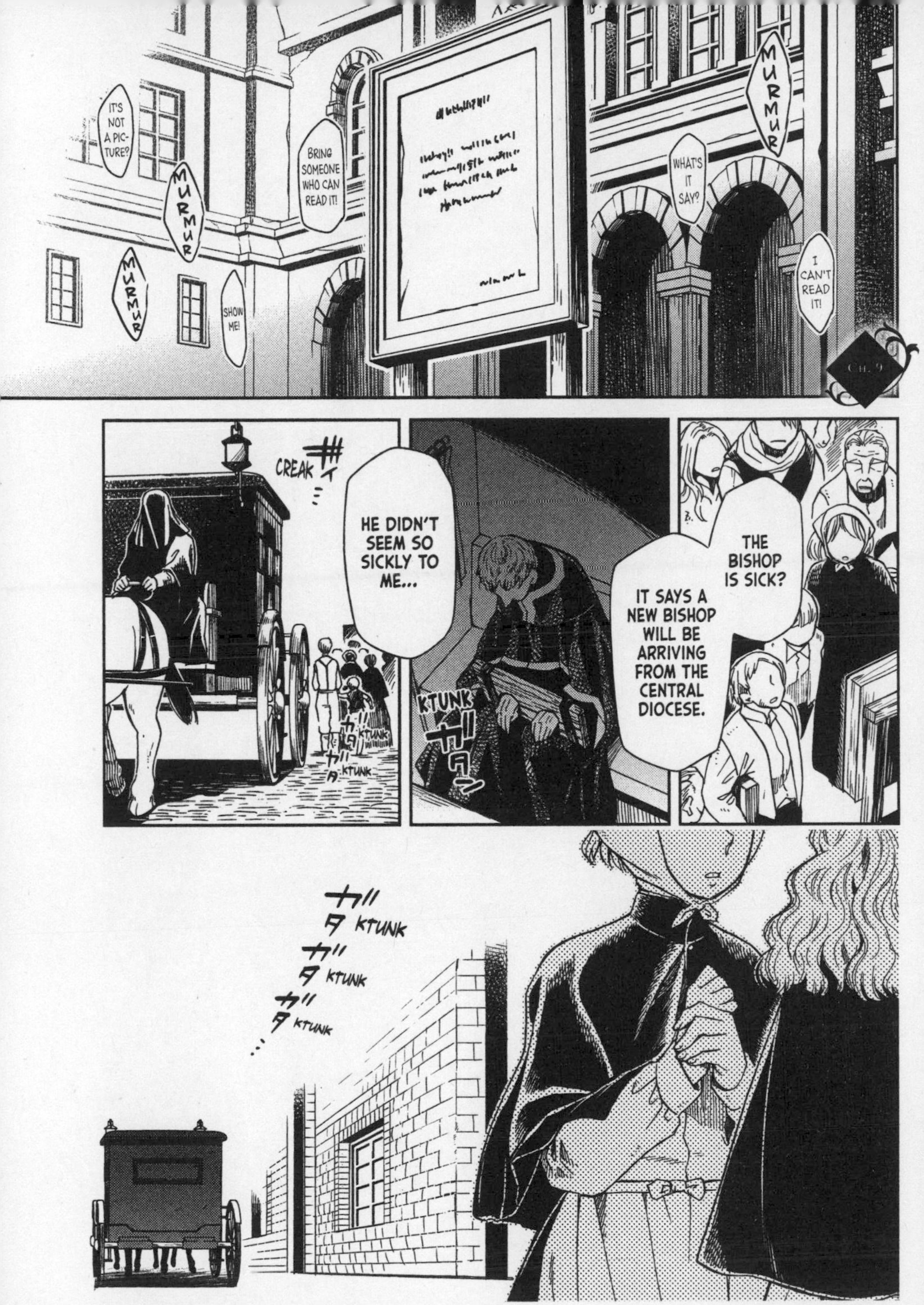
Ch. 9
MURMUR
WHAT'S IT SAY?
I CAN'T READ IT!
BRING SOMEONE WHO CAN READ IT!
IT'S NOT A PICTURE?
MURMUR
MURMUR
SHOW ME!
THE BISHOP IS SICK?
IT SAYS A NEW BISHOP WILL BE ARRIVING FROM THE CENTRAL DIOCESE.
HE DIDN'T SEEM SO SICKLY TO ME...
KTUNK
CREAK
KTUNK
KTUNK
KTUNK
KTUNK
KTUNK

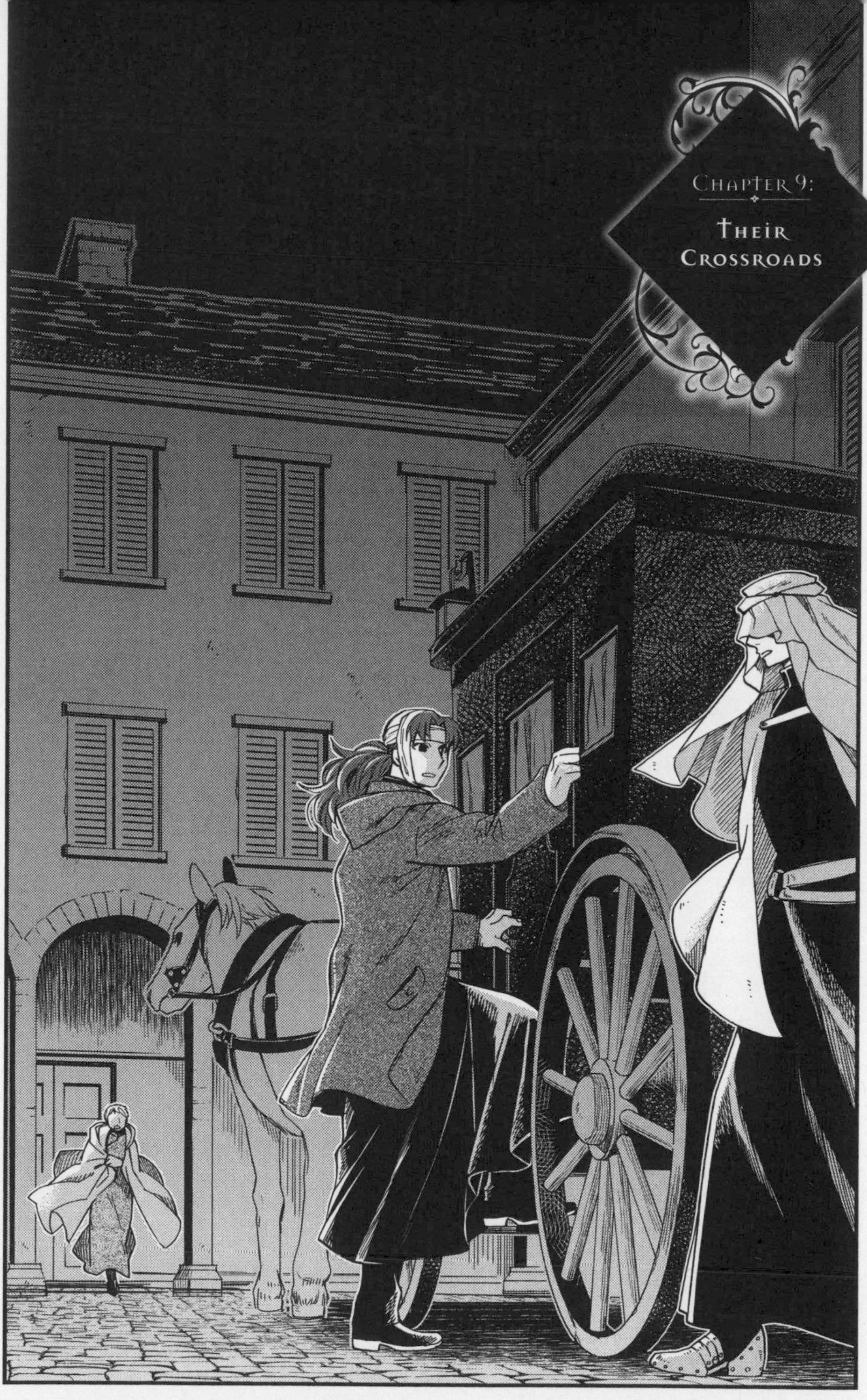
Chapter 9:
Their Crossroads

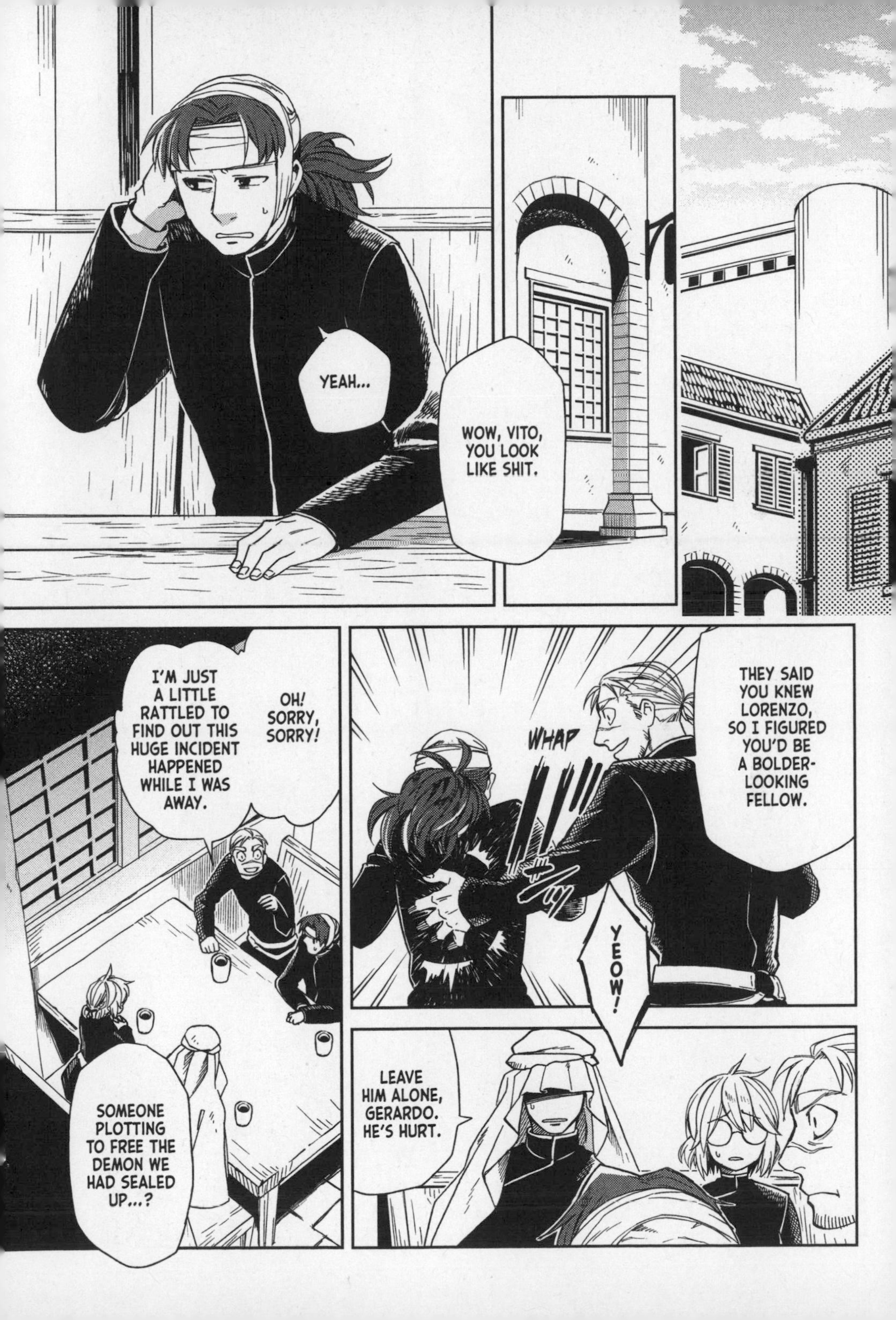
WOW, VITO, YOU LOOK LIKE SHIT.
YEAH...
THEY SAID YOU KNEW LORENZO, SO I FIGURED YOU'D BE A BOLDER-LOOKING FELLOW.
WHAP
YEOW!
LEAVE HIM ALONE, GERARDO. HE'S HURT.
OH! SORRY, SORRY!
I'M JUST A LITTLE RATTLED TO FIND OUT THIS HUGE INCIDENT HAPPENED WHILE I WAS AWAY.
SOMEONE PLOTTING TO FREE THE DEMON WE HAD SEALED UP...?

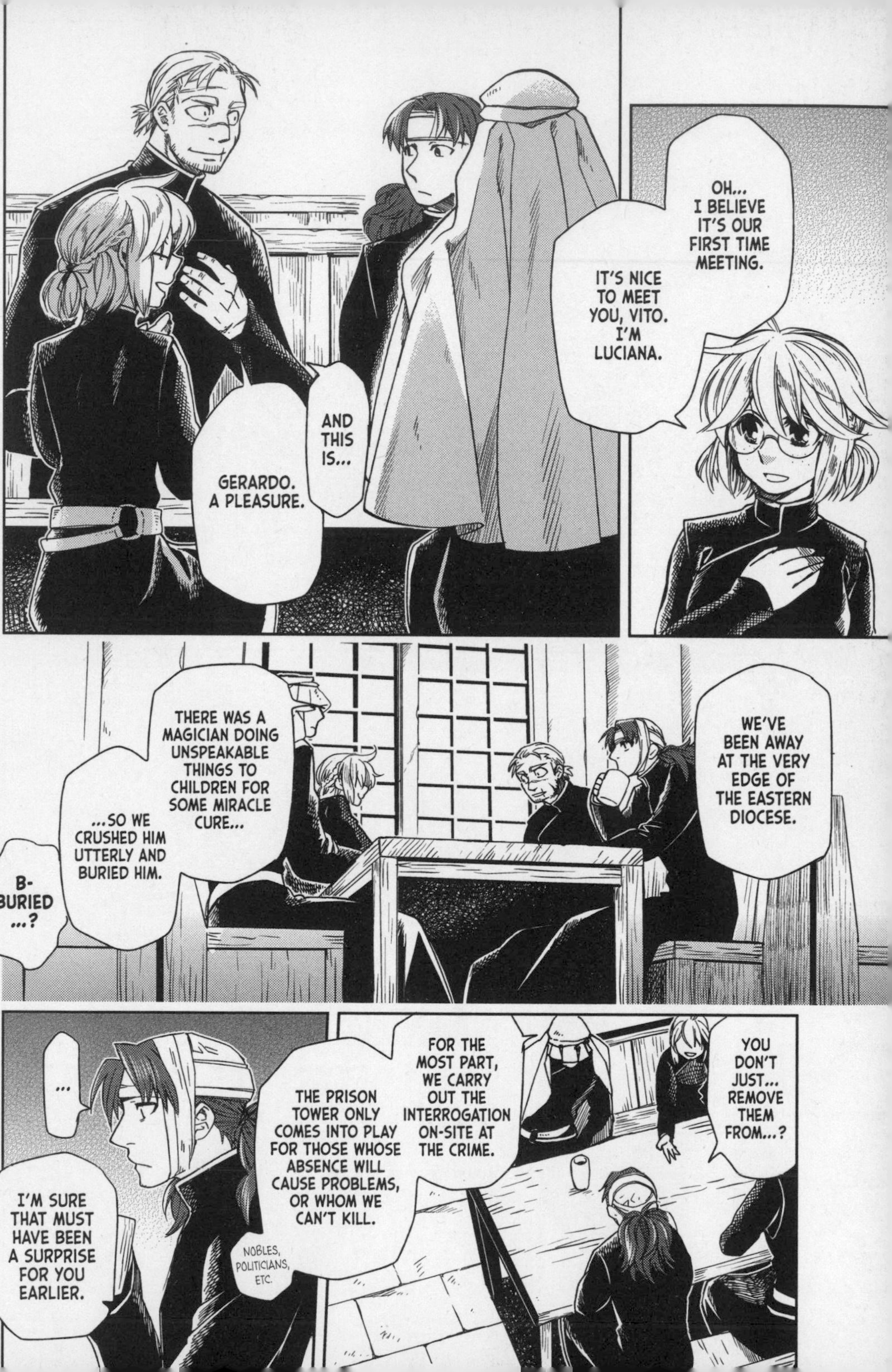
OH... I BELIEVE IT'S OUR FIRST TIME MEETING.
IT'S NICE TO MEET YOU, VITO. I'M LUCIANA.
AND THIS IS...
GERARDO. A PLEASURE.
WE'VE BEEN AWAY AT THE VERY EDGE OF THE EASTERN DIOCESE.
THERE WAS A MAGICIAN DOING UNSPEAKABLE THINGS TO CHILDREN FOR SOME MIRACLE CURE...
...SO WE CRUSHED HIM UTTERLY AND BURIED HIM.
B-BURIED...?
YOU DON'T JUST... REMOVE THEM FROM...?
FOR THE MOST PART, WE CARRY OUT THE INTERROGATION ON-SITE AT THE CRIME.
THE PRISON TOWER ONLY COMES INTO PLAY FOR THOSE WHOSE ABSENCE WILL CAUSE PROBLEMS, OR WHOM WE CAN'T KILL.
NOBLES, POLITICIANS, ETC.
...
I'M SURE THAT MUST HAVE BEEN A SURPRISE FOR YOU EARLIER.

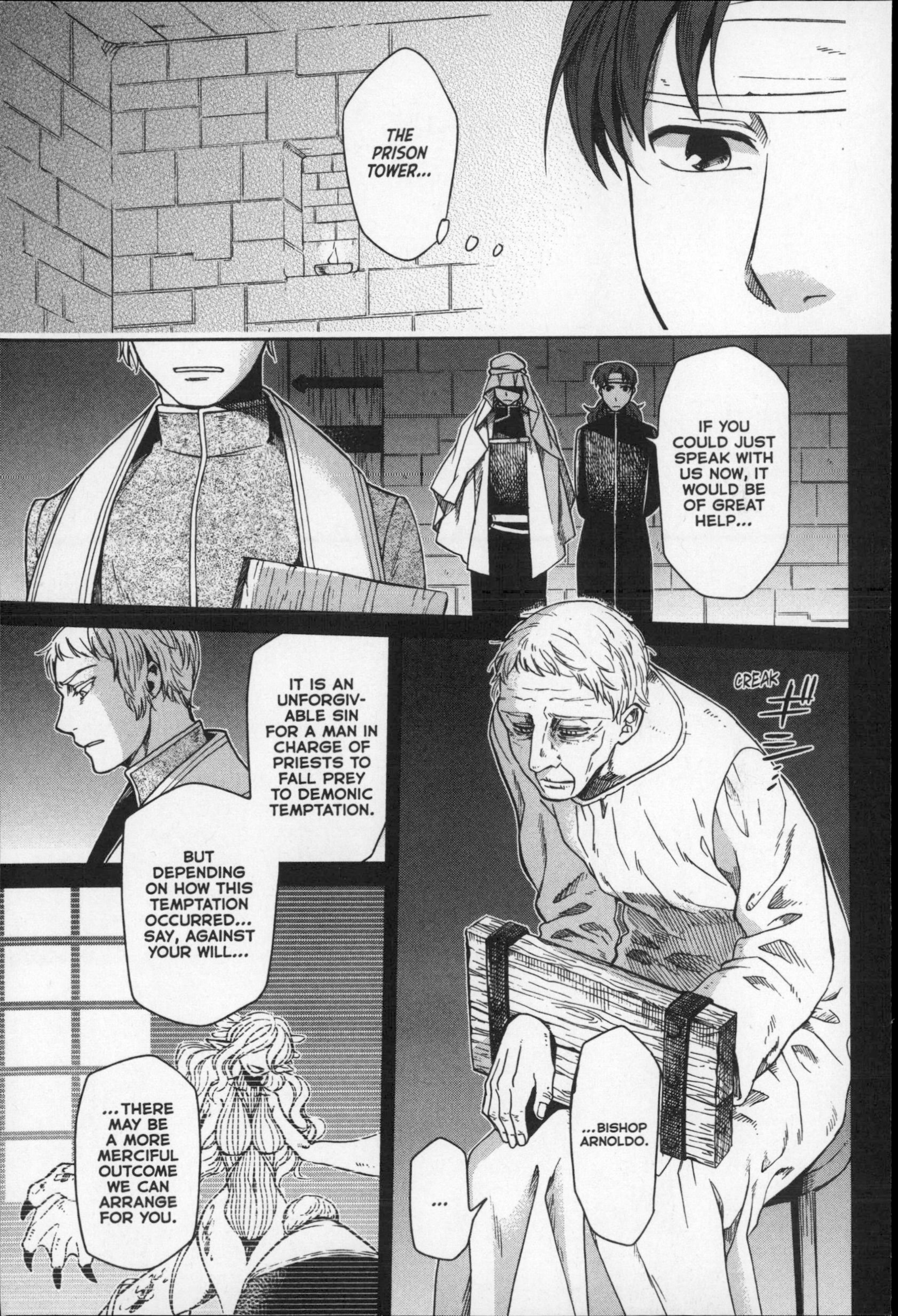
THE PRISON TOWER...
IF YOU COULD JUST SPEAK WITH US NOW, IT WOULD BE OF GREAT HELP...
CREAK
...BISHOP ARNOLDO.
...
IT IS AN UNFORGIVABLE SIN FOR A MAN IN CHARGE OF PRIESTS TO FALL PREY TO DEMONIC TEMPTATION.
BUT DEPENDING ON HOW THIS TEMPTATION OCCURRED... SAY, AGAINST YOUR WILL...
...THERE MAY BE A MORE MERCIFUL OUTCOME WE CAN ARRANGE FOR YOU.

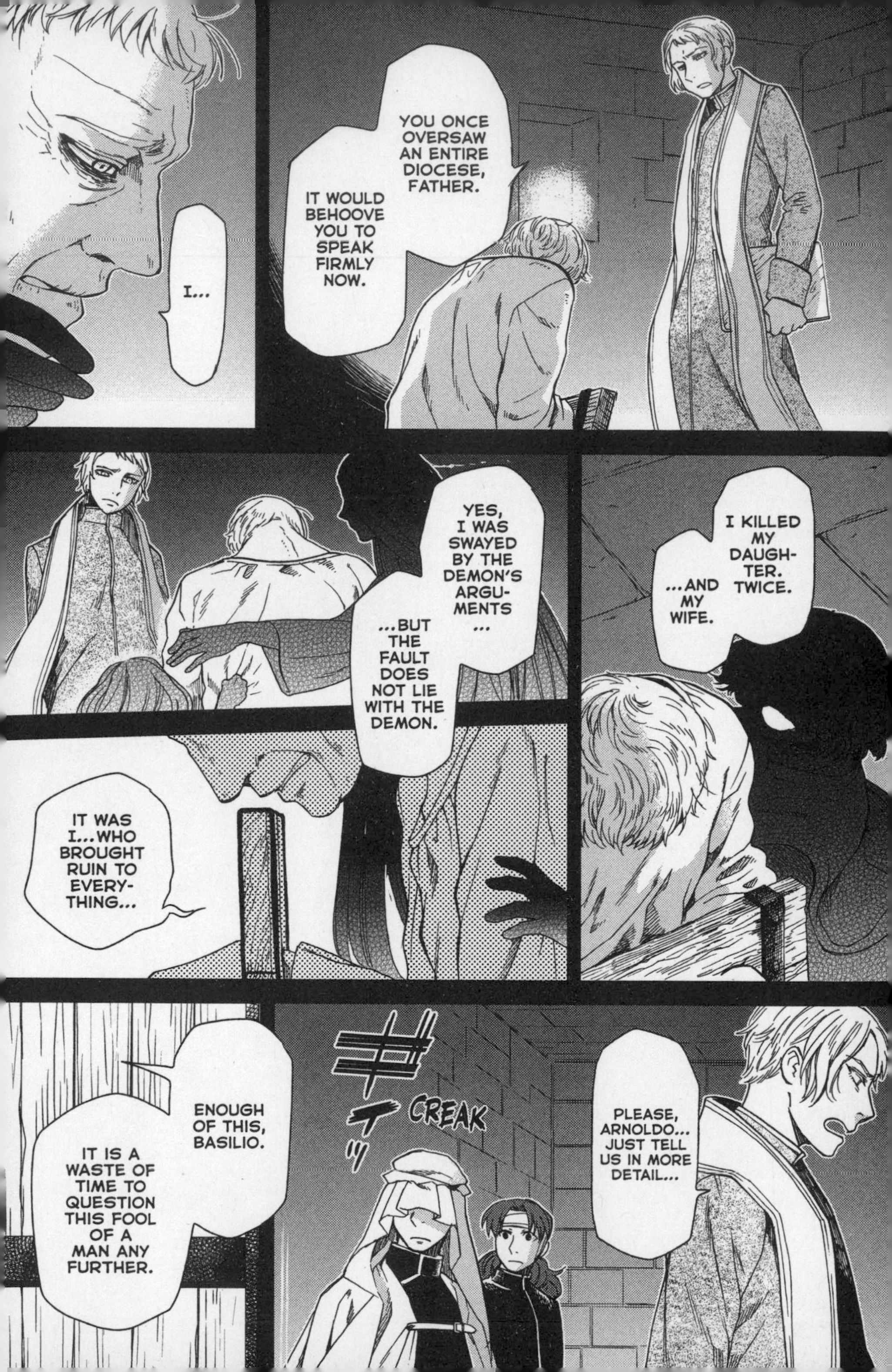
YOU ONCE OVERSAW AN ENTIRE DIOCESE, FATHER.
IT WOULD BEHOOVE YOU TO SPEAK FIRMLY NOW.
I...
I KILLED MY DAUGHTER. TWICE.
...AND MY WIFE.
YES, I WAS SWAYED BY THE DEMON'S ARGUMENTS...
...BUT THE FAULT DOES NOT LIE WITH THE DEMON.
IT WAS I...WHO BROUGHT RUIN TO EVERYTHING...
PLEASE, ARNOLDO... JUST TELL US IN MORE DETAIL...
CREAK
ENOUGH OF THIS, BASILIO.
IT IS A WASTE OF TIME TO QUESTION THIS FOOL OF A MAN ANY FURTHER.

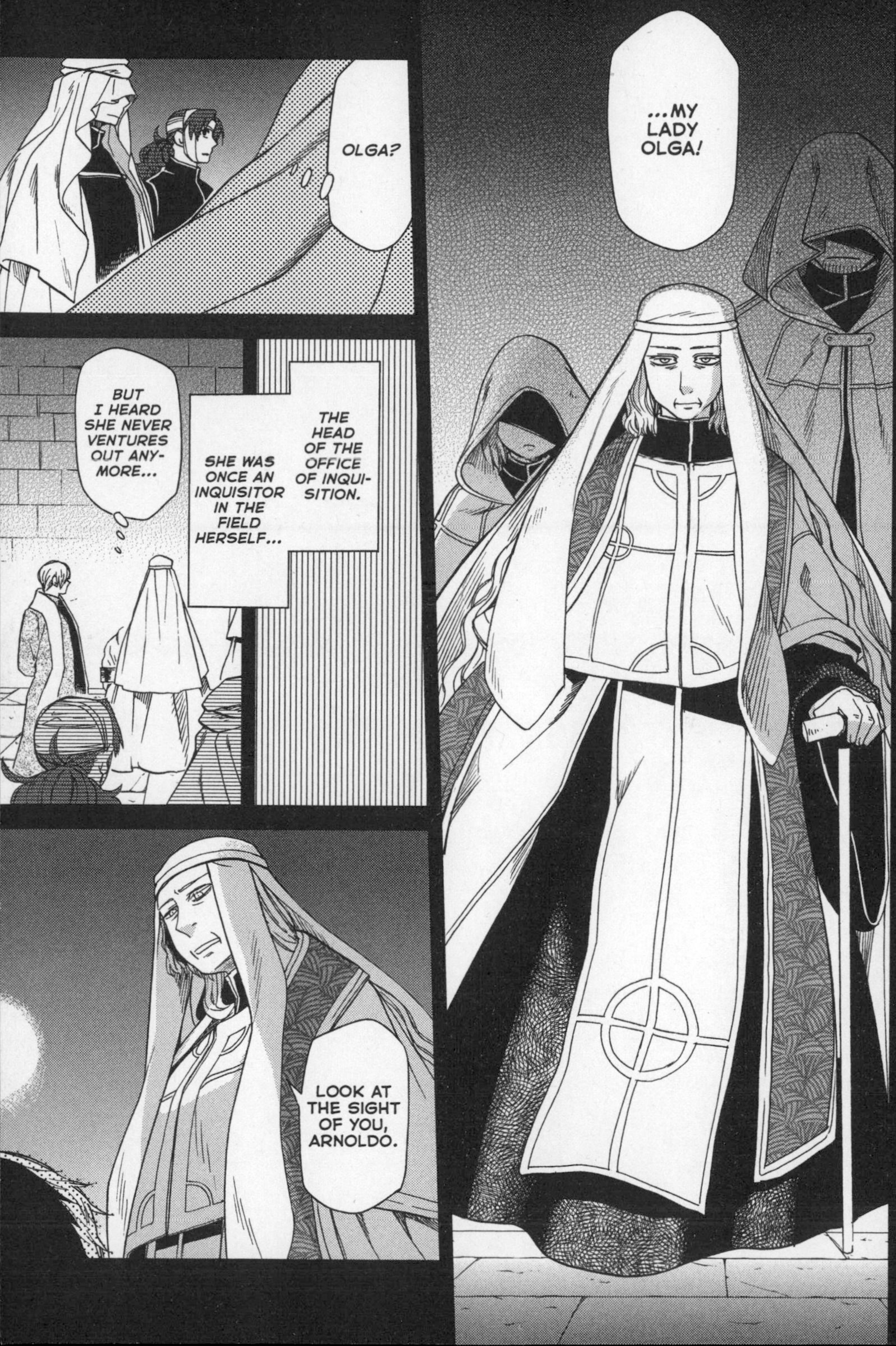
...MY LADY OLGA!
OLGA?
THE HEAD OF THE OFFICE OF INQUISITION.
SHE WAS ONCE AN INQUISITOR IN THE FIELD HERSELF...
BUT I HEARD SHE NEVER VENTURES OUT ANY-MORE...
LOOK AT THE SIGHT OF YOU, ARNOLDO.

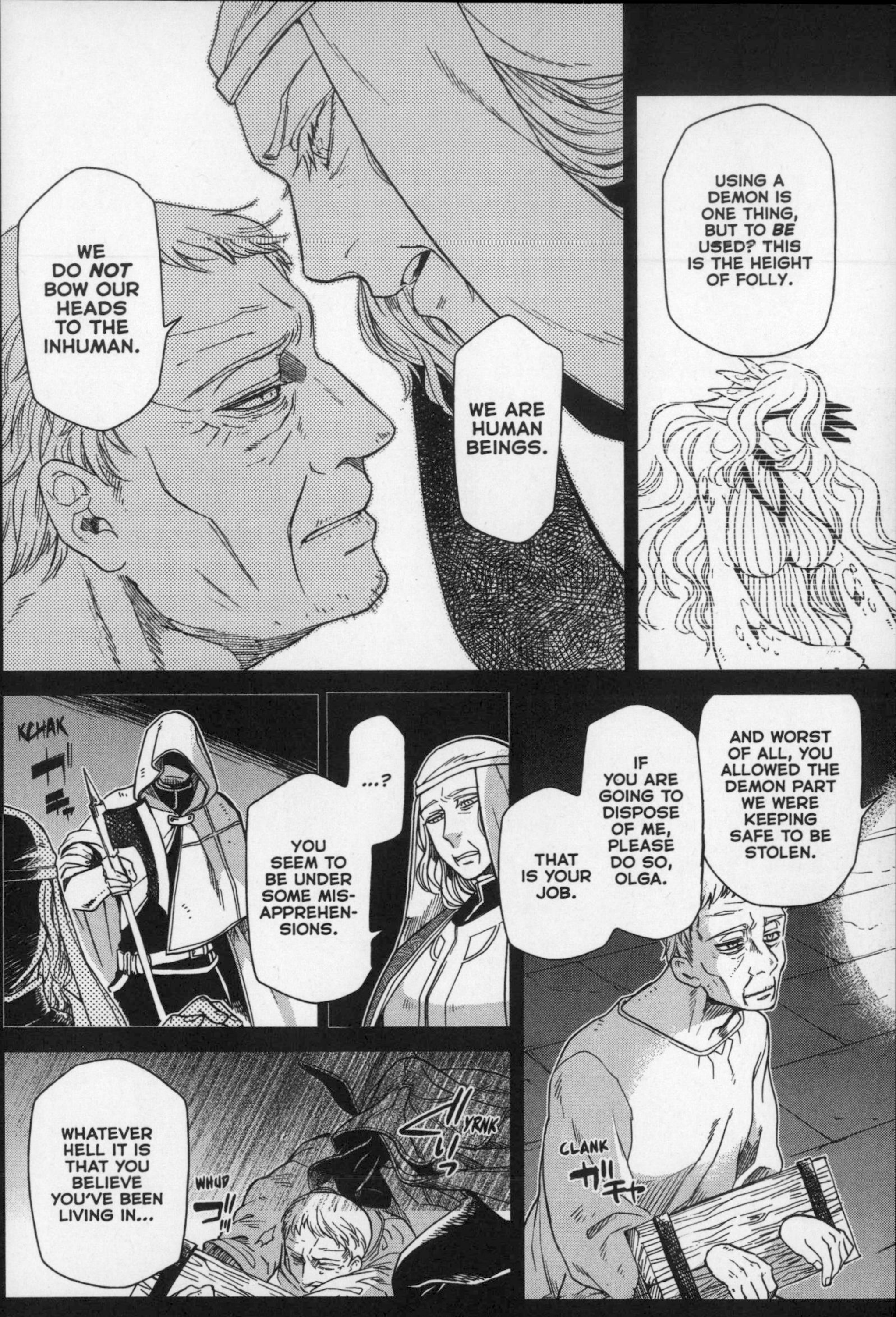
USING A DEMON IS ONE THING, BUT TO *BE* USED? THIS IS THE HEIGHT OF FOLLY.
WE ARE HUMAN BEINGS.
WE DO *NOT* BOW OUR HEADS TO THE INHUMAN.
AND WORST OF ALL, YOU ALLOWED THE DEMON PART WE WERE KEEPING SAFE TO BE STOLEN.
IF YOU ARE GOING TO DISPOSE OF ME, PLEASE DO SO, OLGA.
THAT IS YOUR JOB.
CLANK
...?
YOU SEEM TO BE UNDER SOME MIS-APPREHENSIONS.
KCHAK
YRNK
WHATEVER HELL IT IS THAT YOU BELIEVE YOU'VE BEEN LIVING IN...
WHUD

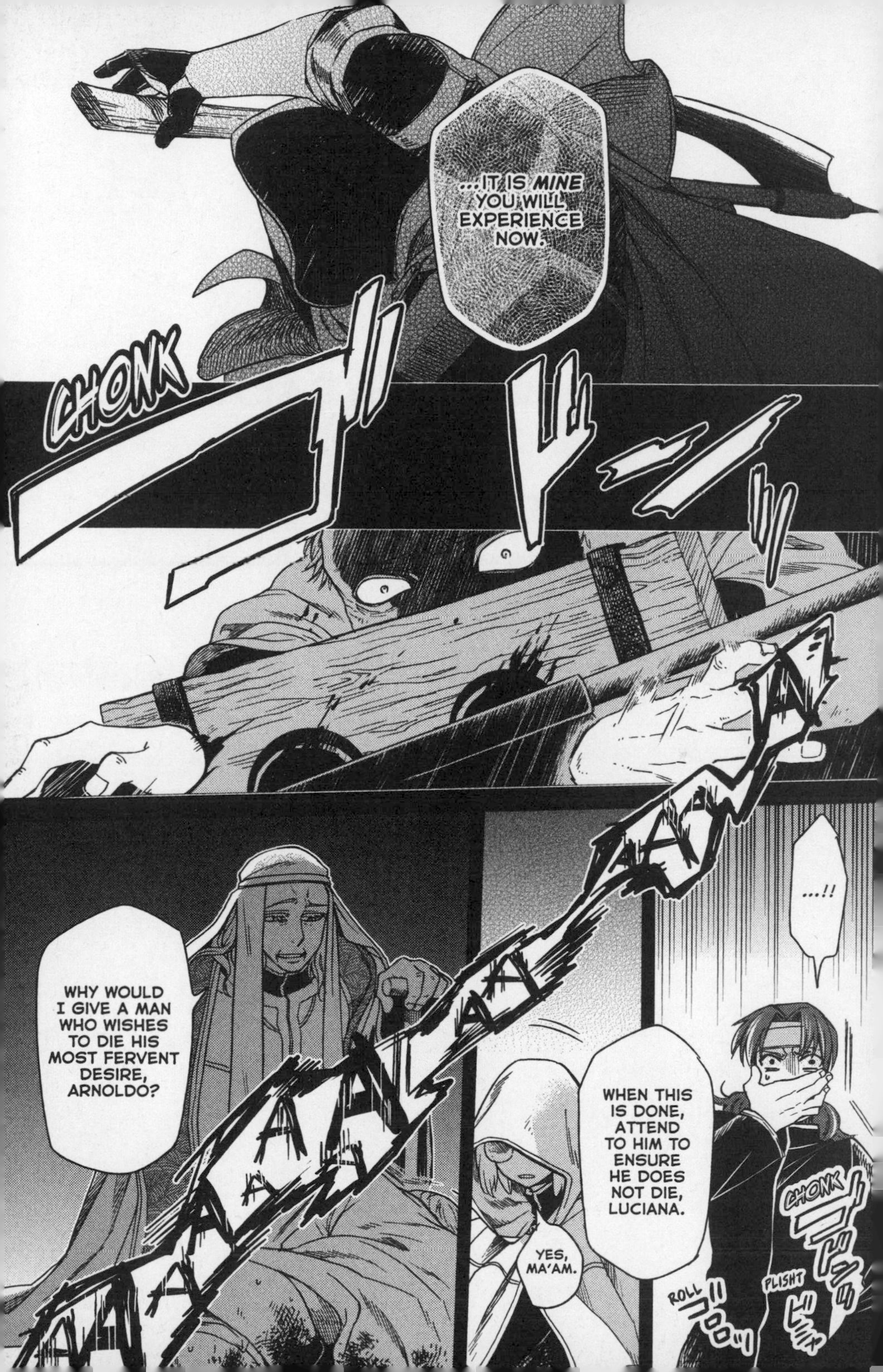
...IT IS MINE YOU WILL EXPERIENCE NOW.
CHONK
...!!
WHEN THIS IS DONE, ATTEND TO HIM TO ENSURE HE DOES NOT DIE, LUCIANA.
YES, MA'AM.
CHONK
PLISHT
ROLL
WHY WOULD I GIVE A MAN WHO WISHES TO DIE HIS MOST FERVENT DESIRE, ARNOLDO?

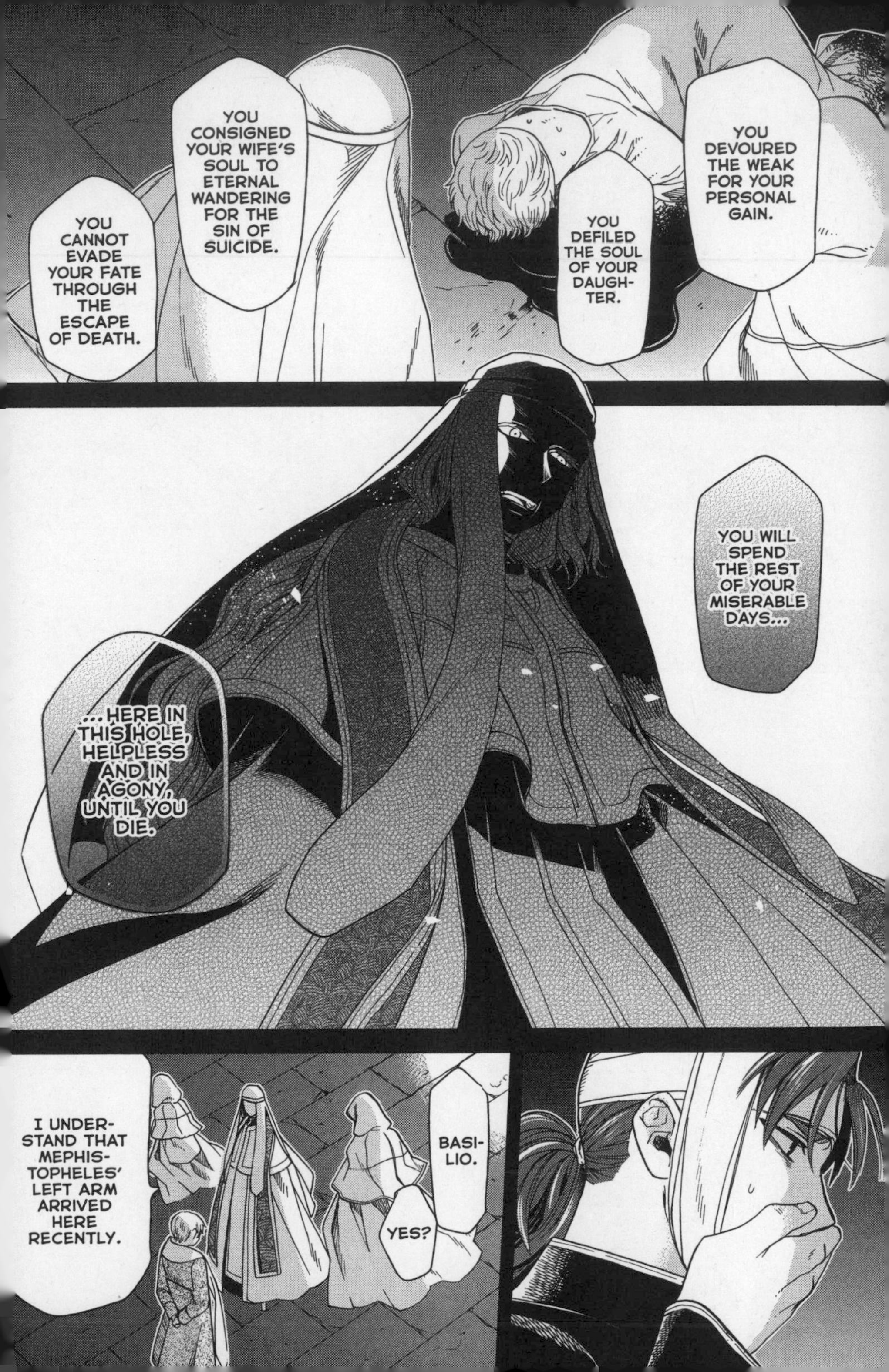
YOU DEVOURED THE WEAK FOR YOUR PERSONAL GAIN.
YOU DEFILED THE SOUL OF YOUR DAUGH-TER.
YOU CONSIGNED YOUR WIFE'S SOUL TO ETERNAL WANDERING FOR THE SIN OF SUICIDE.
YOU CANNOT EVADE YOUR FATE THROUGH THE ESCAPE OF DEATH.
YOU WILL SPEND THE REST OF YOUR MISERABLE DAYS...
...HERE IN THIS HOLE, HELPLESS AND IN AGONY, UNTIL YOU DIE.
BASI-LIO.
YES?
I UNDER-STAND THAT MEPHIS-TOPHELES' LEFT ARM ARRIVED HERE RECENTLY.

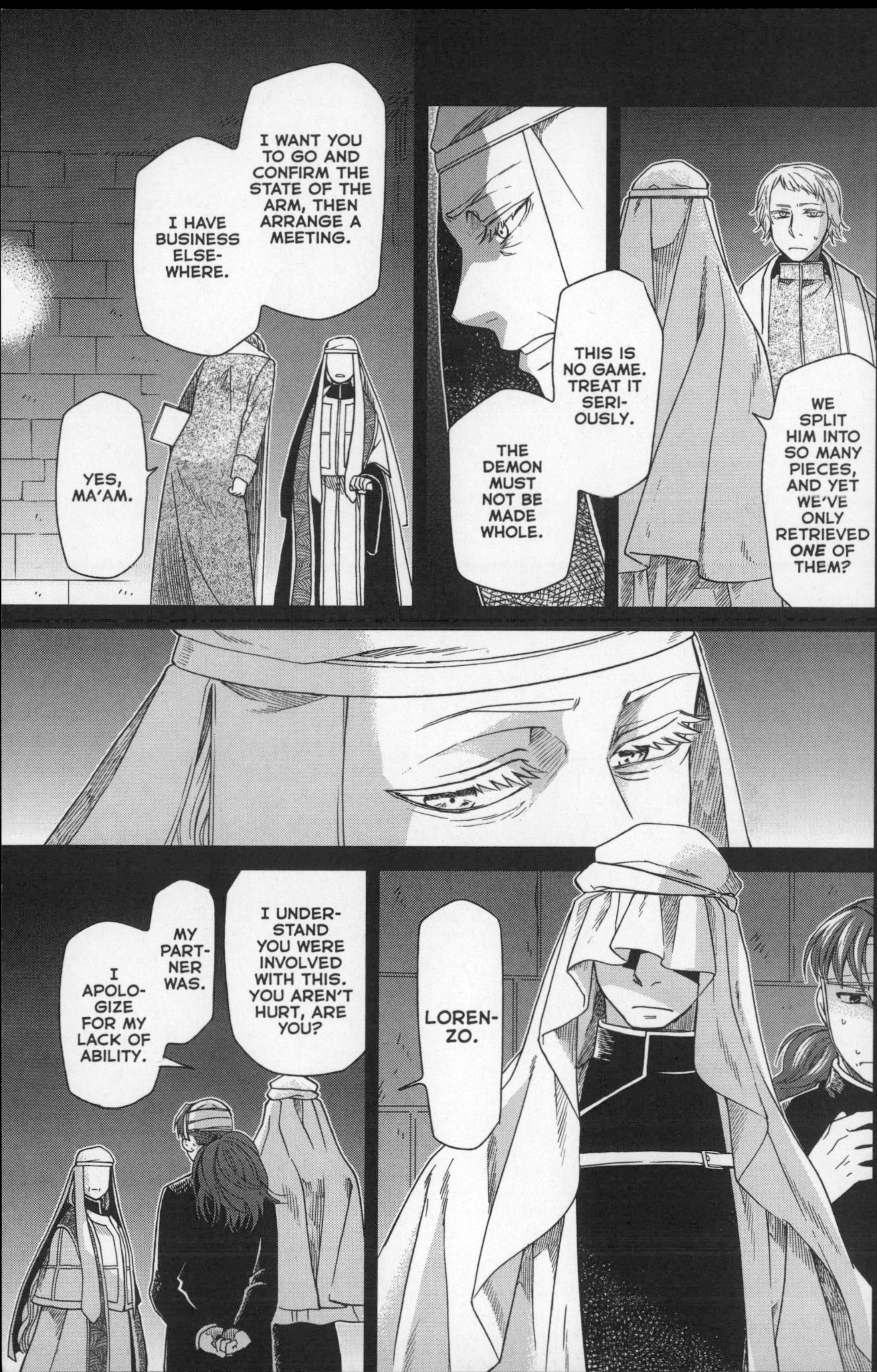
WE SPLIT HIM INTO SO MANY PIECES, AND YET WE'VE ONLY RETRIEVED *ONE* OF THEM?
THIS IS NO GAME. TREAT IT SERIOUSLY.
THE DEMON MUST NOT BE MADE WHOLE.
I WANT YOU TO GO AND CONFIRM THE STATE OF THE ARM, THEN ARRANGE A MEETING.
I HAVE BUSINESS ELSEWHERE.
YES, MA'AM.
LORENZO.
I UNDERSTAND YOU WERE INVOLVED WITH THIS. YOU AREN'T HURT, ARE YOU?
MY PARTNER WAS.
I APOLOGIZE FOR MY LACK OF ABILITY.

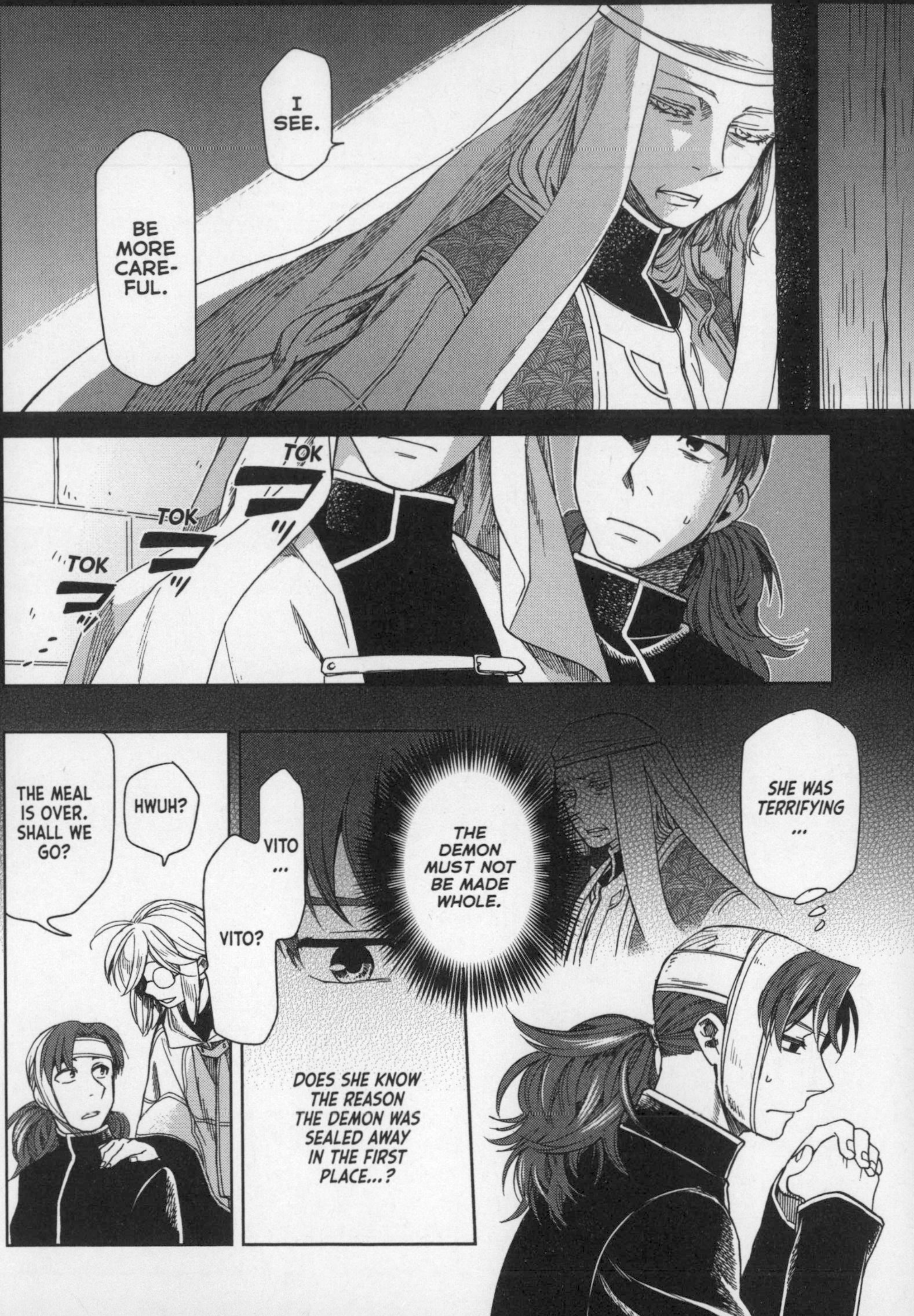
I SEE.
BE MORE CARE-FUL.
TOK
TOK
TOK
SHE WAS TERRIFYING ...
THE DEMON MUST NOT BE MADE WHOLE.
DOES SHE KNOW THE REASON THE DEMON WAS SEALED AWAY IN THE FIRST PLACE...?
VITO ...
VITO?
HWUH?
THE MEAL IS OVER. SHALL WE GO?

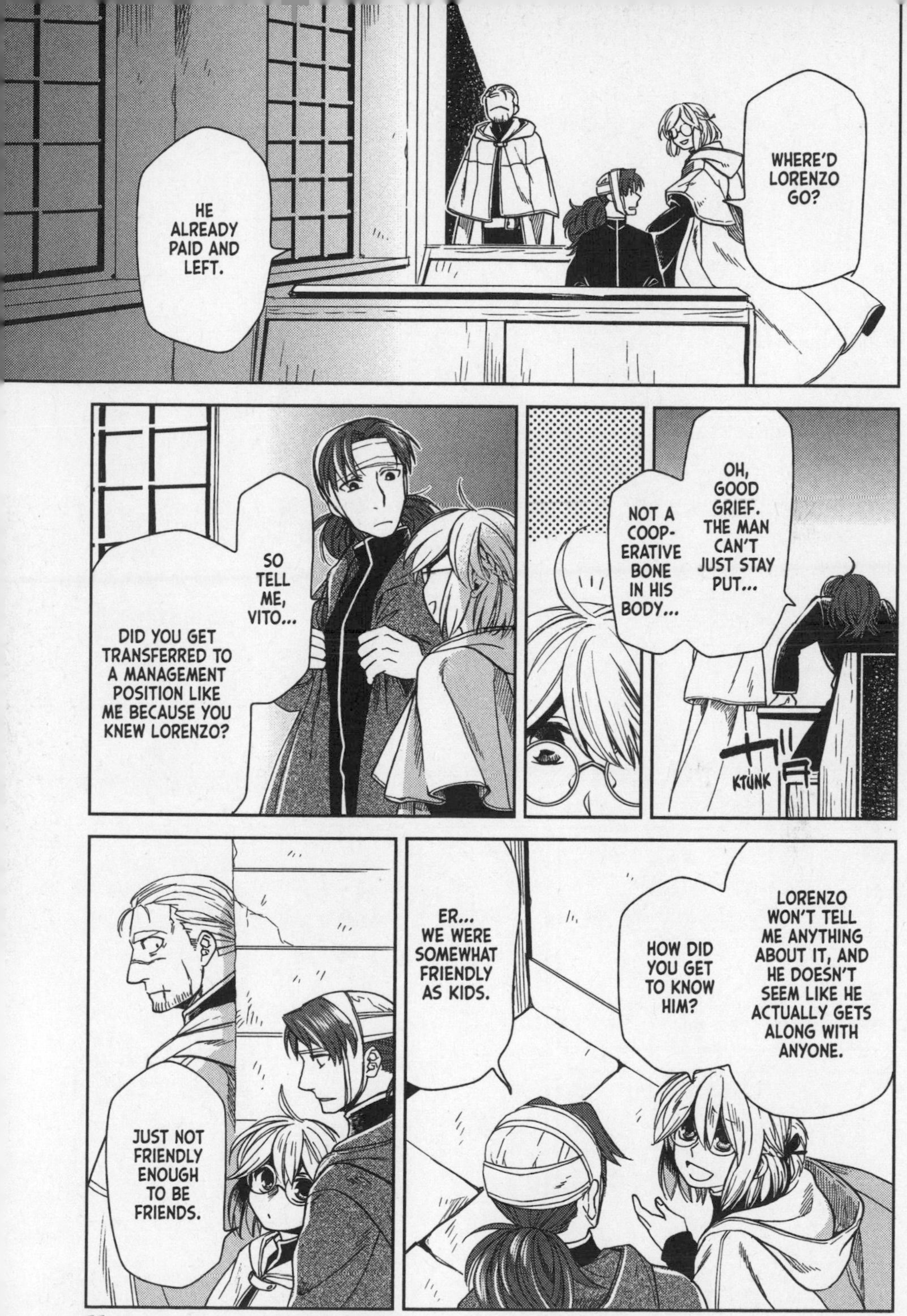
WHERE'D LORENZO GO?
HE ALREADY PAID AND LEFT.
OH, GOOD GRIEF. THE MAN CAN'T JUST STAY PUT...
NOT A COOP-ERATIVE BONE IN HIS BODY...
KTUNK
SO TELL ME, VITO...
DID YOU GET TRANSFERRED TO A MANAGEMENT POSITION LIKE ME BECAUSE YOU KNEW LORENZO?
LORENZO WON'T TELL ME ANYTHING ABOUT IT, AND HE DOESN'T SEEM LIKE HE ACTUALLY GETS ALONG WITH ANYONE.
HOW DID YOU GET TO KNOW HIM?
ER... WE WERE SOMEWHAT FRIENDLY AS KIDS.
JUST NOT FRIENDLY ENOUGH TO BE FRIENDS.

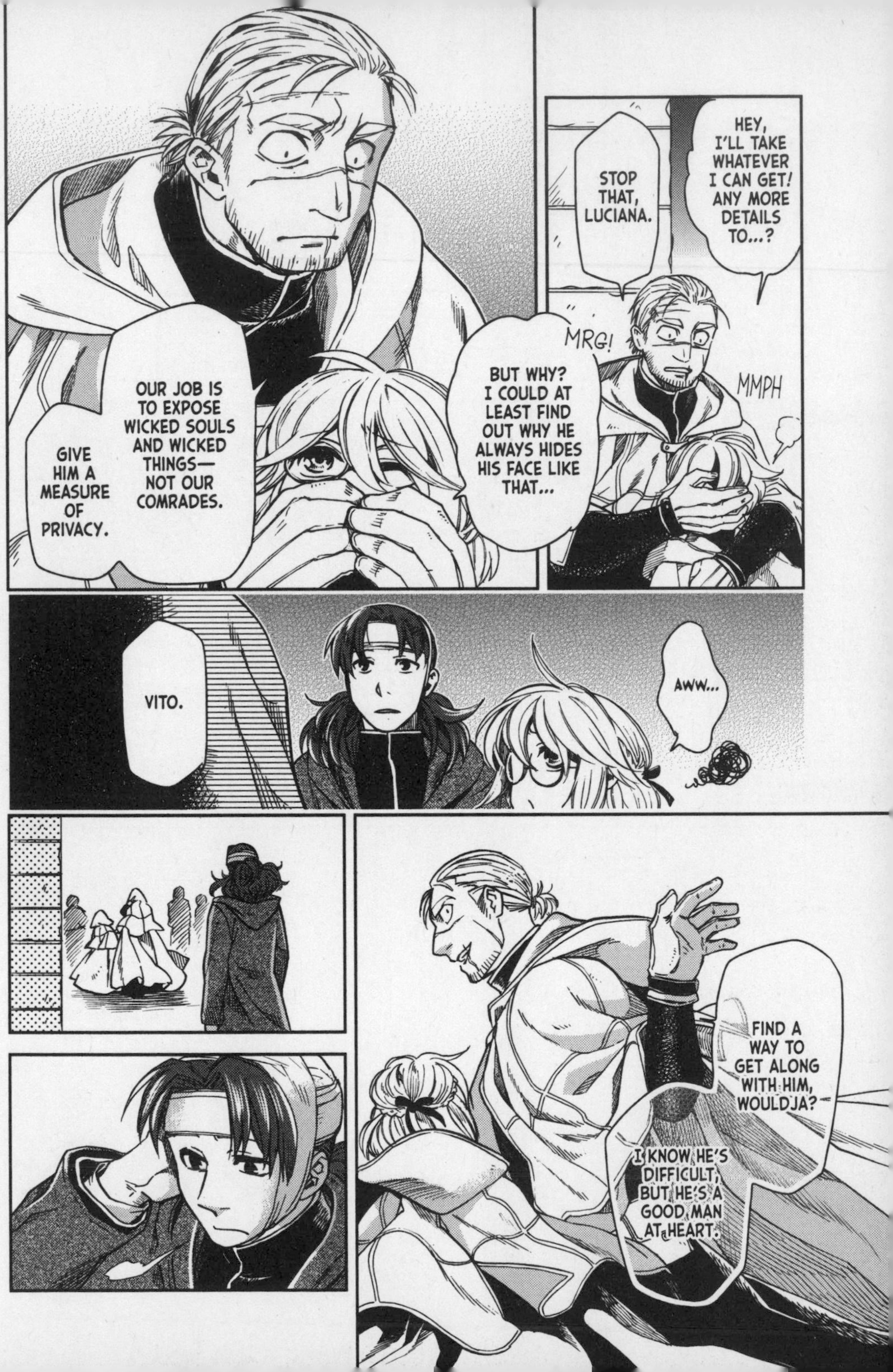
HEY, I'LL TAKE WHATEVER I CAN GET! ANY MORE DETAILS TO...?
STOP THAT, LUCIANA.
MRG!
MMPH
BUT WHY? I COULD AT LEAST FIND OUT WHY HE ALWAYS HIDES HIS FACE LIKE THAT...
OUR JOB IS TO EXPOSE WICKED SOULS AND WICKED THINGS— NOT OUR COMRADES.
GIVE HIM A MEASURE OF PRIVACY.
AWW...
VITO.
FIND A WAY TO GET ALONG WITH HIM, WOULDJA?
I KNOW HE'S DIFFICULT, BUT HE'S A GOOD MAN AT HEART.

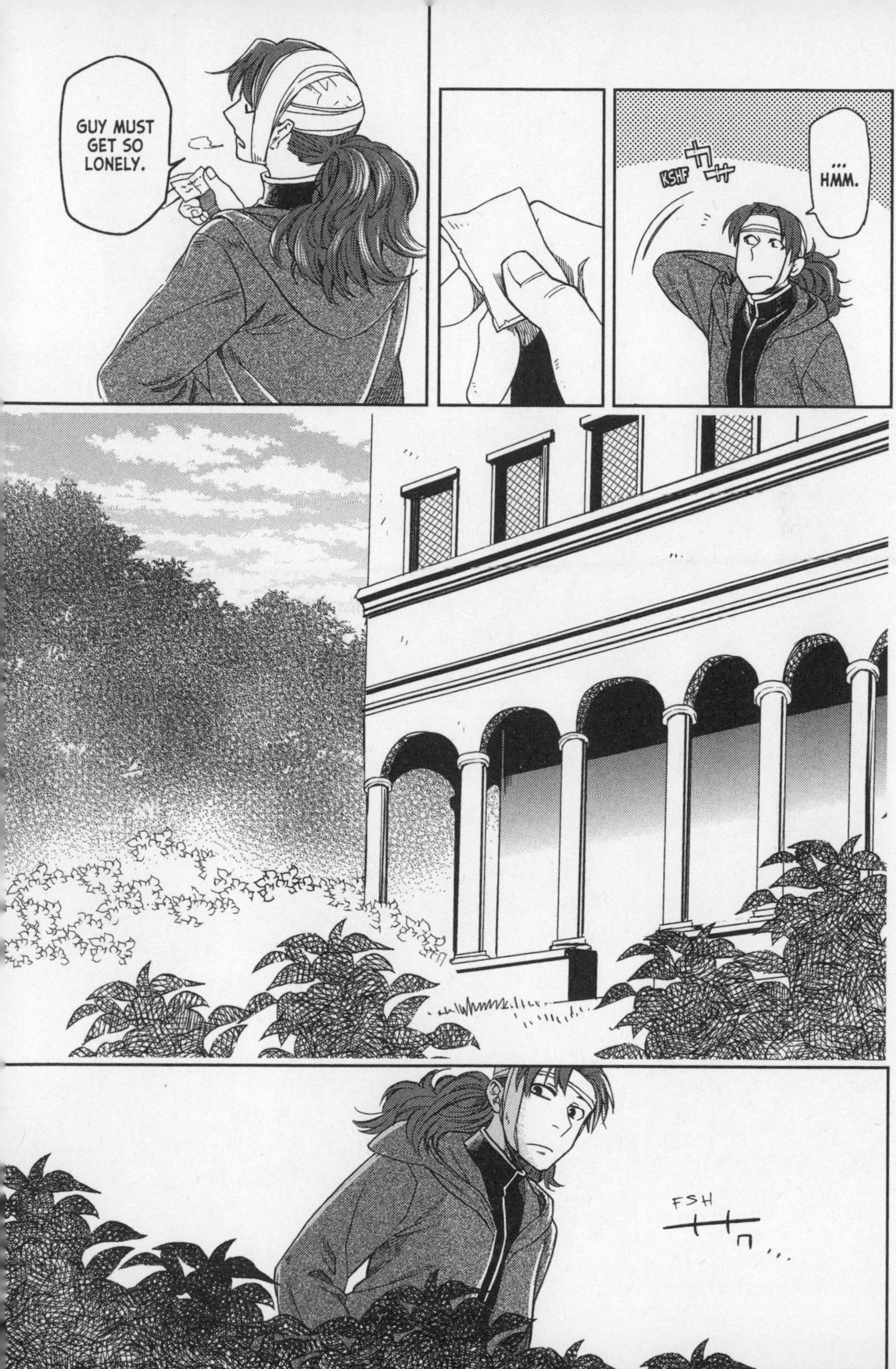
... HMM.
KSHF
GUY MUST GET SO LONELY.
FSH

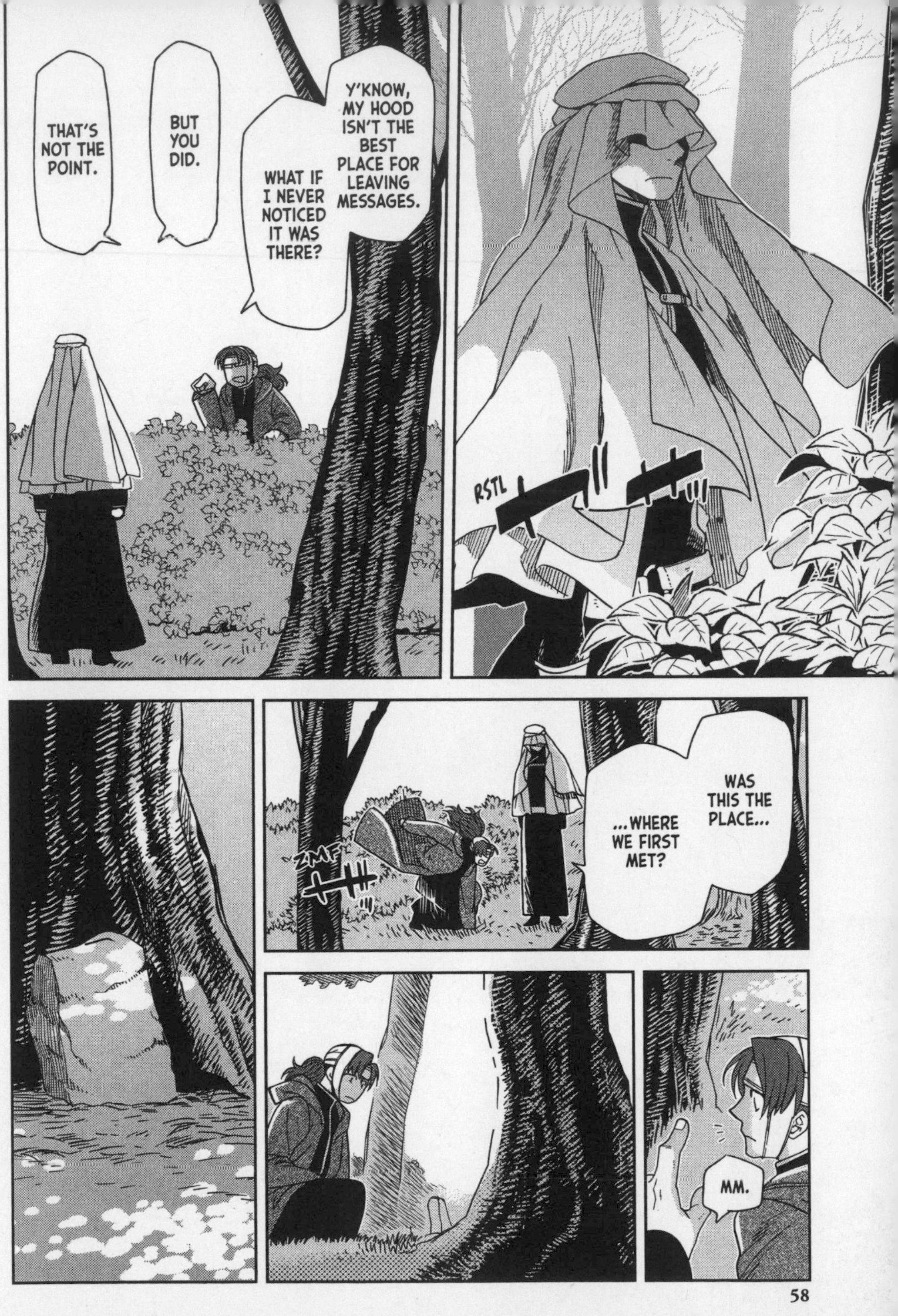
RSTL
Y'KNOW, MY HOOD ISN'T THE BEST PLACE FOR LEAVING MESSAGES.
WHAT IF I NEVER NOTICED IT WAS THERE?
BUT YOU DID.
THAT'S NOT THE POINT.
WAS THIS THE PLACE...
...WHERE WE FIRST MET?
ZMF
MM.

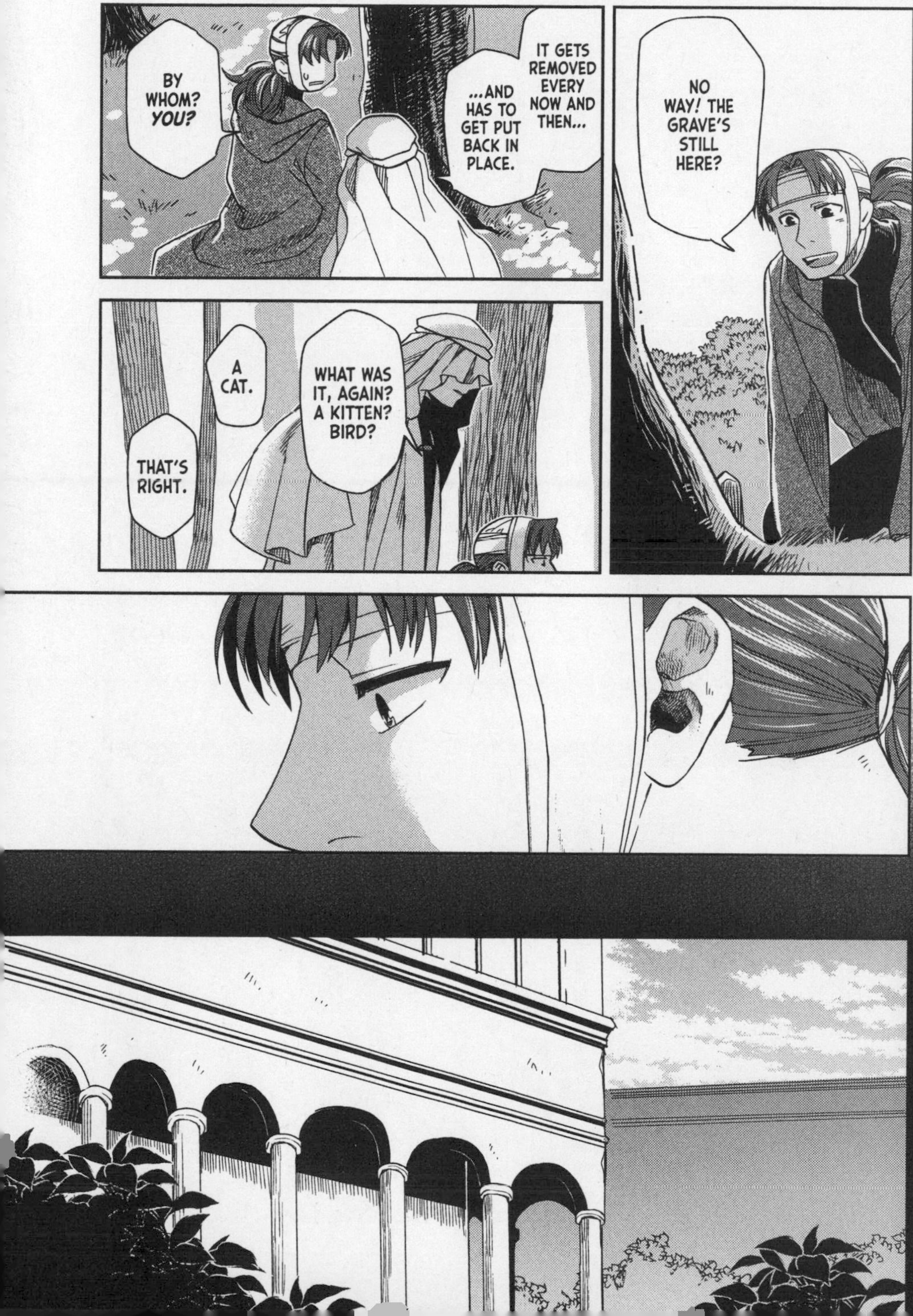
NO WAY! THE GRAVE'S STILL HERE?
IT GETS REMOVED EVERY NOW AND THEN...
...AND HAS TO GET PUT BACK IN PLACE.
BY WHOM? *YOU?*
WHAT WAS IT, AGAIN? A KITTEN? BIRD?
A CAT.
THAT'S RIGHT.

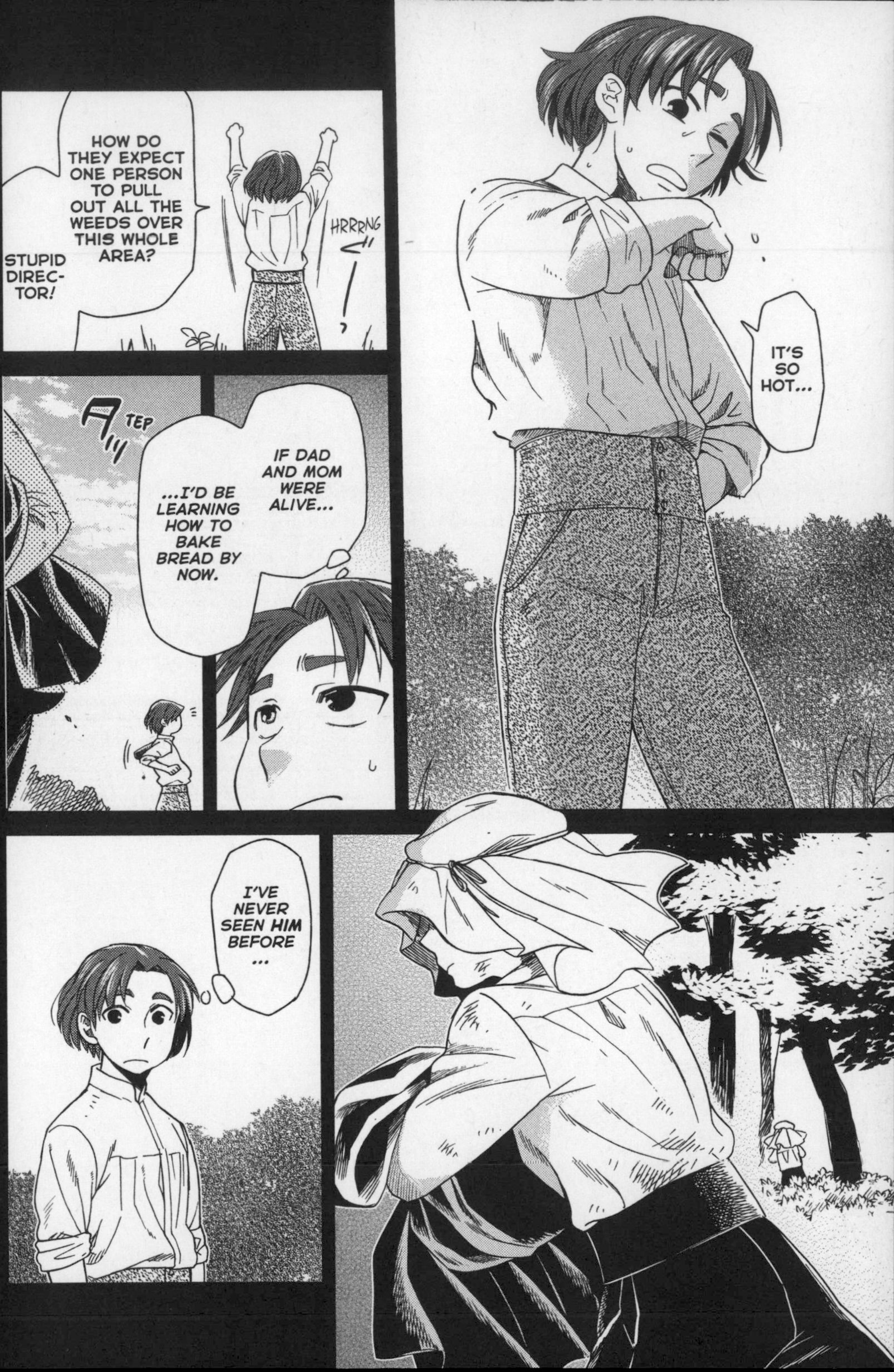
IT'S SO HOT...
HOW DO THEY EXPECT ONE PERSON TO PULL OUT ALL THE WEEDS OVER THIS WHOLE AREA?
HRRRNG
STUPID DIRECTOR!
IF DAD AND MOM WERE ALIVE...
...I'D BE LEARNING HOW TO BAKE BREAD BY NOW.
TEP
I'VE NEVER SEEN HIM BEFORE ...

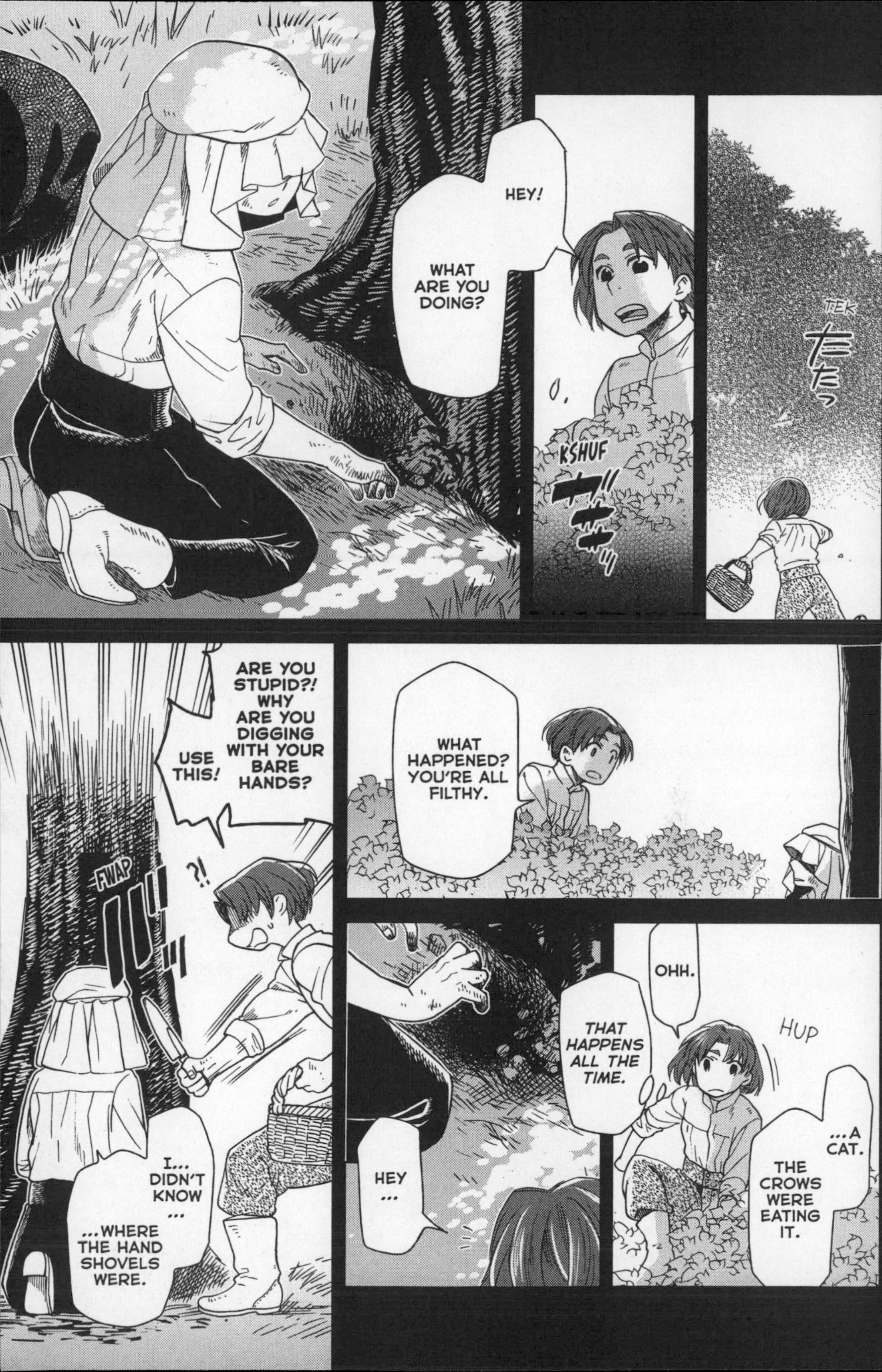
TEK
たたっ
HEY!
WHAT ARE YOU DOING?
KSHUF
WHAT HAPPENED? YOU'RE ALL FILTHY.
...A CAT.
THE CROWS WERE EATING IT.
HUP
OHH.
THAT HAPPENS ALL THE TIME.
HEY ...
ARE YOU STUPID?! WHY ARE YOU DIGGING WITH YOUR BARE HANDS?
USE THIS!
FWAP
?!
I... DIDN'T KNOW ...
...WHERE THE HAND SHOVELS WERE.

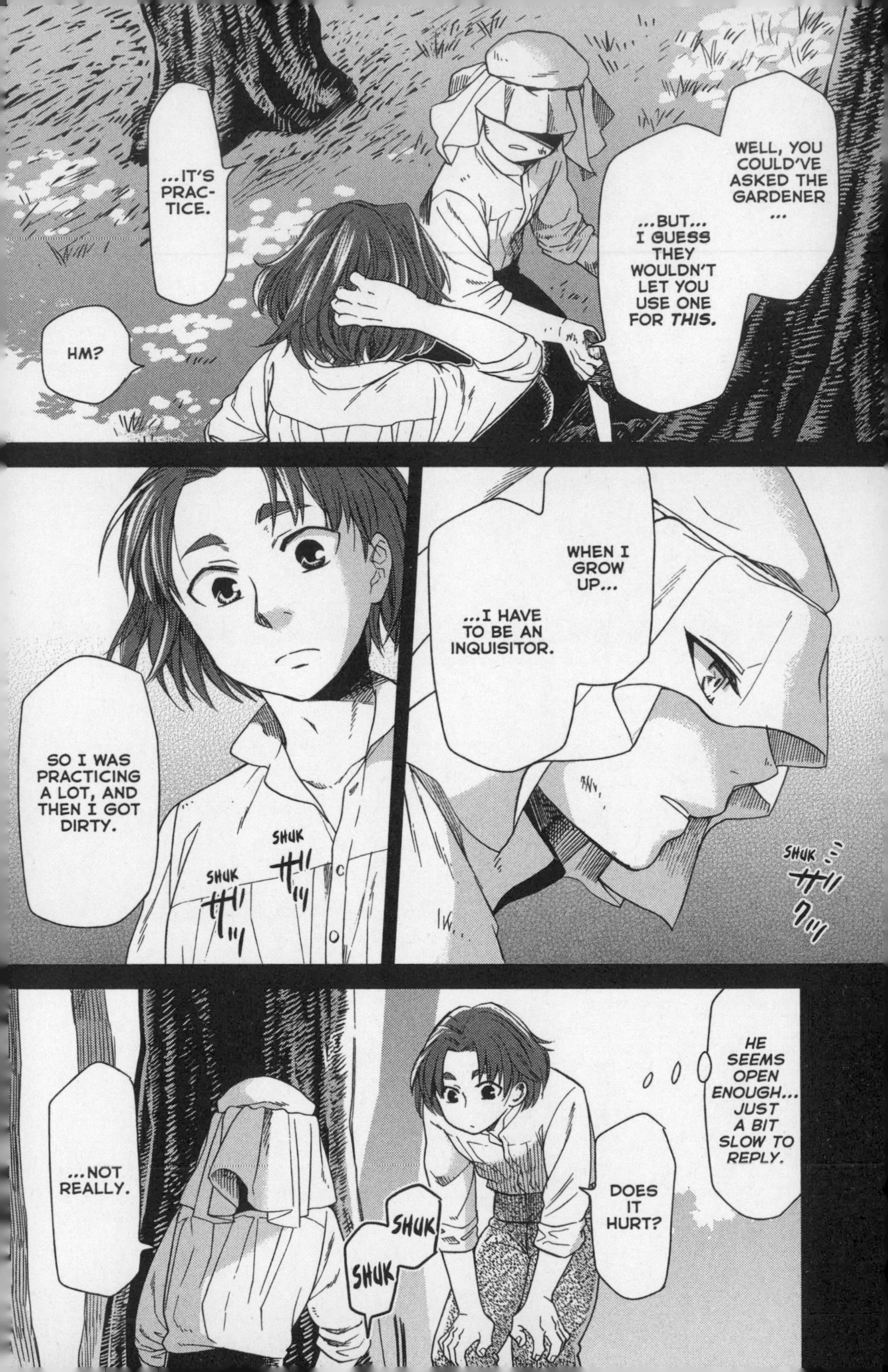
WELL, YOU COULD'VE ASKED THE GARDENER...
...BUT... I GUESS THEY WOULDN'T LET YOU USE ONE FOR *THIS.*
...IT'S PRACTICE.
HM?
WHEN I GROW UP...
...I HAVE TO BE AN INQUISITOR.
SHUK
SO I WAS PRACTICING A LOT, AND THEN I GOT DIRTY.
SHUK
SHUK
HE SEEMS OPEN ENOUGH... JUST A BIT SLOW TO REPLY.
DOES IT HURT?
...NOT REALLY.
SHUK
SHUK

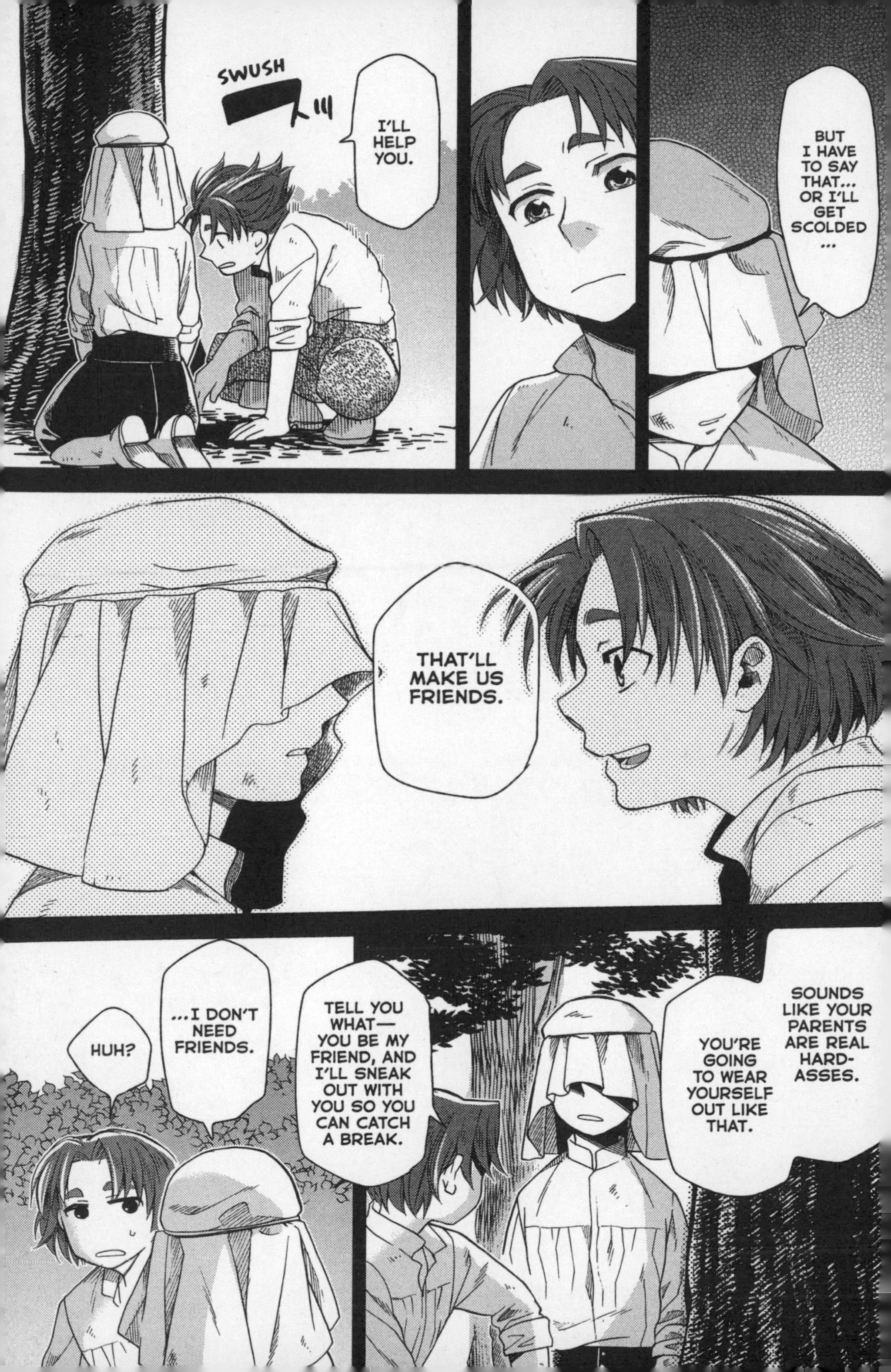

BUT I HAVE TO SAY THAT... OR I'LL GET SCOLDED...
SWUSH
I'LL HELP YOU.
THAT'LL MAKE US FRIENDS.
SOUNDS LIKE YOUR PARENTS ARE REAL HARD-ASSES.
YOU'RE GOING TO WEAR YOURSELF OUT LIKE THAT.
TELL YOU WHAT— YOU BE MY FRIEND, AND I'LL SNEAK OUT WITH YOU SO YOU CAN CATCH A BREAK.
...I DON'T NEED FRIENDS.
HUH?

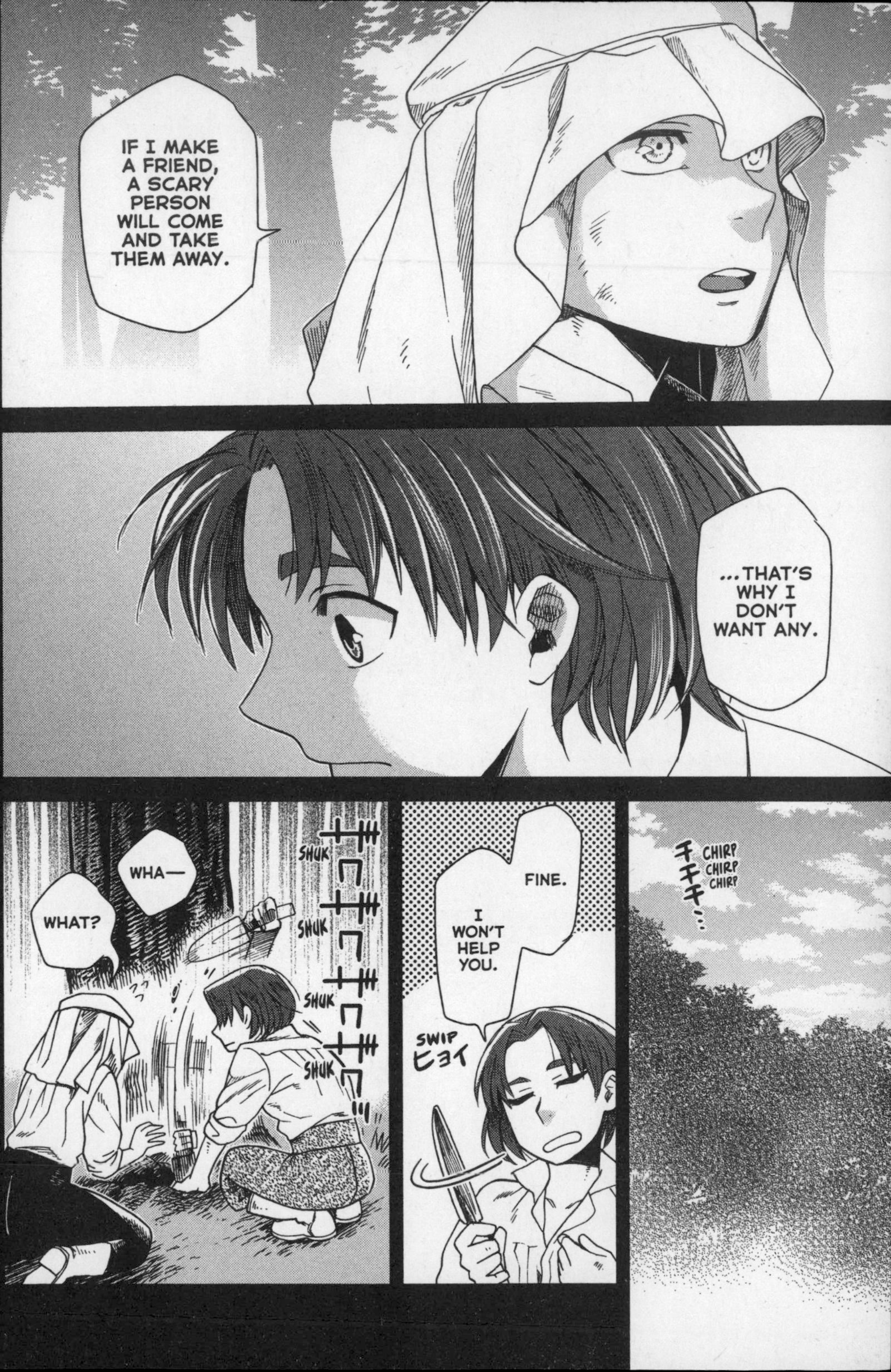
IF I MAKE A FRIEND, A SCARY PERSON WILL COME AND TAKE THEM AWAY.
...THAT'S WHY I DON'T WANT ANY.
チチチ…
CHIRP CHIRP CHIRP
FINE.
I WON'T HELP YOU.
SWIP
ヒョイ
SHUK
SHUK
SHUK
SHUK
WHA—
WHAT?

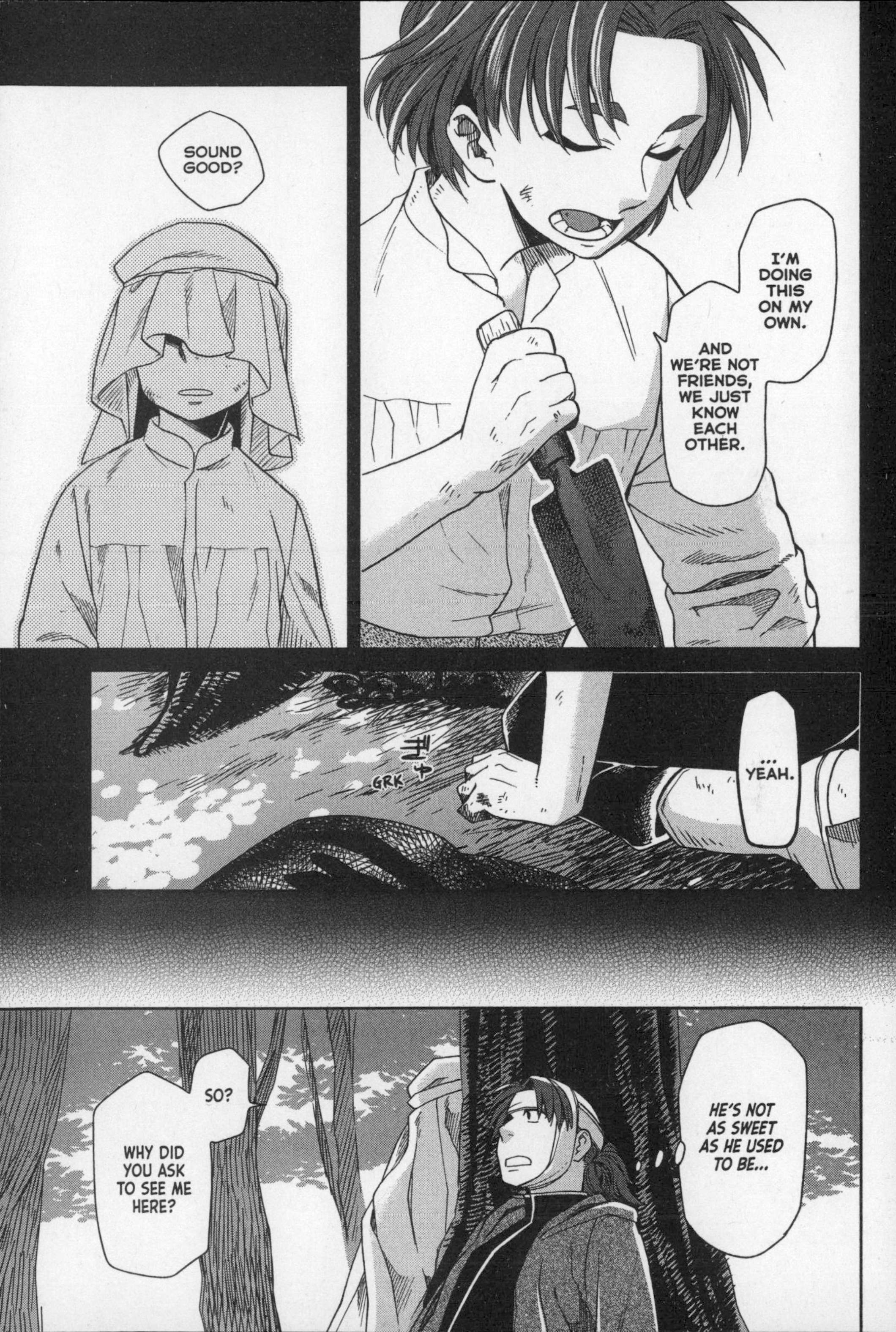
I'M DOING THIS ON MY OWN.
AND WE'RE NOT FRIENDS, WE JUST KNOW EACH OTHER.
SOUND GOOD?
...YEAH.
GRK
HE'S NOT AS SWEET AS HE USED TO BE...
SO?
WHY DID YOU ASK TO SEE ME HERE?

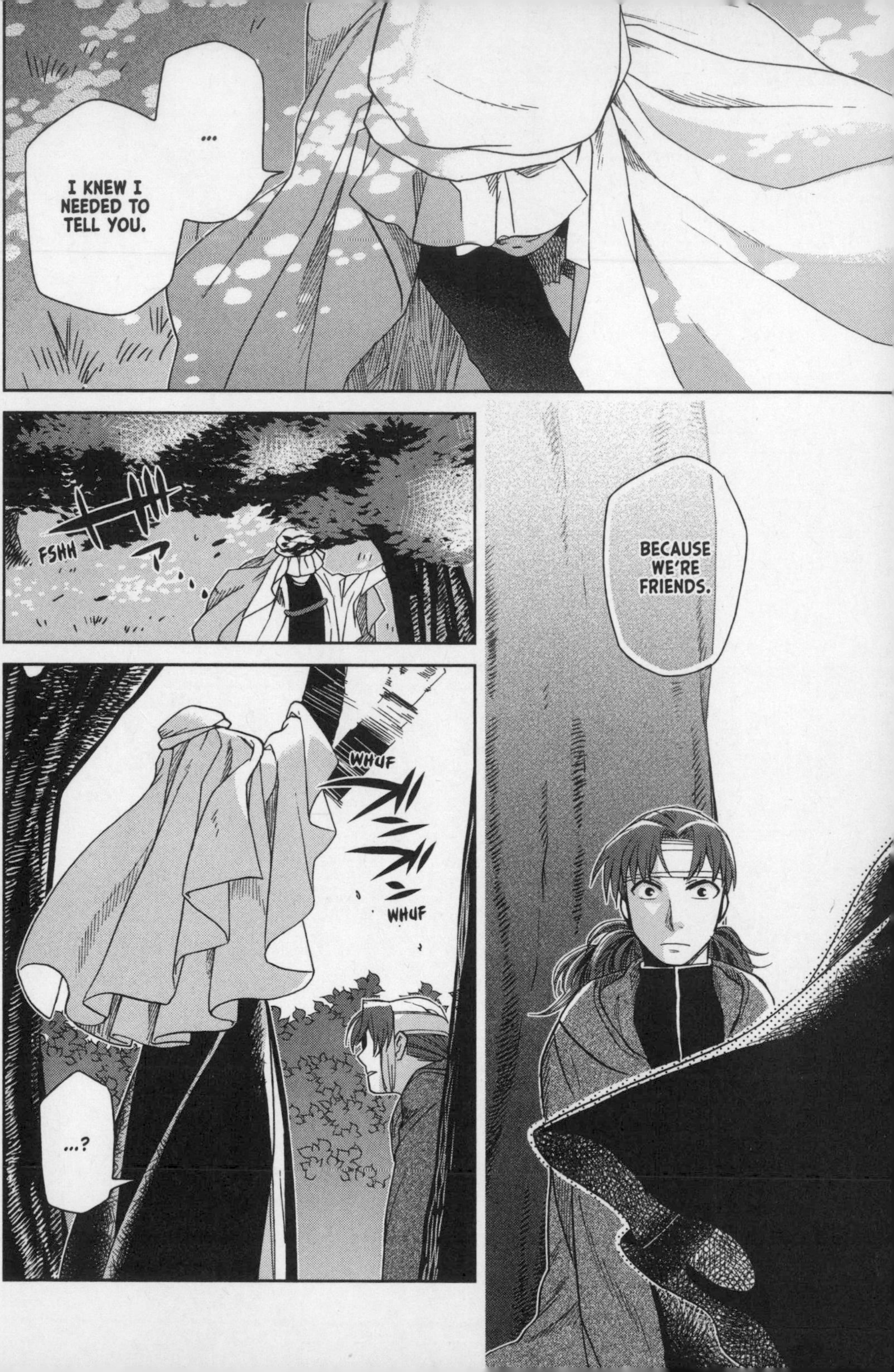
...
I KNEW I NEEDED TO TELL YOU.
BECAUSE WE'RE FRIENDS.
FSHH
WHUF
WHUF
...?

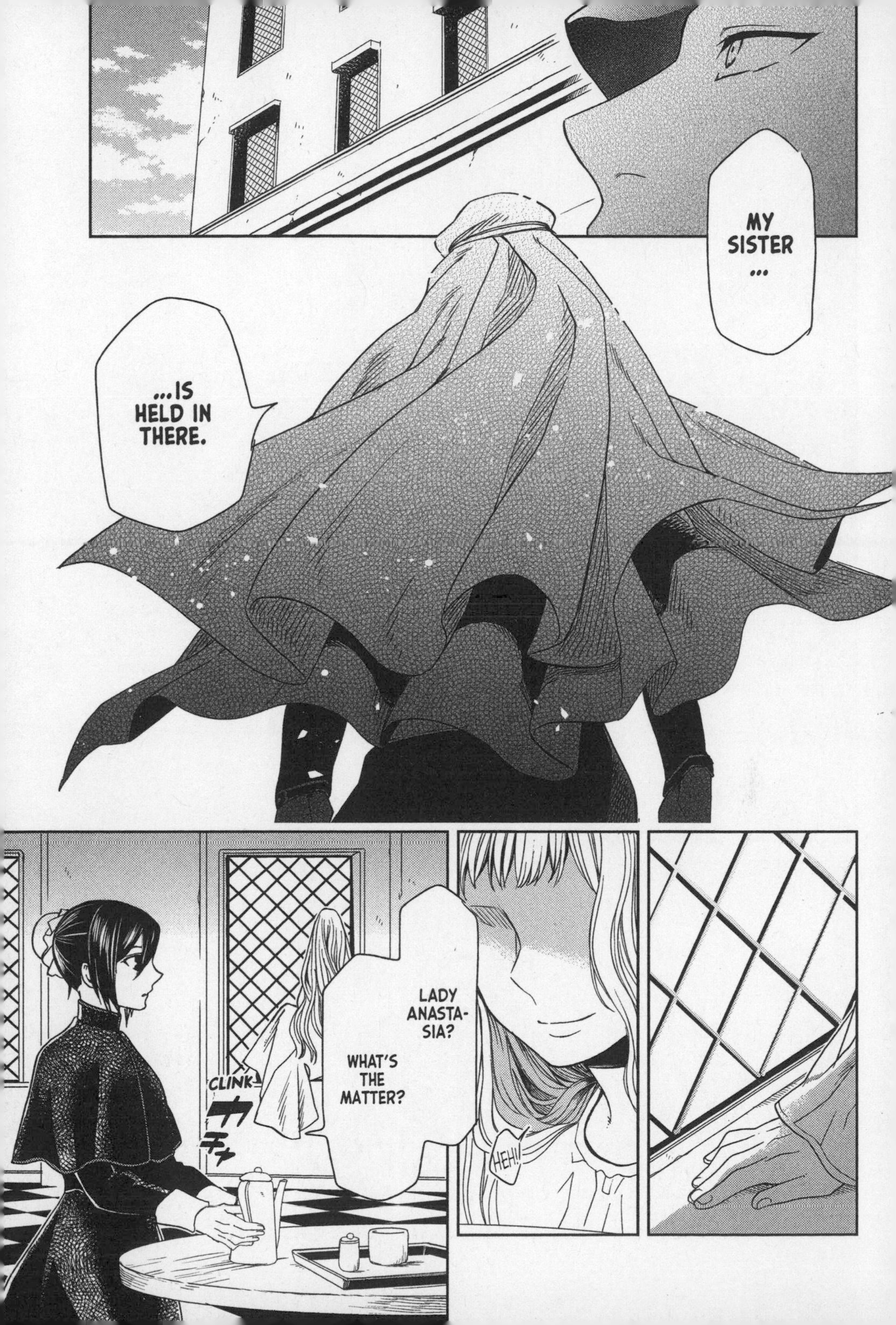
MY SISTER ...
...IS HELD IN THERE.
HEH!
LADY ANASTASIA?
WHAT'S THE MATTER?
CLINK
カチャ

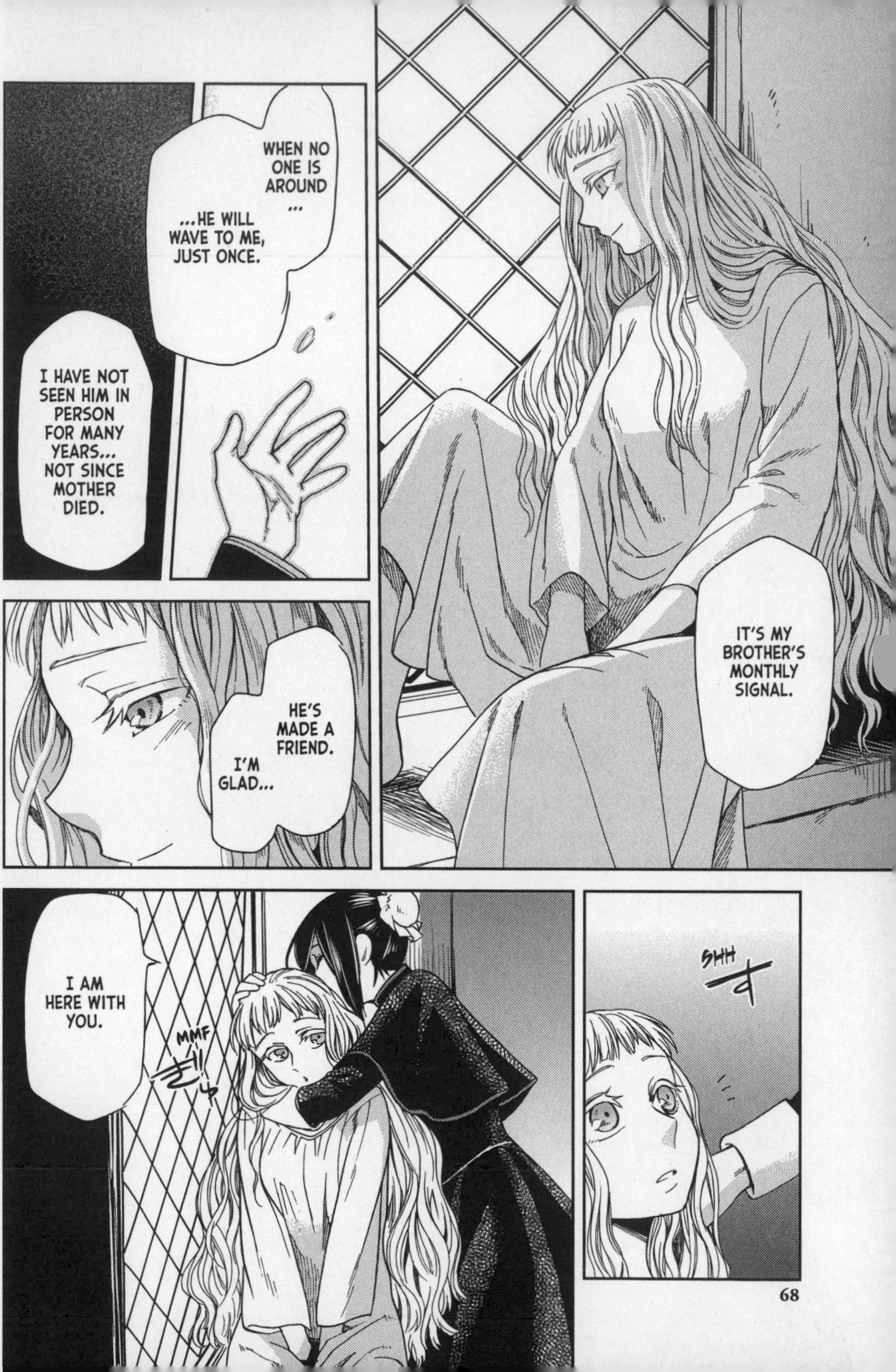
IT'S MY BROTHER'S MONTHLY SIGNAL.
WHEN NO ONE IS AROUND...
...HE WILL WAVE TO ME, JUST ONCE.
I HAVE NOT SEEN HIM IN PERSON FOR MANY YEARS... NOT SINCE MOTHER DIED.
HE'S MADE A FRIEND.
I'M GLAD...
SHH
I AM HERE WITH YOU.
MMF

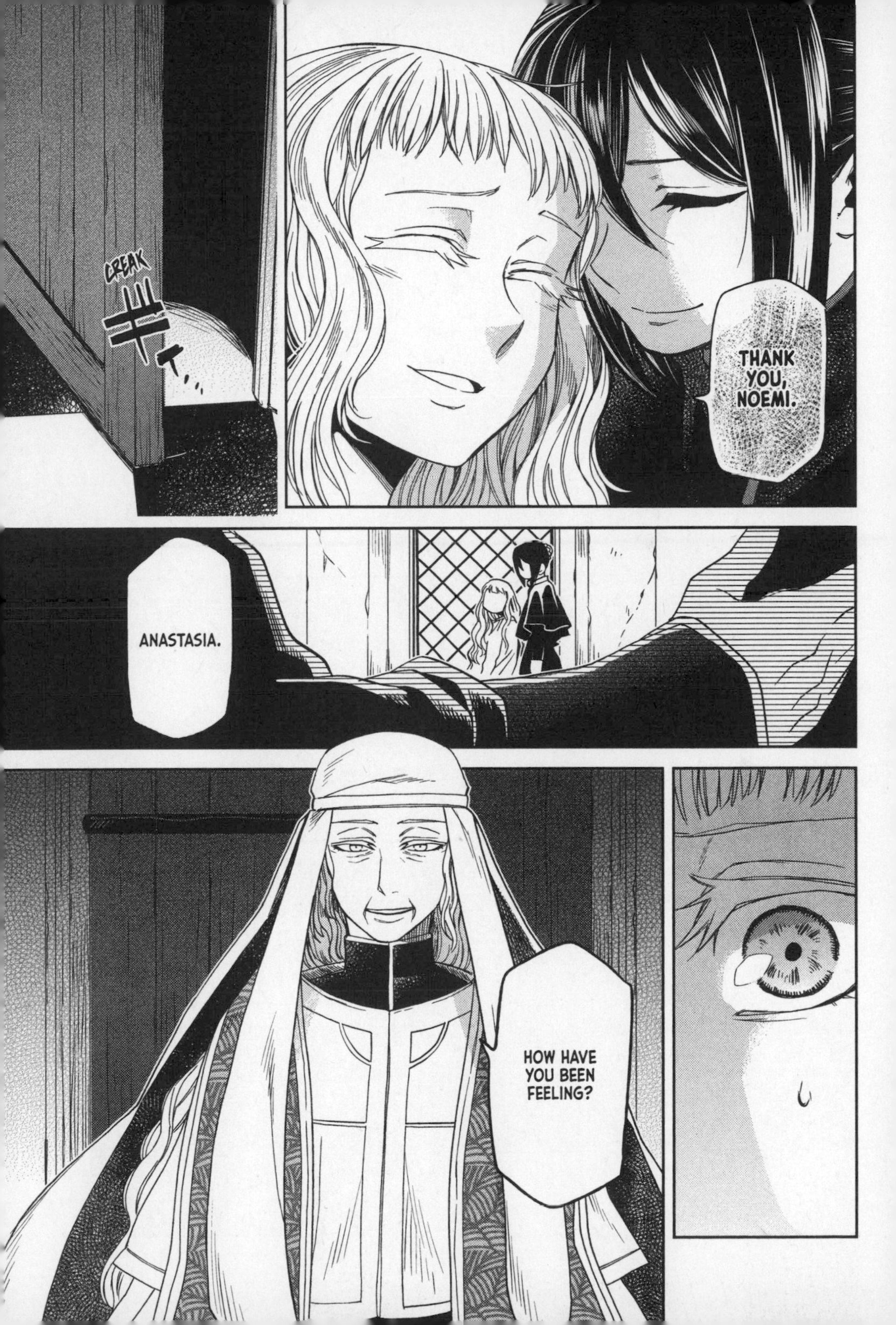
THANK YOU, NOEMI.
CREAK
ANASTASIA.
HOW HAVE YOU BEEN FEELING?

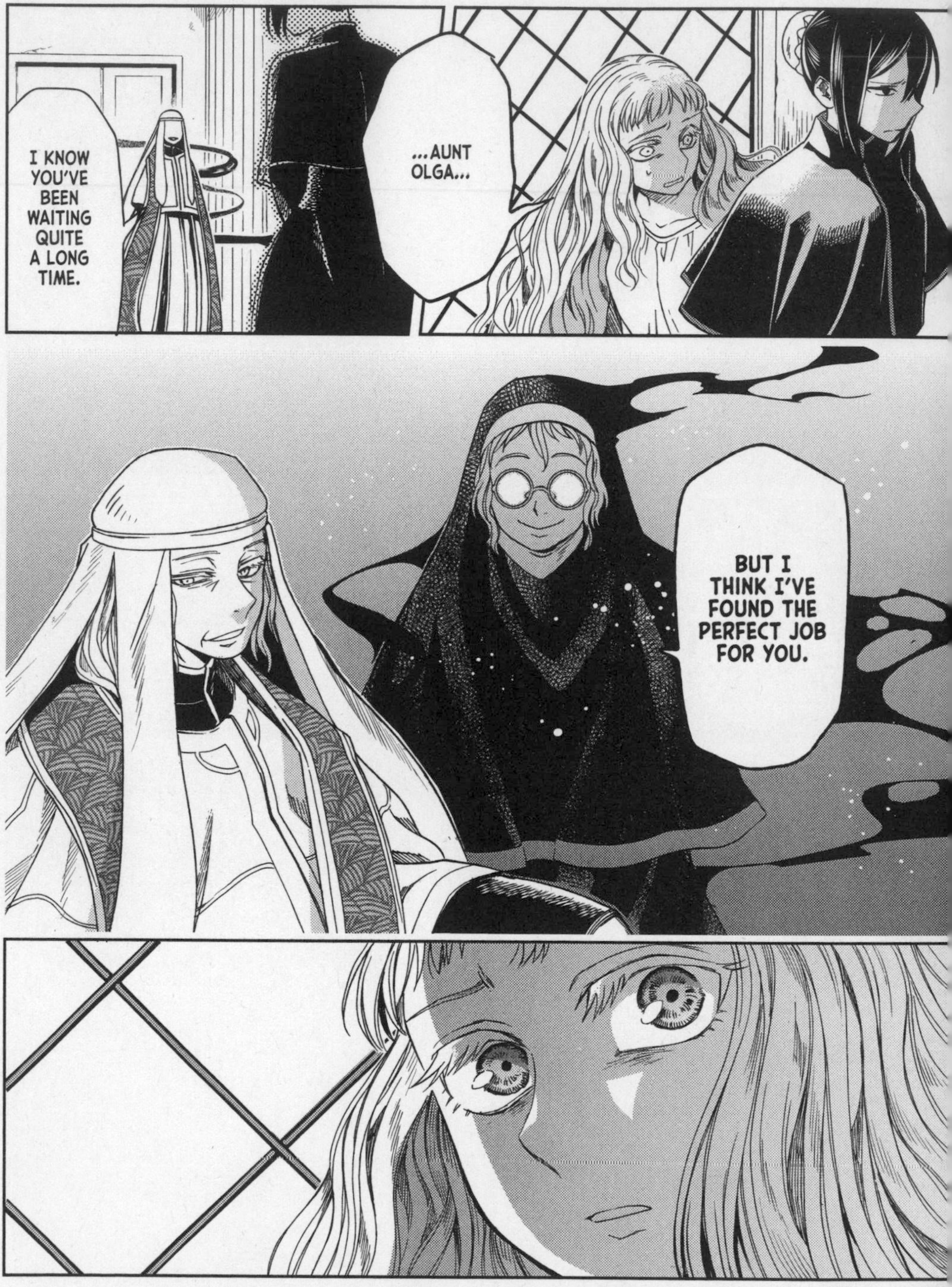
...AUNT OLGA...
I KNOW YOU'VE BEEN WAITING QUITE A LONG TIME.
BUT I THINK I'VE FOUND THE PERFECT JOB FOR YOU.

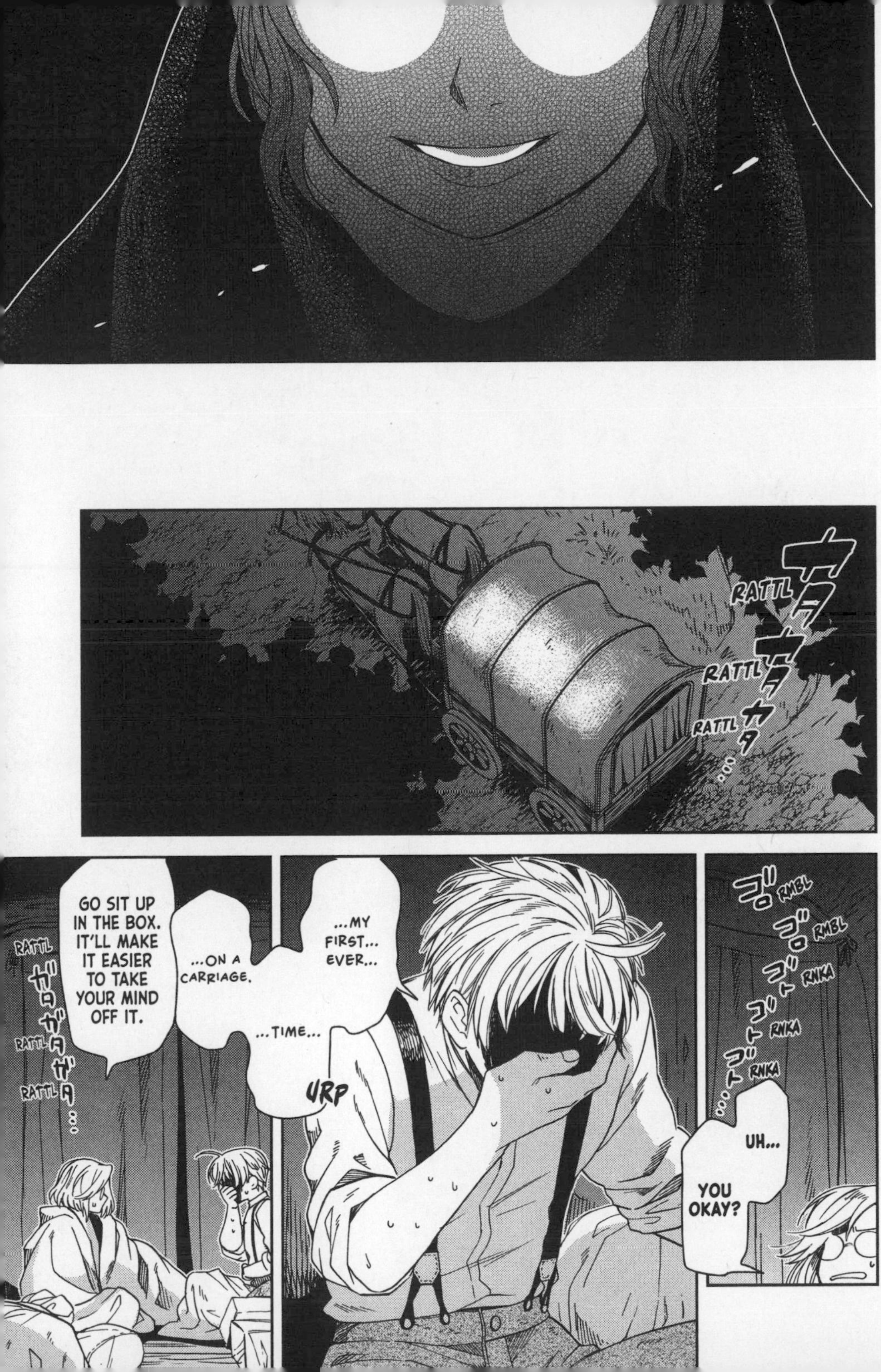

カタカタカタ…
RATTL
RATTL
RATTL
ゴロ RMBL
ゴロ RMBL
ゴト RNKA
ゴト RNKA
ゴト… RNKA
UH...
YOU OKAY?
...MY FIRST... EVER...
...TIME...
URP
...ON A CARRIAGE.
GO SIT UP IN THE BOX. IT'LL MAKE IT EASIER TO TAKE YOUR MIND OFF IT.
ガタガタ… RATTL
RATTL
RATTL

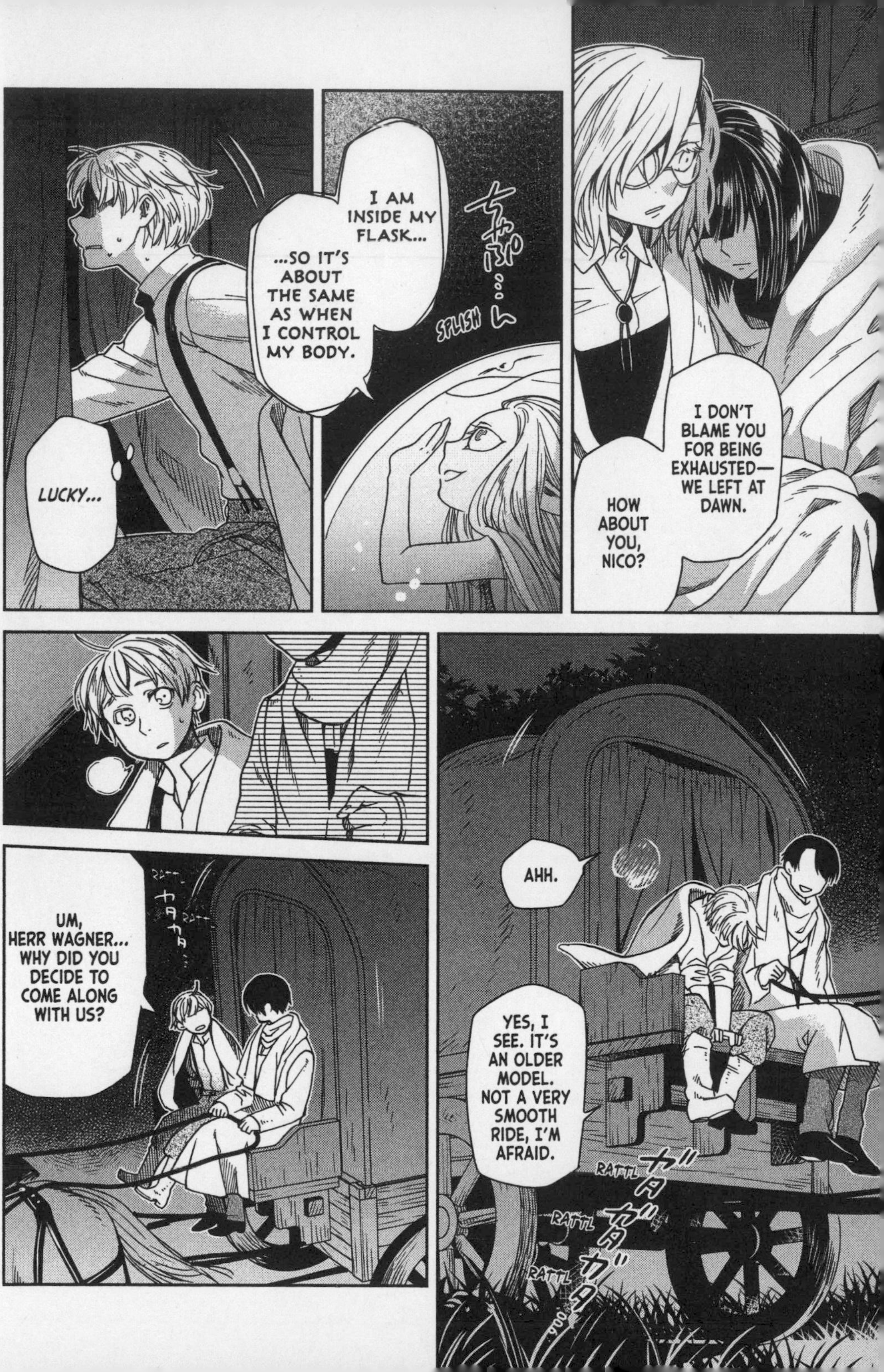
I DON'T BLAME YOU FOR BEING EXHAUSTED— WE LEFT AT DAWN.
HOW ABOUT YOU, NICO?
I AM INSIDE MY FLASK...
...SO IT'S ABOUT THE SAME AS WHEN I CONTROL MY BODY.
SPLISH
LUCKY...
AHH.
YES, I SEE. IT'S AN OLDER MODEL. NOT A VERY SMOOTH RIDE, I'M AFRAID.
RATTL
RATTL
RATTL
UM, HERR WAGNER... WHY DID YOU DECIDE TO COME ALONG WITH US?
RATTL
RATTL

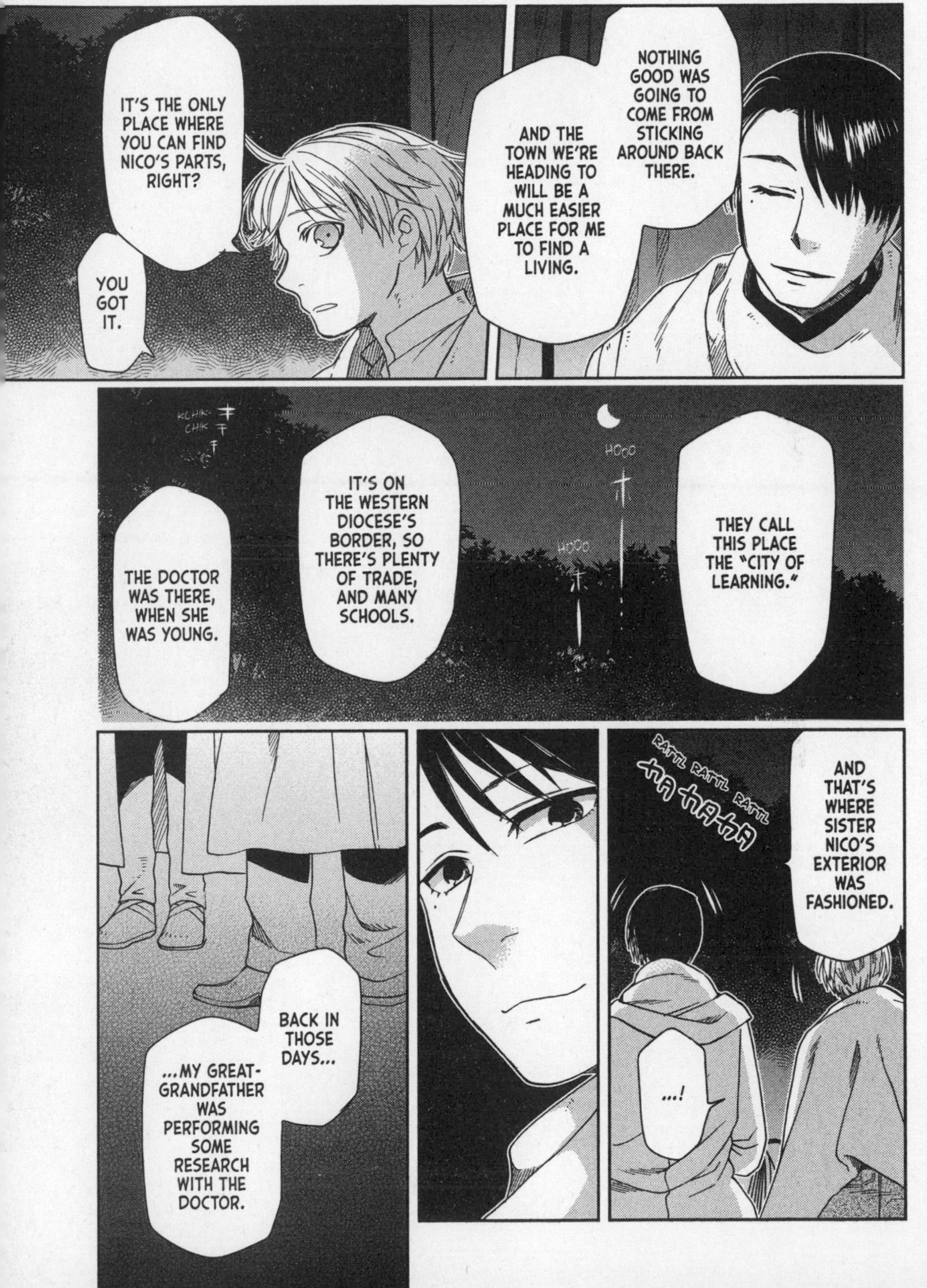
NOTHING GOOD WAS GOING TO COME FROM STICKING AROUND BACK THERE.
AND THE TOWN WE'RE HEADING TO WILL BE A MUCH EASIER PLACE FOR ME TO FIND A LIVING.
IT'S THE ONLY PLACE WHERE YOU CAN FIND NICO'S PARTS, RIGHT?
YOU GOT IT.
THEY CALL THIS PLACE THE "CITY OF LEARNING."
HOOO
HOOO
IT'S ON THE WESTERN DIOCESE'S BORDER, SO THERE'S PLENTY OF TRADE, AND MANY SCHOOLS.
KCHIK-CHIK
THE DOCTOR WAS THERE, WHEN SHE WAS YOUNG.
RATTL RATTL RATTL
AND THAT'S WHERE SISTER NICO'S EXTERIOR WAS FASHIONED.
...!
BACK IN THOSE DAYS...
...MY GREAT-GRANDFATHER WAS PERFORMING SOME RESEARCH WITH THE DOCTOR.

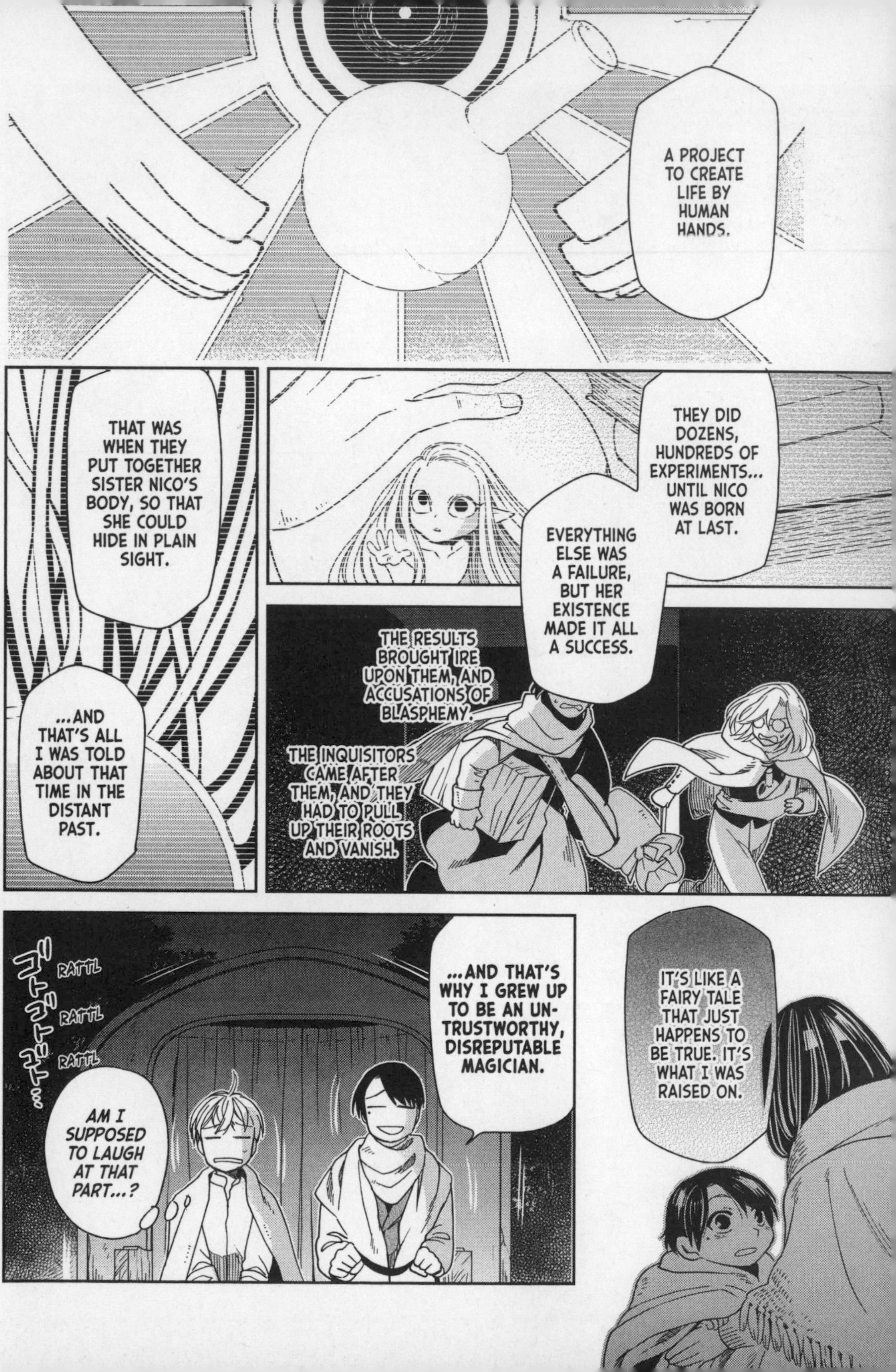
A PROJECT TO CREATE LIFE BY HUMAN HANDS.
THEY DID DOZENS, HUNDREDS OF EXPERIMENTS... UNTIL NICO WAS BORN AT LAST.
EVERYTHING ELSE WAS A FAILURE, BUT HER EXISTENCE MADE IT ALL A SUCCESS.
THE RESULTS BROUGHT IRE UPON THEM, AND ACCUSATIONS OF BLASPHEMY.
THE INQUISITORS CAME AFTER THEM, AND THEY HAD TO PULL UP THEIR ROOTS AND VANISH.
THAT WAS WHEN THEY PUT TOGETHER SISTER NICO'S BODY, SO THAT SHE COULD HIDE IN PLAIN SIGHT.
...AND THAT'S ALL I WAS TOLD ABOUT THAT TIME IN THE DISTANT PAST.
IT'S LIKE A FAIRY TALE THAT JUST HAPPENS TO BE TRUE. IT'S WHAT I WAS RAISED ON.
RATTL
RATTL
RATTL
...AND THAT'S WHY I GREW UP TO BE AN UN-TRUSTWORTHY, DISREPUTABLE MAGICIAN.
AM I SUPPOSED TO LAUGH AT THAT PART...?

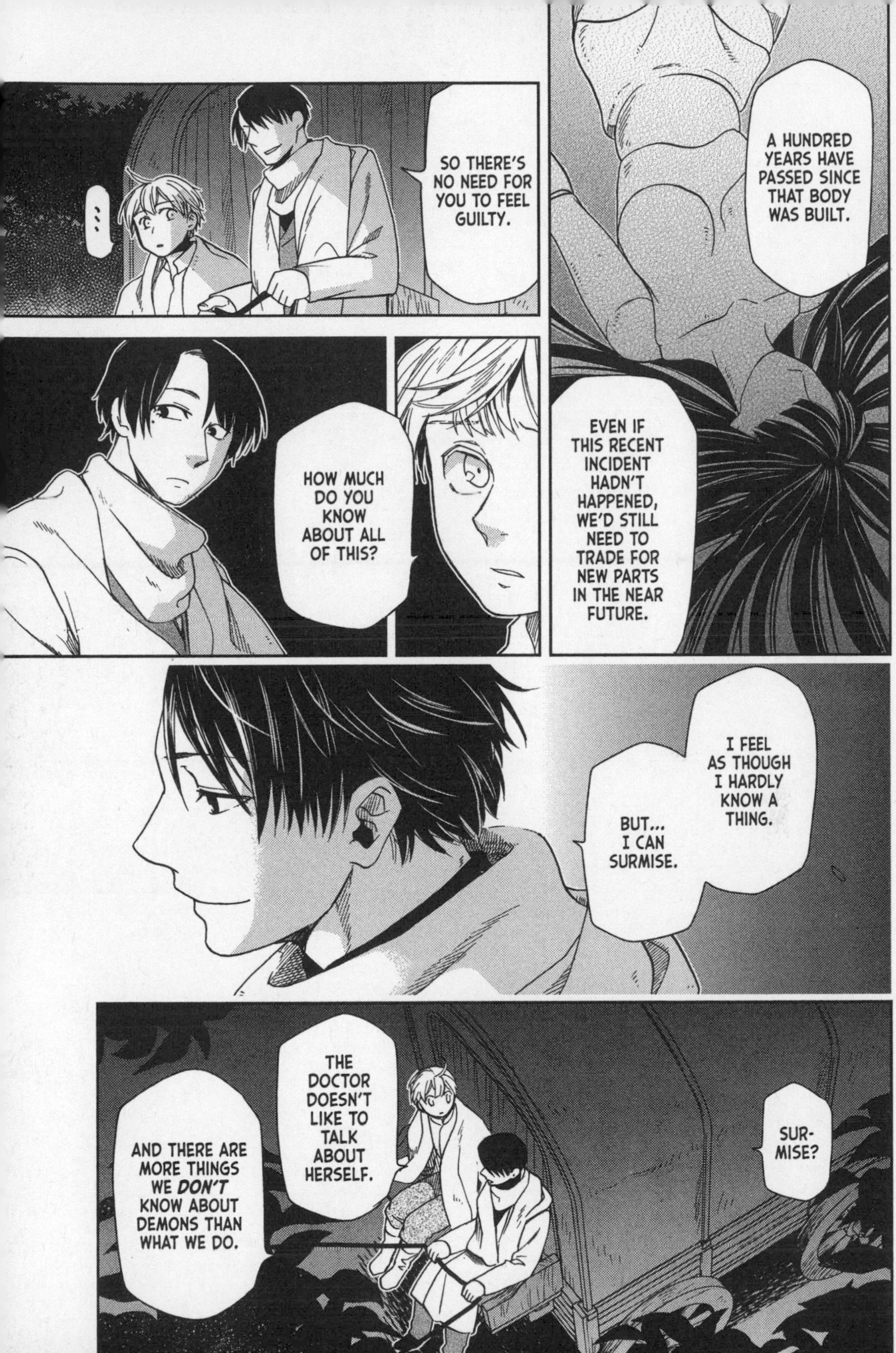
A HUNDRED YEARS HAVE PASSED SINCE THAT BODY WAS BUILT.
EVEN IF THIS RECENT INCIDENT HADN'T HAPPENED, WE'D STILL NEED TO TRADE FOR NEW PARTS IN THE NEAR FUTURE.
SO THERE'S NO NEED FOR YOU TO FEEL GUILTY.
...
HOW MUCH DO YOU KNOW ABOUT ALL OF THIS?
I FEEL AS THOUGH I HARDLY KNOW A THING.
BUT... I CAN SURMISE.
SUR-MISE?
THE DOCTOR DOESN'T LIKE TO TALK ABOUT HERSELF.
AND THERE ARE MORE THINGS WE *DON'T* KNOW ABOUT DEMONS THAN WHAT WE DO.

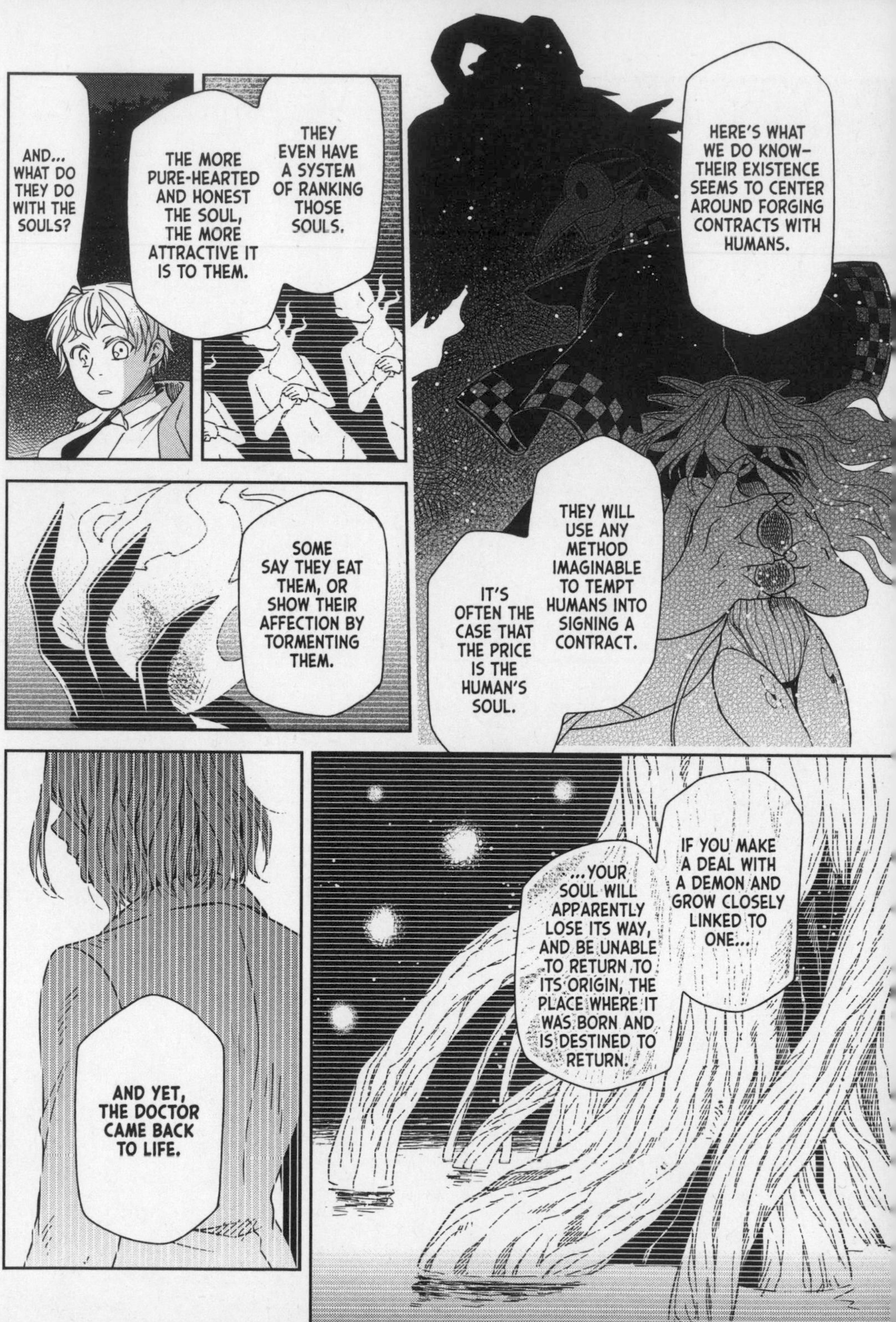
HERE'S WHAT WE DO KNOW—THEIR EXISTENCE SEEMS TO CENTER AROUND FORGING CONTRACTS WITH HUMANS.
THEY WILL USE ANY METHOD IMAGINABLE TO TEMPT HUMANS INTO SIGNING A CONTRACT.
IT'S OFTEN THE CASE THAT THE PRICE IS THE HUMAN'S SOUL.
THEY EVEN HAVE A SYSTEM OF RANKING THOSE SOULS.
THE MORE PURE-HEARTED AND HONEST THE SOUL, THE MORE ATTRACTIVE IT IS TO THEM.
AND... WHAT DO THEY DO WITH THE SOULS?
SOME SAY THEY EAT THEM, OR SHOW THEIR AFFECTION BY TORMENTING THEM.
IF YOU MAKE A DEAL WITH A DEMON AND GROW CLOSELY LINKED TO ONE...
...YOUR SOUL WILL APPARENTLY LOSE ITS WAY, AND BE UNABLE TO RETURN TO ITS ORIGIN, THE PLACE WHERE IT WAS BORN AND IS DESTINED TO RETURN.
AND YET, THE DOCTOR CAME BACK TO LIFE.

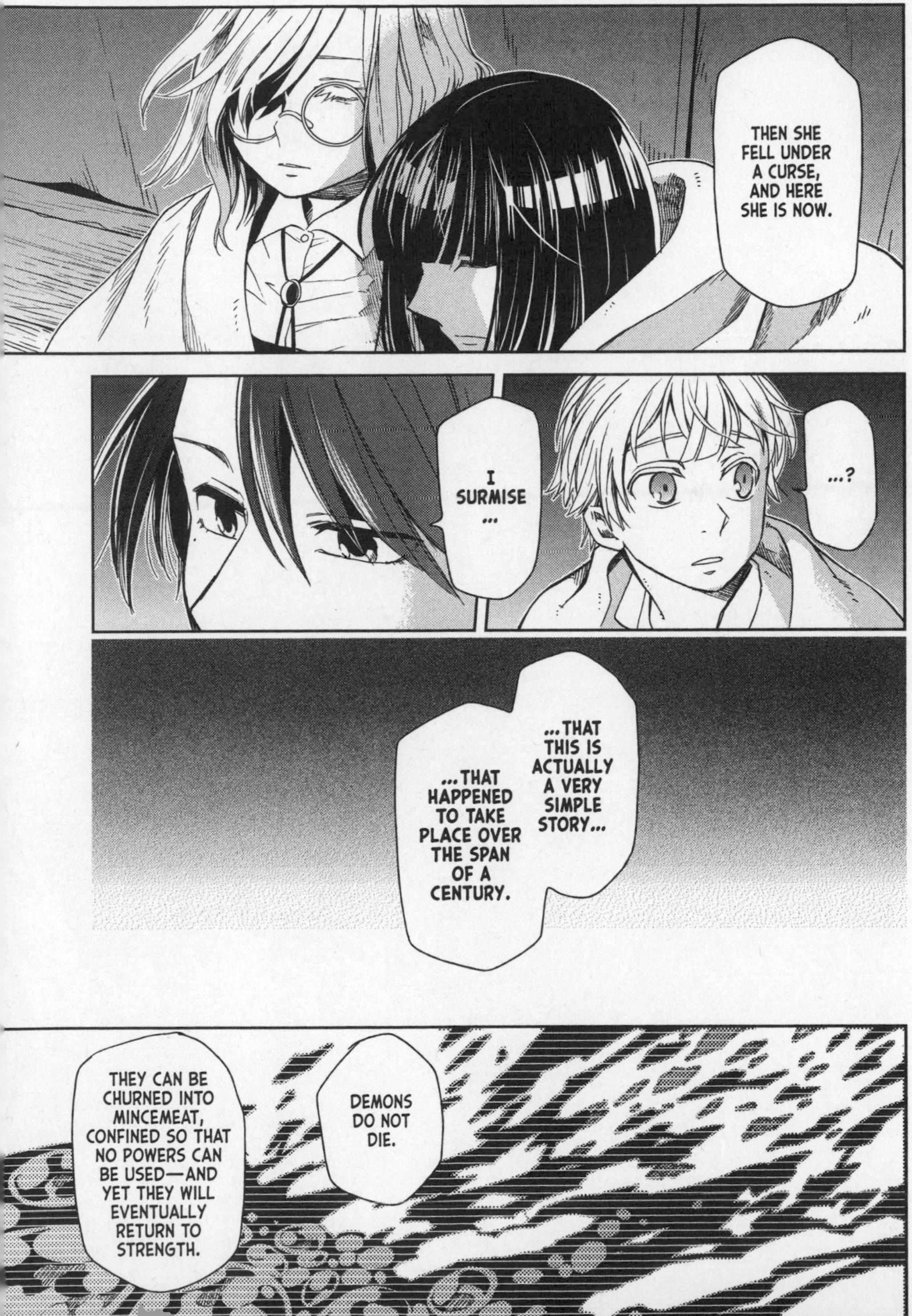
THEN SHE FELL UNDER A CURSE, AND HERE SHE IS NOW.
...?
I SURMISE ...
...THAT THIS IS ACTUALLY A VERY SIMPLE STORY...
...THAT HAPPENED TO TAKE PLACE OVER THE SPAN OF A CENTURY.
DEMONS DO NOT DIE.
THEY CAN BE CHURNED INTO MINCEMEAT, CONFINED SO THAT NO POWERS CAN BE USED—AND YET THEY WILL EVENTUALLY RETURN TO STRENGTH.

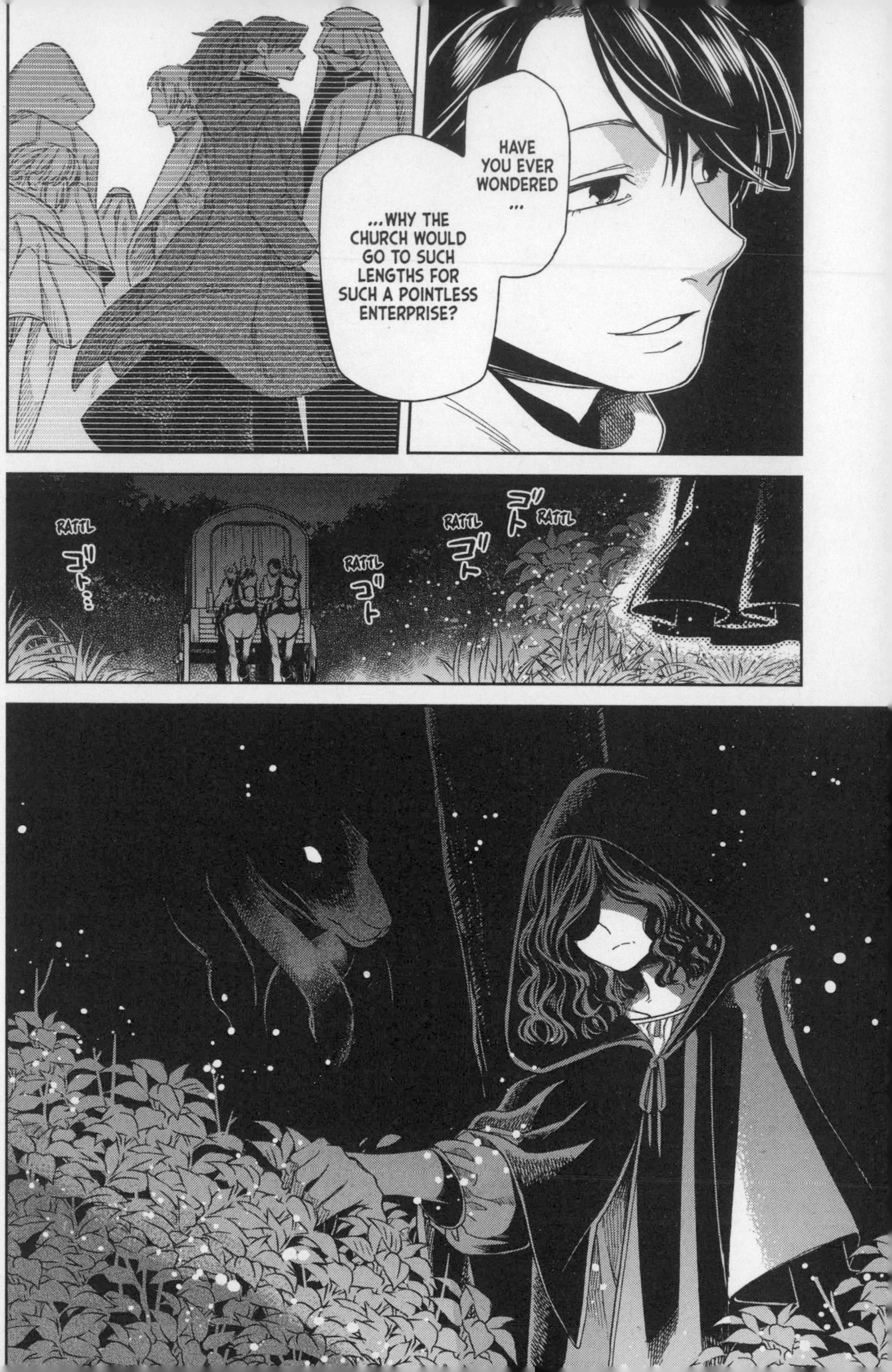
HAVE YOU EVER WONDERED ...
...WHY THE CHURCH WOULD GO TO SUCH LENGTHS FOR SUCH A POINTLESS ENTERPRISE?
RATTL
ゴト
RATTL
ゴト
RATTL
ゴト
RATTL
ゴト…

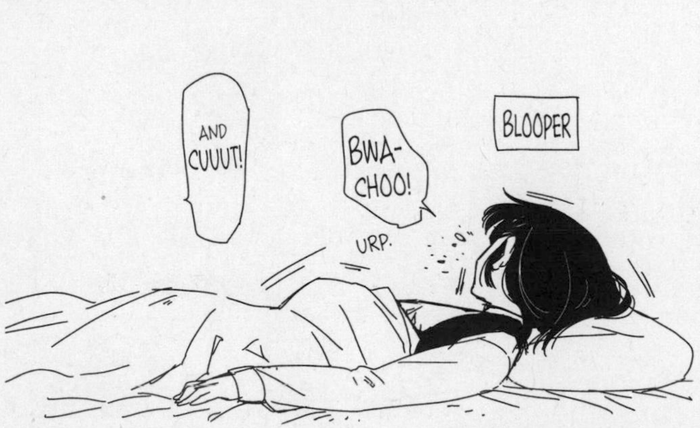
BLOOPER
BWA-CHOO!
URP.
AND CUUUT!

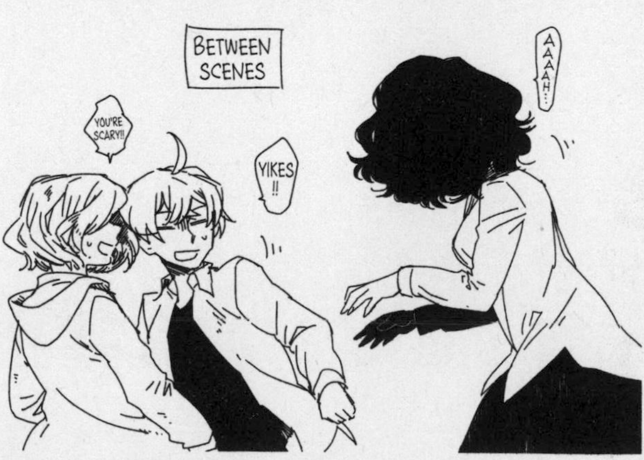
BETWEEN SCENES
AAAAH...
YIKES!!
YOU'RE SCARY!!

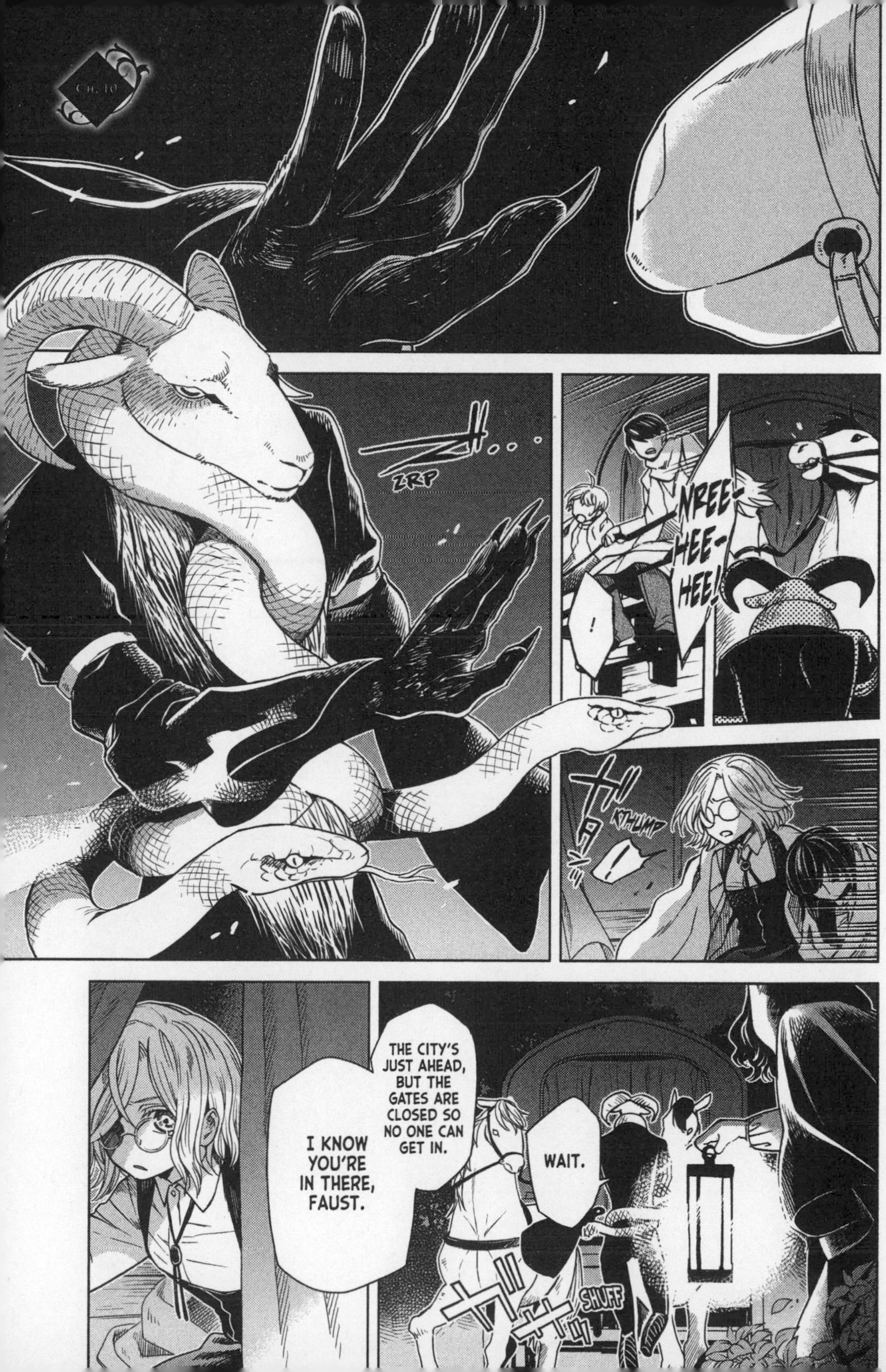
Ch. 10
NREE-HEE-HEE!
!
KTHUMP
!
ZRP
WAIT.
THE CITY'S JUST AHEAD, BUT THE GATES ARE CLOSED SO NO ONE CAN GET IN.
SHUFF
I KNOW YOU'RE IN THERE, FAUST.

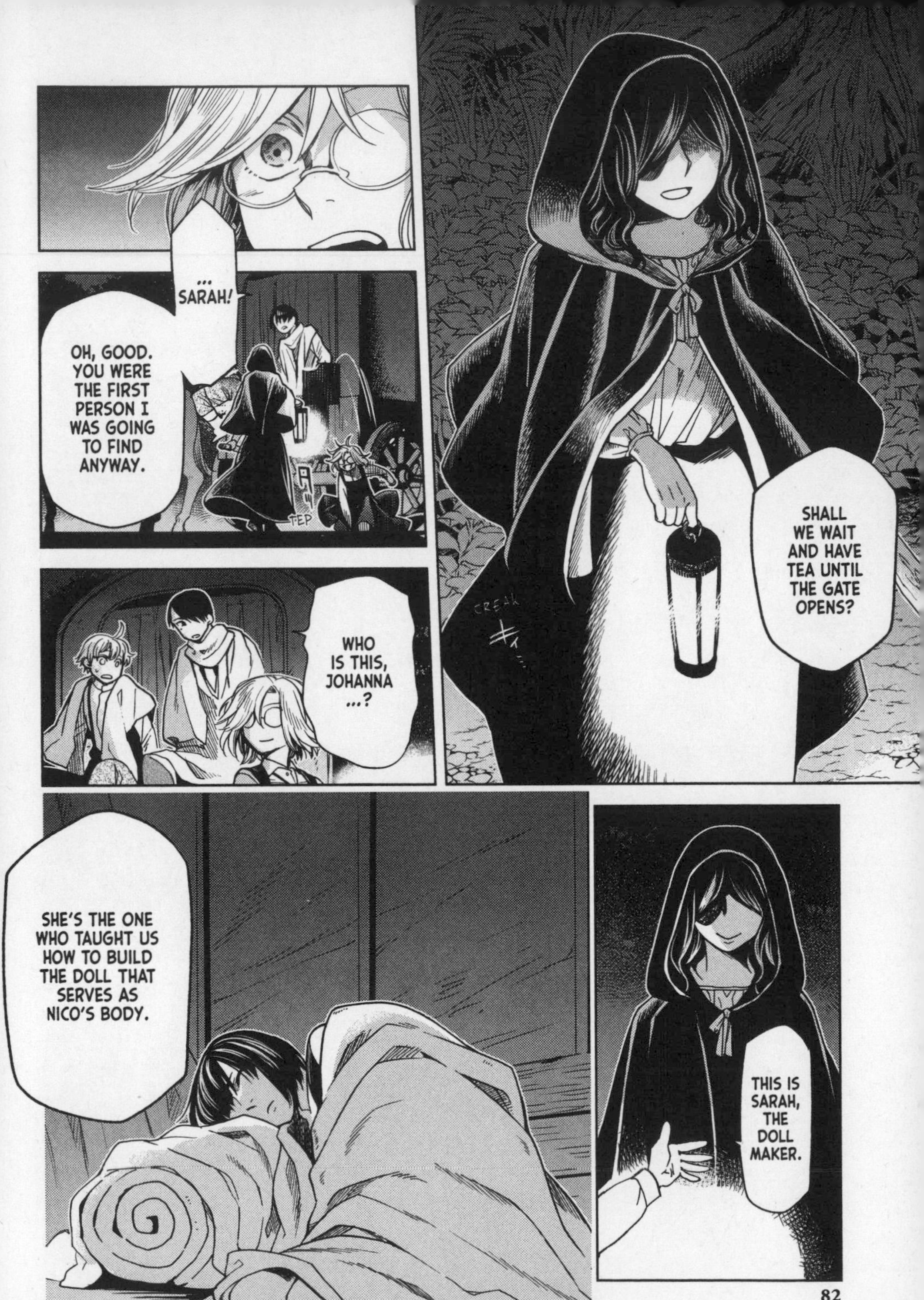
SHALL WE WAIT AND HAVE TEA UNTIL THE GATE OPENS?
CREAK
...SARAH!
OH, GOOD. YOU WERE THE FIRST PERSON I WAS GOING TO FIND ANYWAY.
TEP
WHO IS THIS, JOHANNA...?
THIS IS SARAH, THE DOLL MAKER.
SHE'S THE ONE WHO TAUGHT US HOW TO BUILD THE DOLL THAT SERVES AS NICO'S BODY.

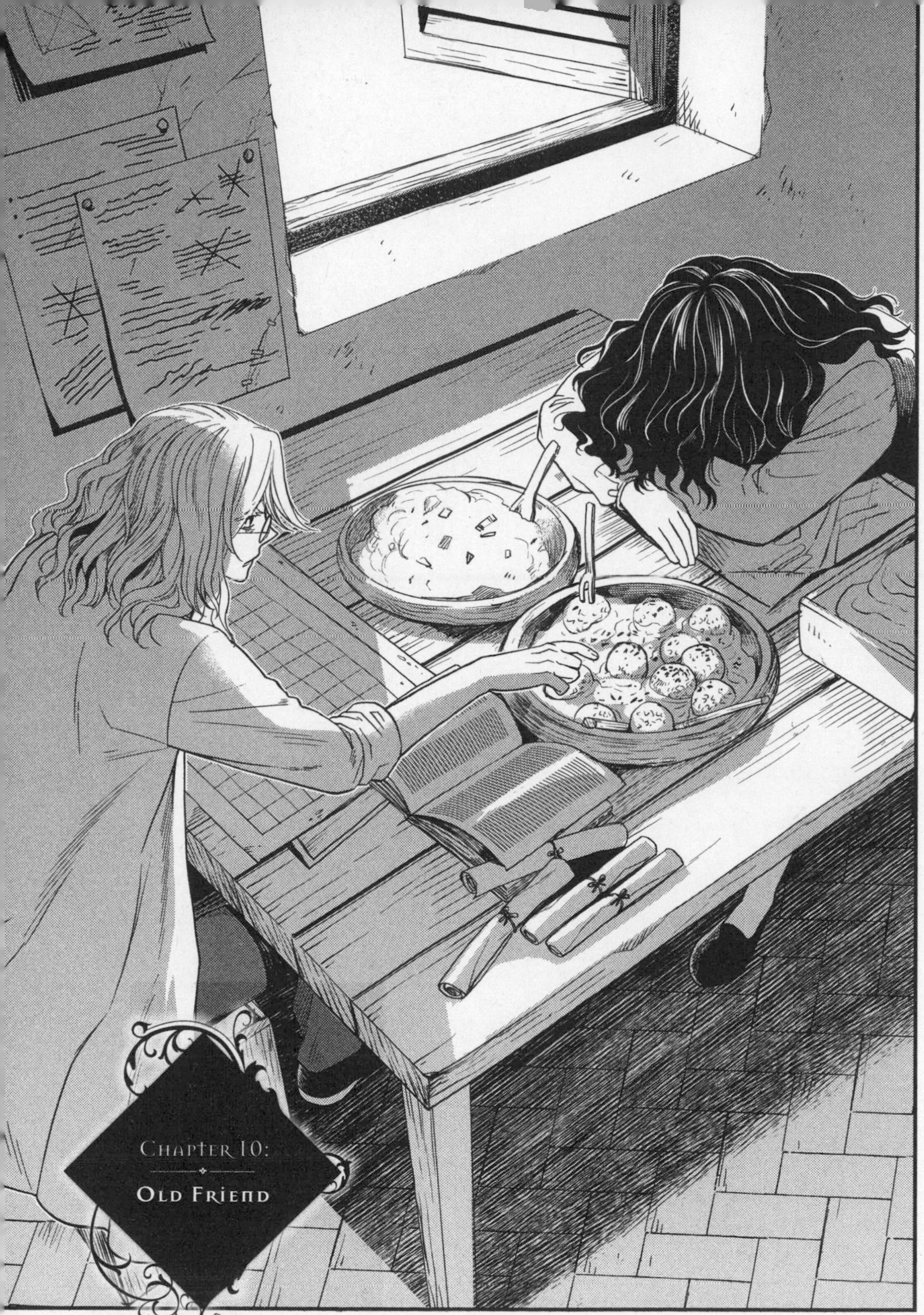
Chapter 10:
Old Friend

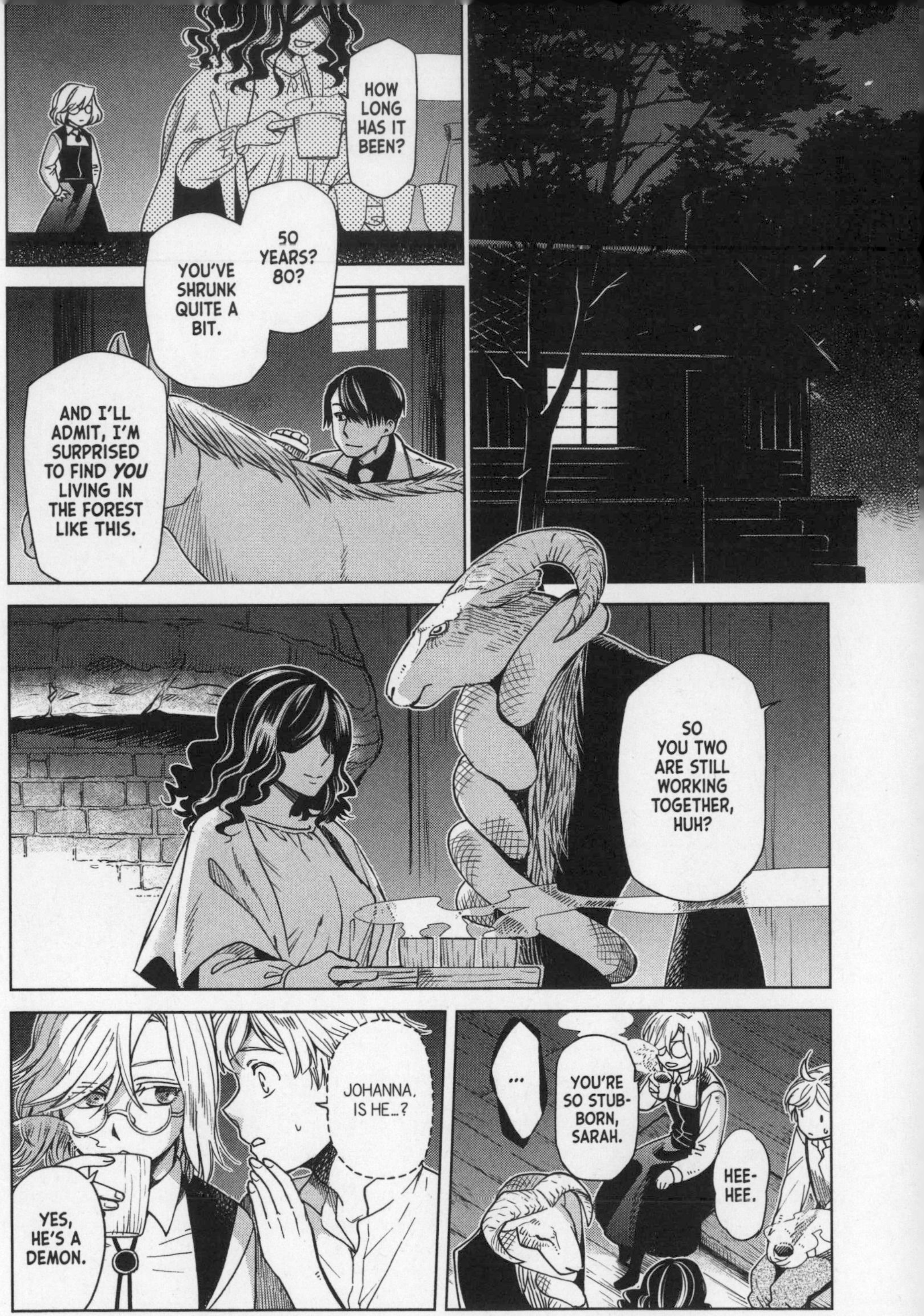
HOW LONG HAS IT BEEN?
50 YEARS? 80?
YOU'VE SHRUNK QUITE A BIT.
AND I'LL ADMIT, I'M SURPRISED TO FIND *YOU* LIVING IN THE FOREST LIKE THIS.
SO YOU TWO ARE STILL WORKING TOGETHER, HUH?
...
YOU'RE SO STUB-BORN, SARAH.
HEE-HEE.
JOHANNA, IS HE...?
YES, HE'S A DEMON.

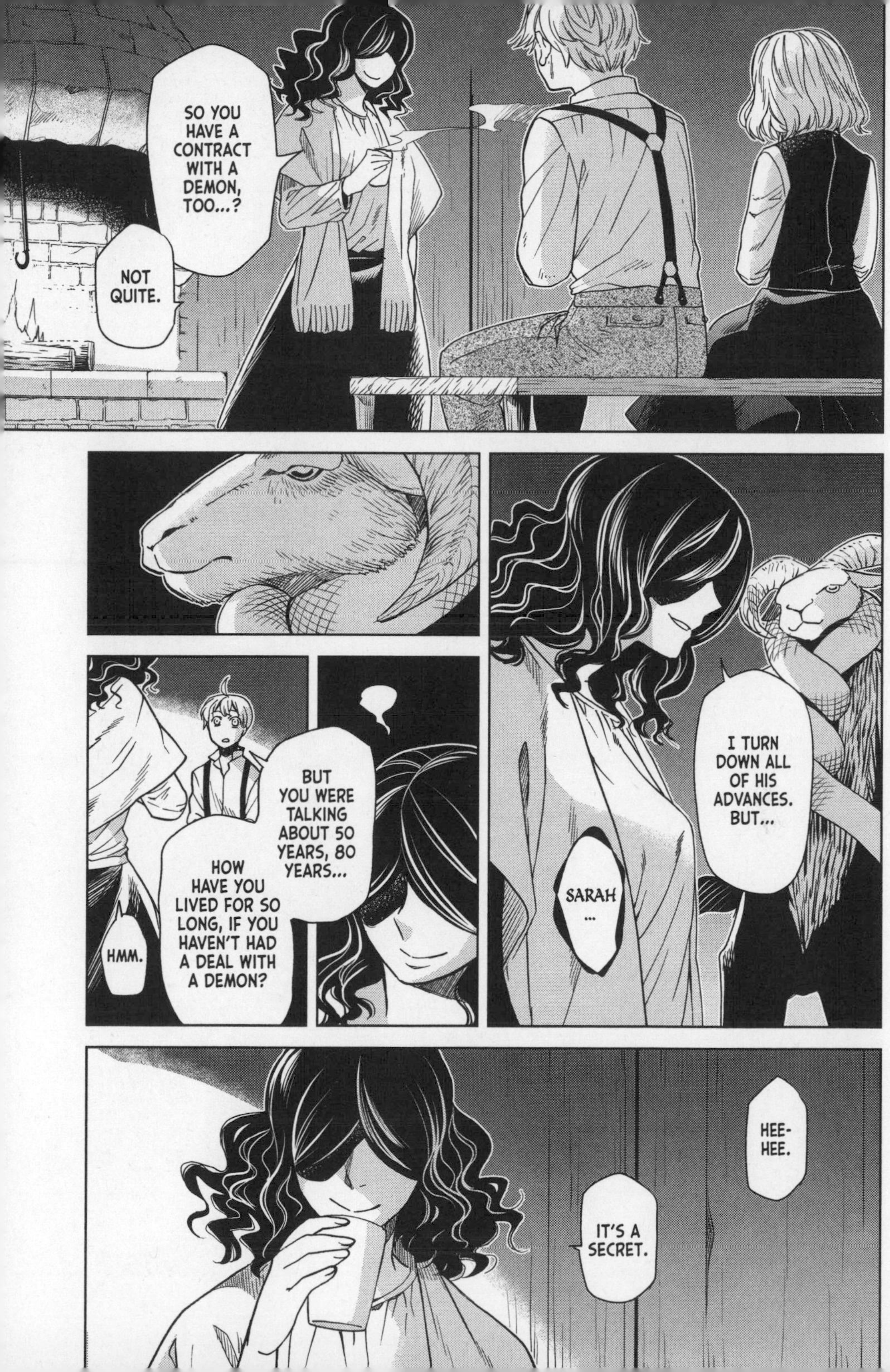
SO YOU HAVE A CONTRACT WITH A DEMON, TOO...?
NOT QUITE.
I TURN DOWN ALL OF HIS ADVANCES. BUT...
SARAH ...
BUT YOU WERE TALKING ABOUT 50 YEARS, 80 YEARS...
HOW HAVE YOU LIVED FOR SO LONG, IF YOU HAVEN'T HAD A DEAL WITH A DEMON?
HMM.
HEE-HEE.
IT'S A SECRET.

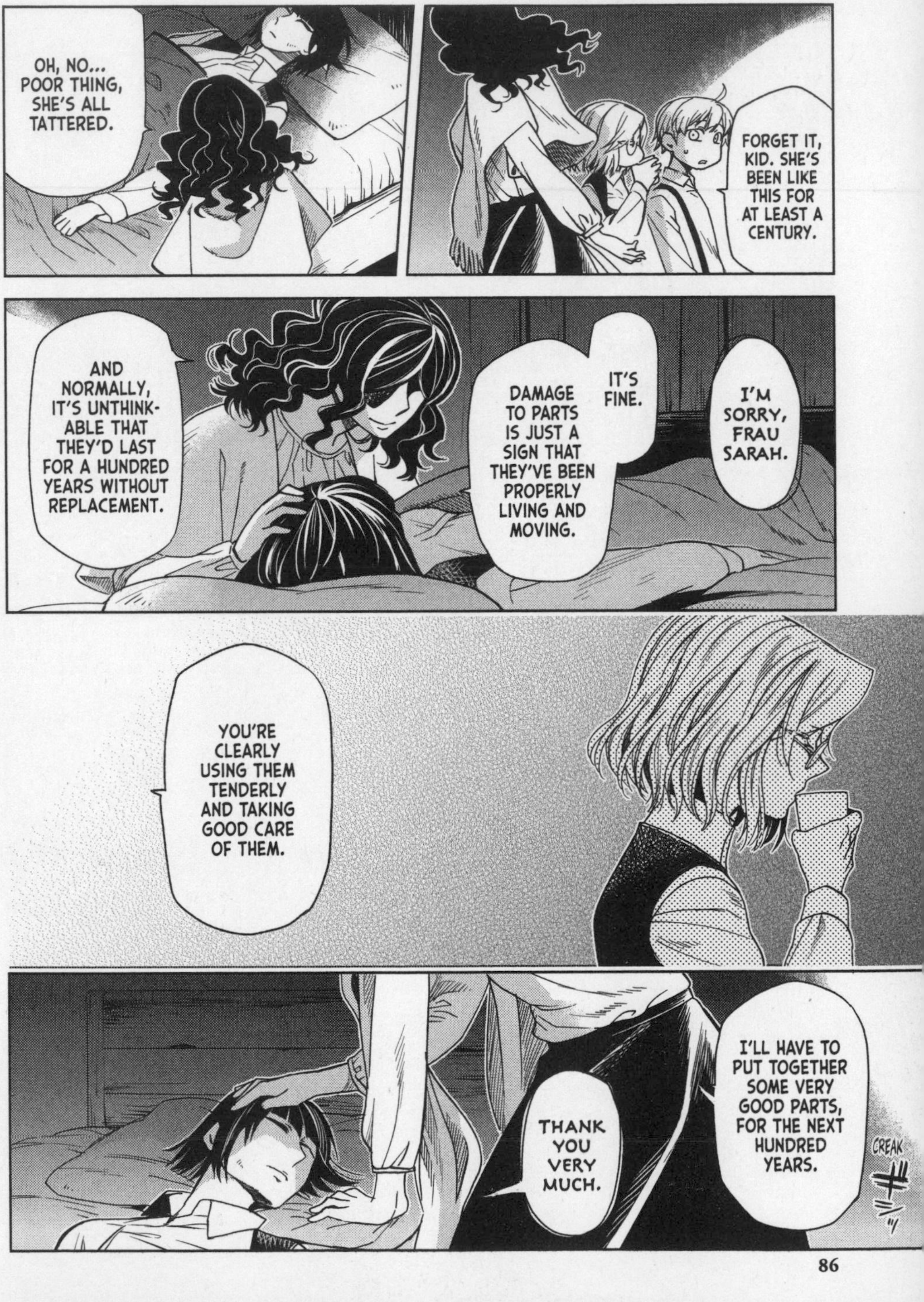
FORGET IT, KID. SHE'S BEEN LIKE THIS FOR AT LEAST A CENTURY.
OH, NO... POOR THING, SHE'S ALL TATTERED.
I'M SORRY, FRAU SARAH.
IT'S FINE.
DAMAGE TO PARTS IS JUST A SIGN THAT THEY'VE BEEN PROPERLY LIVING AND MOVING.
AND NORMALLY, IT'S UNTHINK-ABLE THAT THEY'D LAST FOR A HUNDRED YEARS WITHOUT REPLACEMENT.
YOU'RE CLEARLY USING THEM TENDERLY AND TAKING GOOD CARE OF THEM.
CREAK
I'LL HAVE TO PUT TOGETHER SOME VERY GOOD PARTS, FOR THE NEXT HUNDRED YEARS.
THANK YOU VERY MUCH.

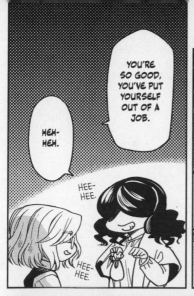

I APPRECIATE IT, SARAH... WILL THIS BE ENOUGH?
I WISH I COULD DO THE MAG-NANIMOUS THING AND REFUSE...
...BUT I'LL ADMIT, I'M GRATEFUL. ORDERS HAVE BEEN DOWN LATELY.
YOU'RE SO GOOD, YOU'VE PUT YOURSELF OUT OF A JOB.
HEH-HEH.
HEE-HEE.
HEE-HEE.
ALL RIGHT, IT'S TIME FOR YOU LOT.
CAN YOU HELP ARRANGE SOME BEDS AND FOOD?
...INNG
FWUP
WHEE
TUNK
TET
TET
TET

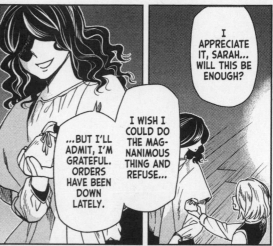

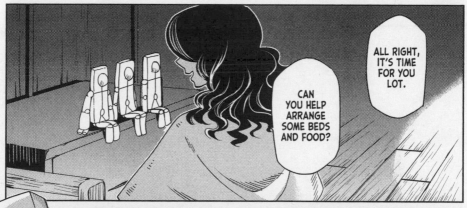

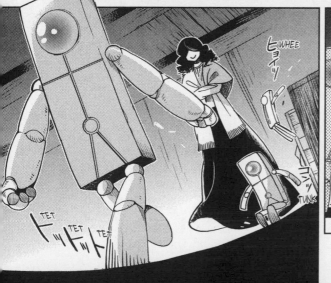

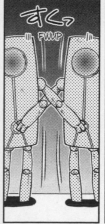

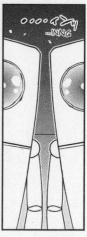

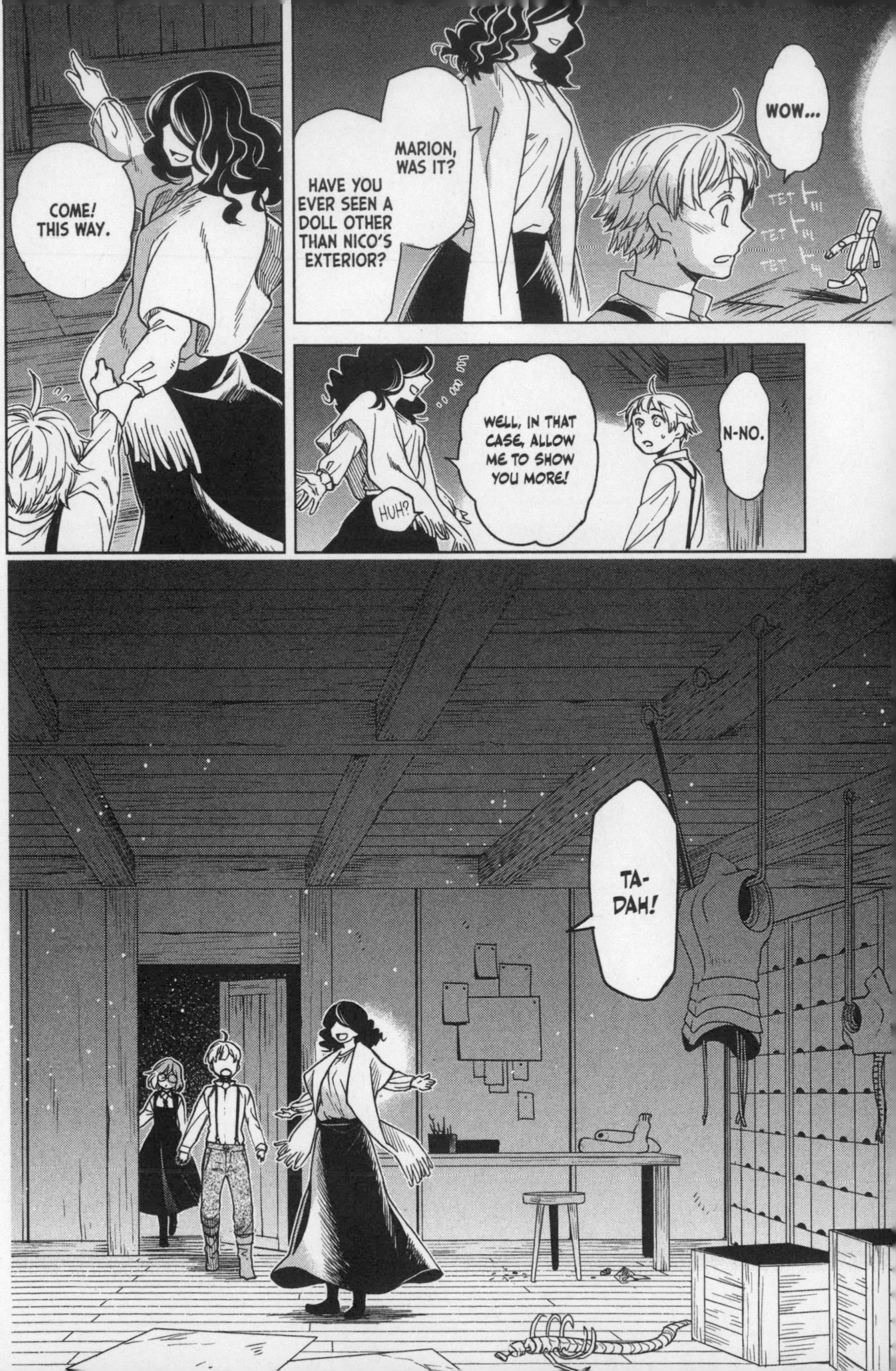
WOW...
TET TET TET
MARION, WAS IT?
HAVE YOU EVER SEEN A DOLL OTHER THAN NICO'S EXTERIOR?
N-NO.
WELL, IN THAT CASE, ALLOW ME TO SHOW YOU MORE!
HUH?
COME! THIS WAY.
TA-DAH!

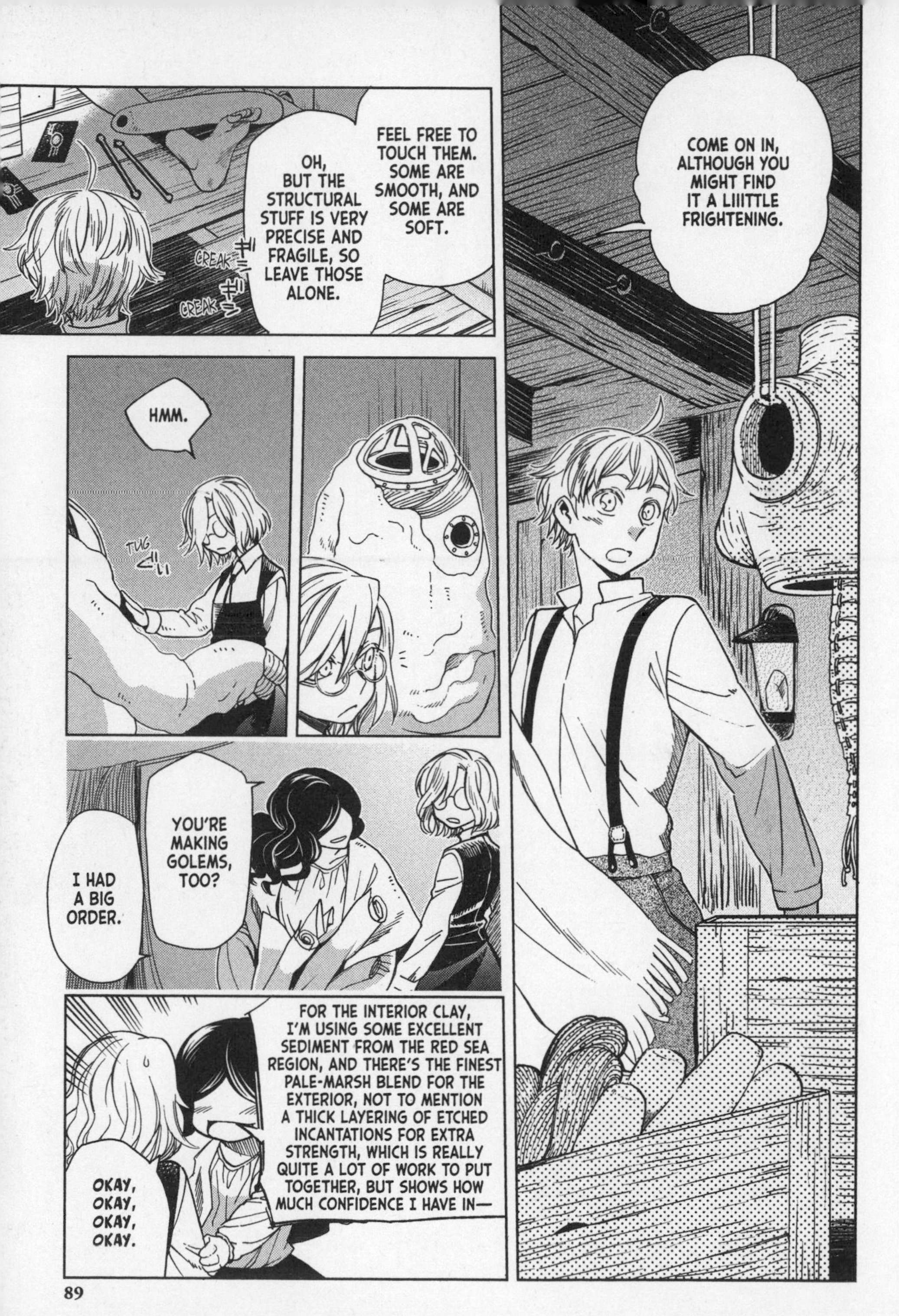
COME ON IN, ALTHOUGH YOU MIGHT FIND IT A LIIITTLE FRIGHTENING.
FEEL FREE TO TOUCH THEM. SOME ARE SMOOTH, AND SOME ARE SOFT.
OH, BUT THE STRUCTURAL STUFF IS VERY PRECISE AND FRAGILE, SO LEAVE THOSE ALONE.
CREAK
CREAK
HMM.
TUG
YOU'RE MAKING GOLEMS, TOO?
I HAD A BIG ORDER.
FOR THE INTERIOR CLAY, I'M USING SOME EXCELLENT SEDIMENT FROM THE RED SEA REGION, AND THERE'S THE FINEST PALE-MARSH BLEND FOR THE EXTERIOR, NOT TO MENTION A THICK LAYERING OF ETCHED INCANTATIONS FOR EXTRA STRENGTH, WHICH IS REALLY QUITE A LOT OF WORK TO PUT TOGETHER, BUT SHOWS HOW MUCH CONFIDENCE I HAVE IN—
OKAY, OKAY, OKAY, OKAY.

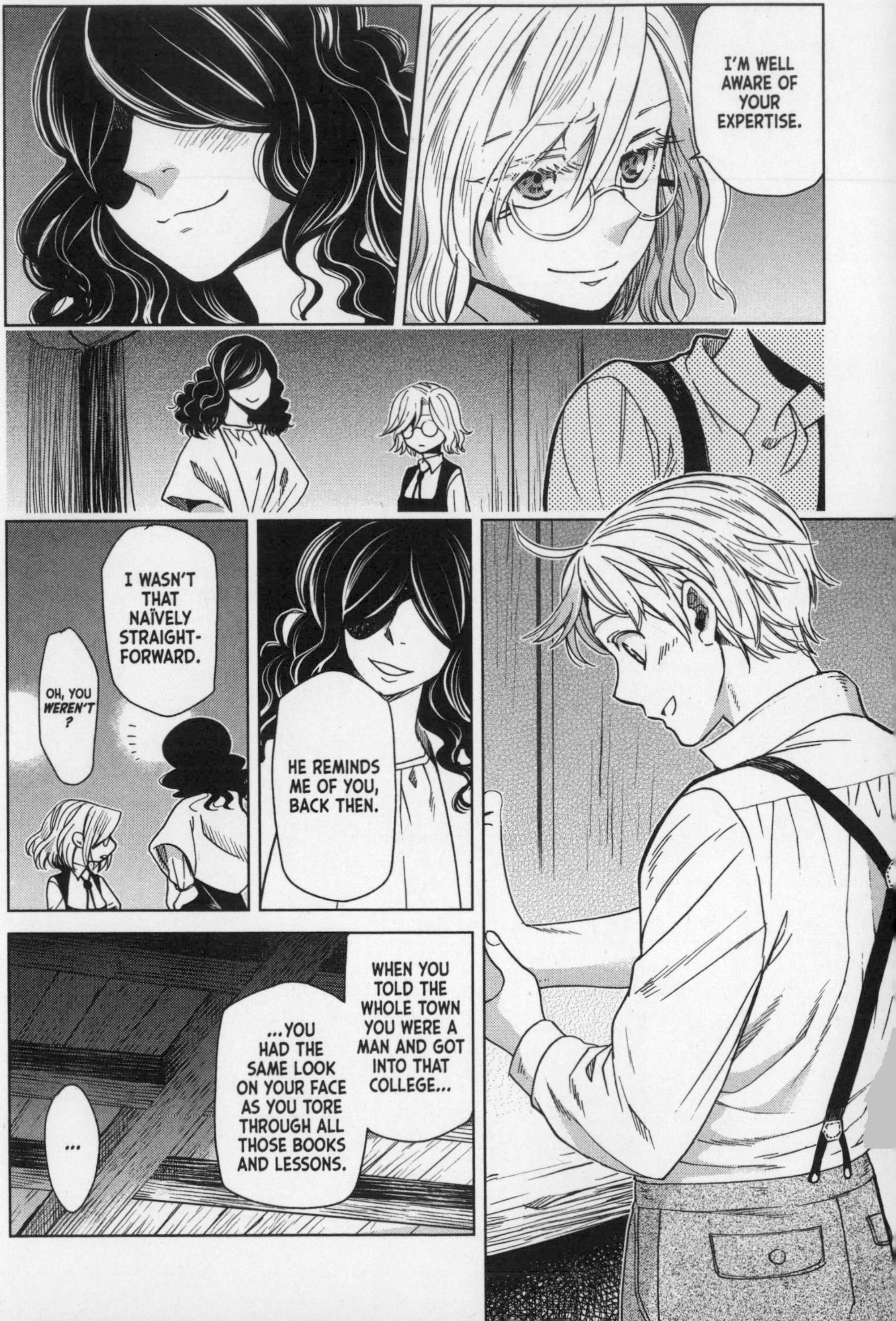
I'M WELL AWARE OF YOUR EXPERTISE.
HE REMINDS ME OF YOU, BACK THEN.
I WASN'T THAT NAÏVELY STRAIGHT-FORWARD.
OH, YOU *WEREN'T*?
WHEN YOU TOLD THE WHOLE TOWN YOU WERE A MAN AND GOT INTO THAT COLLEGE...
...YOU HAD THE SAME LOOK ON YOUR FACE AS YOU TORE THROUGH ALL THOSE BOOKS AND LESSONS.
...

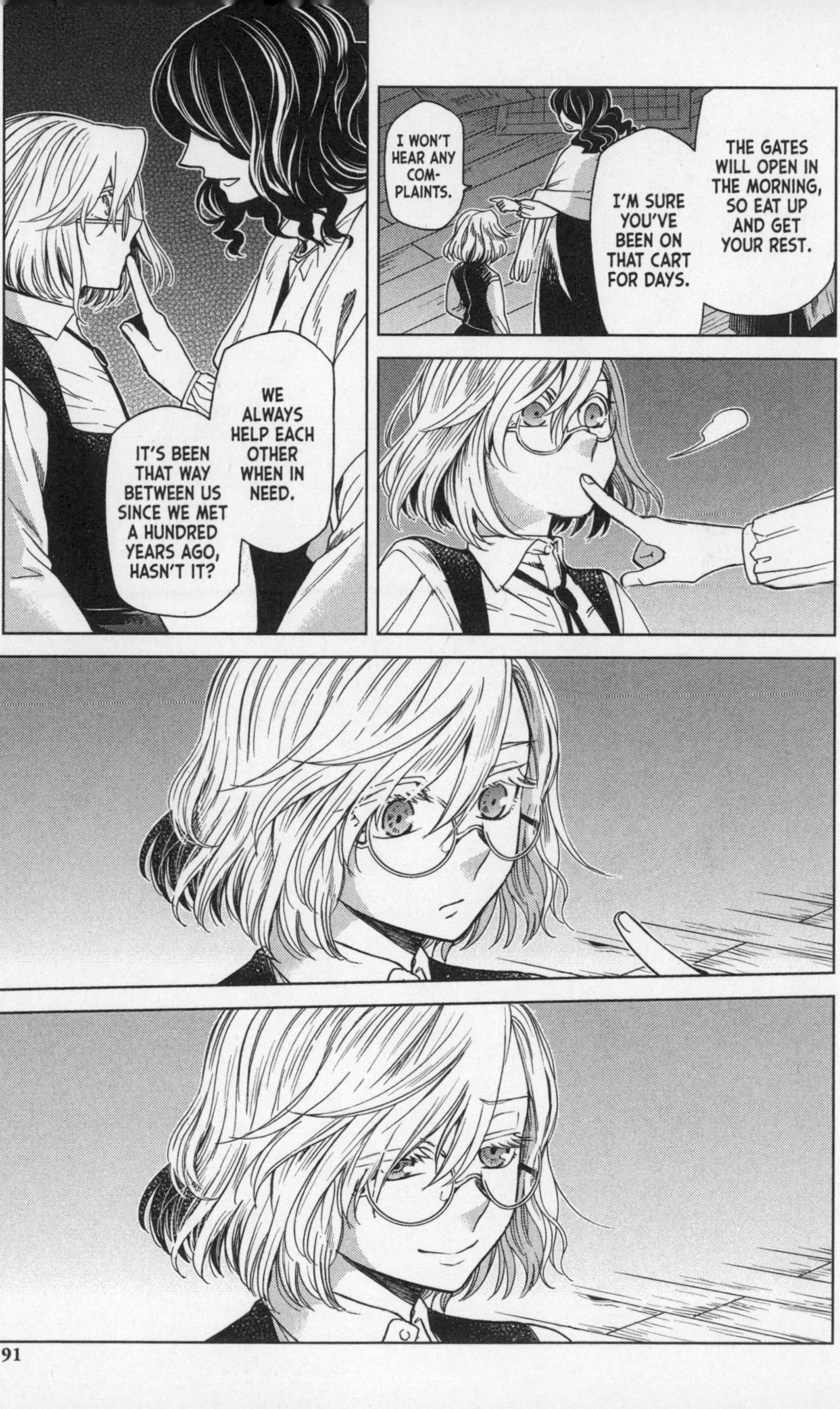
THE GATES WILL OPEN IN THE MORNING, SO EAT UP AND GET YOUR REST.
I'M SURE YOU'VE BEEN ON THAT CART FOR DAYS.
I WON'T HEAR ANY COM-PLAINTS.
WE ALWAYS HELP EACH OTHER WHEN IN NEED.
IT'S BEEN THAT WAY BETWEEN US SINCE WE MET A HUNDRED YEARS AGO, HASN'T IT?

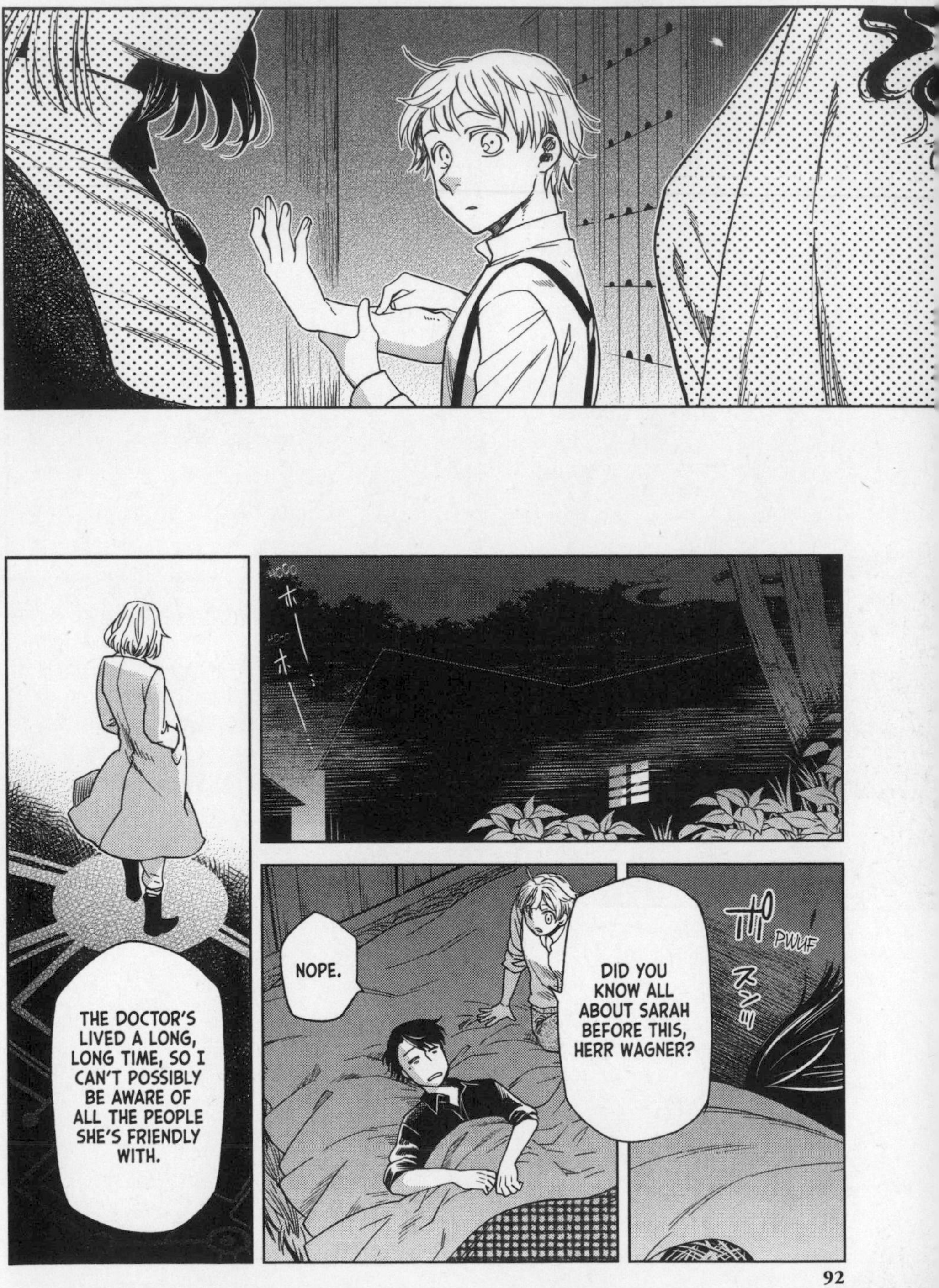
HOOO
HOOO
PWUF
DID YOU KNOW ALL ABOUT SARAH BEFORE THIS, HERR WAGNER?
NOPE.
THE DOCTOR'S LIVED A LONG, LONG TIME, SO I CAN'T POSSIBLY BE AWARE OF ALL THE PEOPLE SHE'S FRIENDLY WITH.

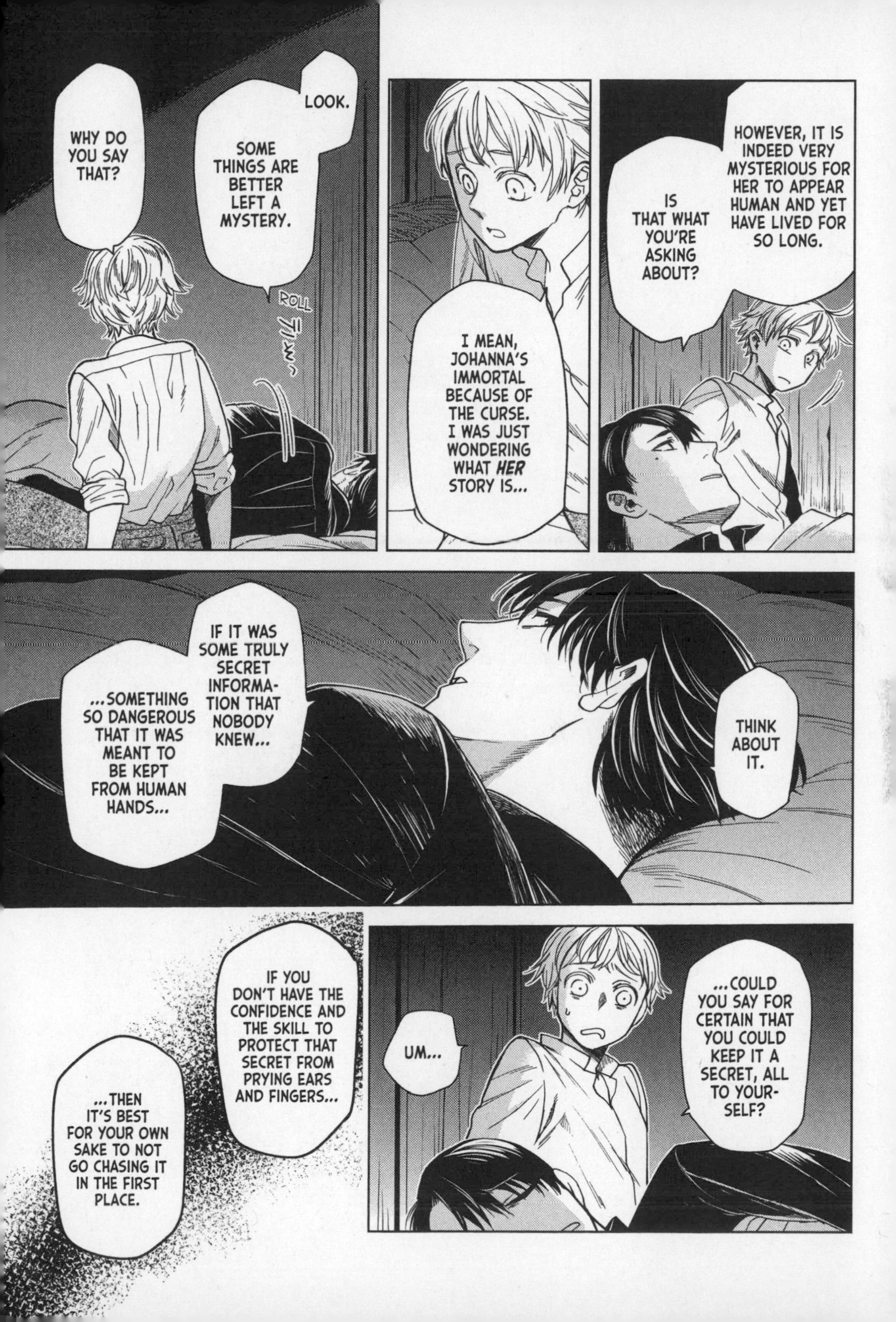
HOWEVER, IT IS INDEED VERY MYSTERIOUS FOR HER TO APPEAR HUMAN AND YET HAVE LIVED FOR SO LONG.
IS THAT WHAT YOU'RE ASKING ABOUT?
I MEAN, JOHANNA'S IMMORTAL BECAUSE OF THE CURSE. I WAS JUST WONDERING WHAT *HER* STORY IS...
LOOK.
SOME THINGS ARE BETTER LEFT A MYSTERY.
WHY DO YOU SAY THAT?
ROLL
THINK ABOUT IT.
IF IT WAS SOME TRULY SECRET INFORMATION THAT NOBODY KNEW...
...SOMETHING SO DANGEROUS THAT IT WAS MEANT TO BE KEPT FROM HUMAN HANDS...
...COULD YOU SAY FOR CERTAIN THAT YOU COULD KEEP IT A SECRET, ALL TO YOURSELF?
UM...
IF YOU DON'T HAVE THE CONFIDENCE AND THE SKILL TO PROTECT THAT SECRET FROM PRYING EARS AND FINGERS...
...THEN IT'S BEST FOR YOUR OWN SAKE TO NOT GO CHASING IT IN THE FIRST PLACE.

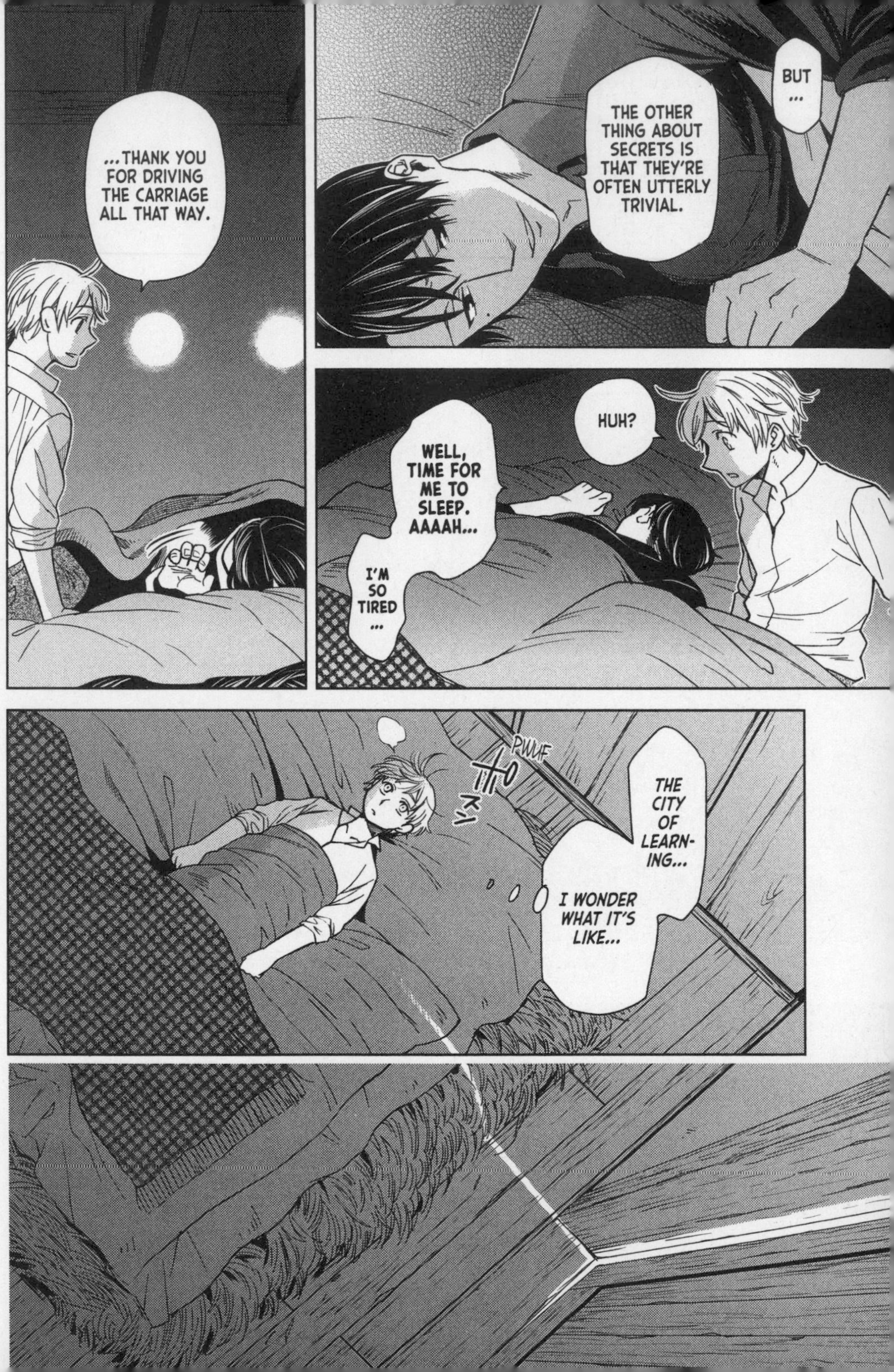
BUT ...
THE OTHER THING ABOUT SECRETS IS THAT THEY'RE OFTEN UTTERLY TRIVIAL.
HUH?
WELL, TIME FOR ME TO SLEEP. AAAAH...
I'M SO TIRED ...
...THANK YOU FOR DRIVING THE CARRIAGE ALL THAT WAY.
PWUF
THE CITY OF LEARNING...
I WONDER WHAT IT'S LIKE...

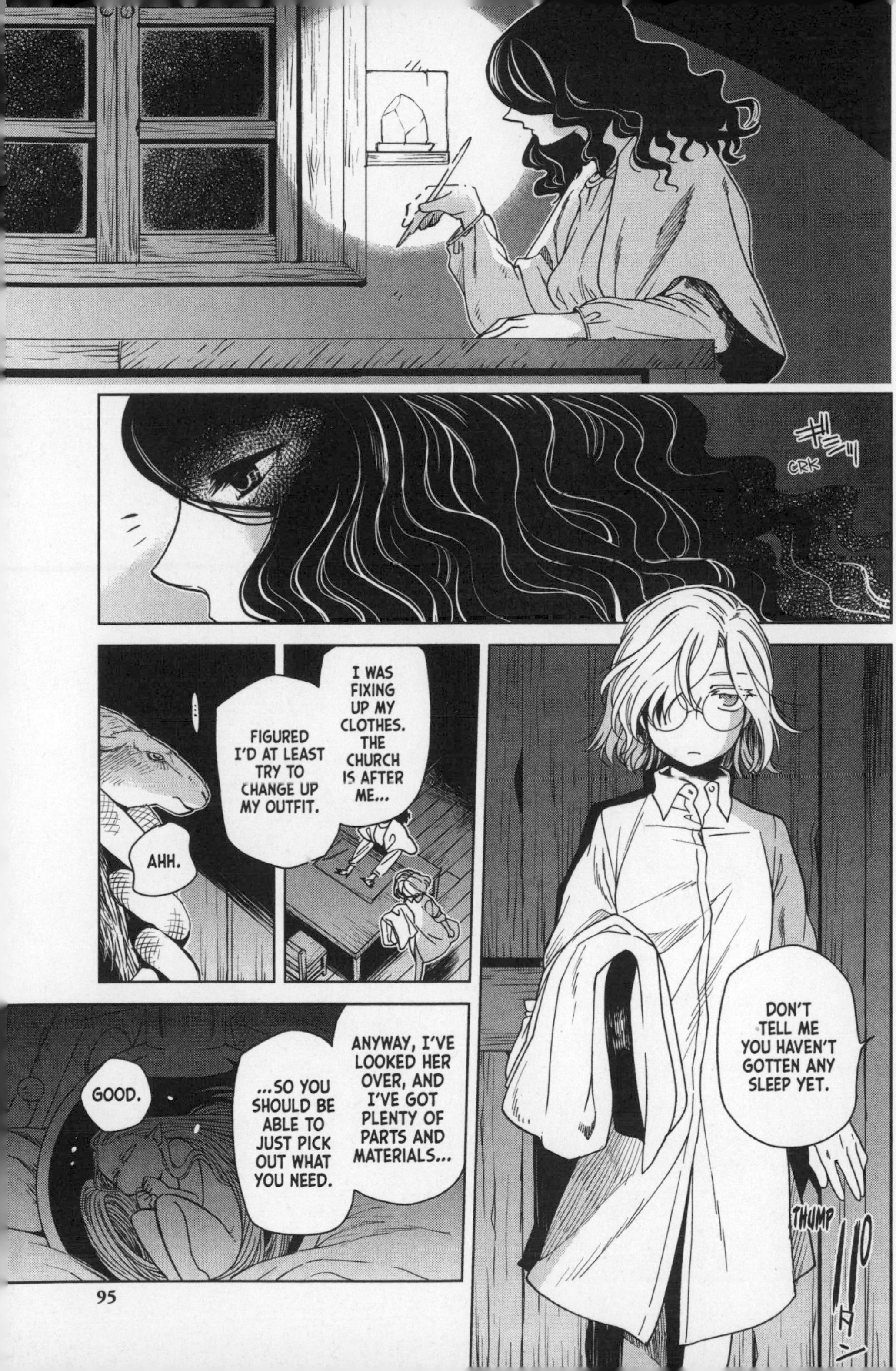
CRK
DON'T TELL ME YOU HAVEN'T GOTTEN ANY SLEEP YET.
THUMP
I WAS FIXING UP MY CLOTHES. THE CHURCH IS AFTER ME...
FIGURED I'D AT LEAST TRY TO CHANGE UP MY OUTFIT.
...
AHH.
ANYWAY, I'VE LOOKED HER OVER, AND I'VE GOT PLENTY OF PARTS AND MATERIALS...
...SO YOU SHOULD BE ABLE TO JUST PICK OUT WHAT YOU NEED.
GOOD.

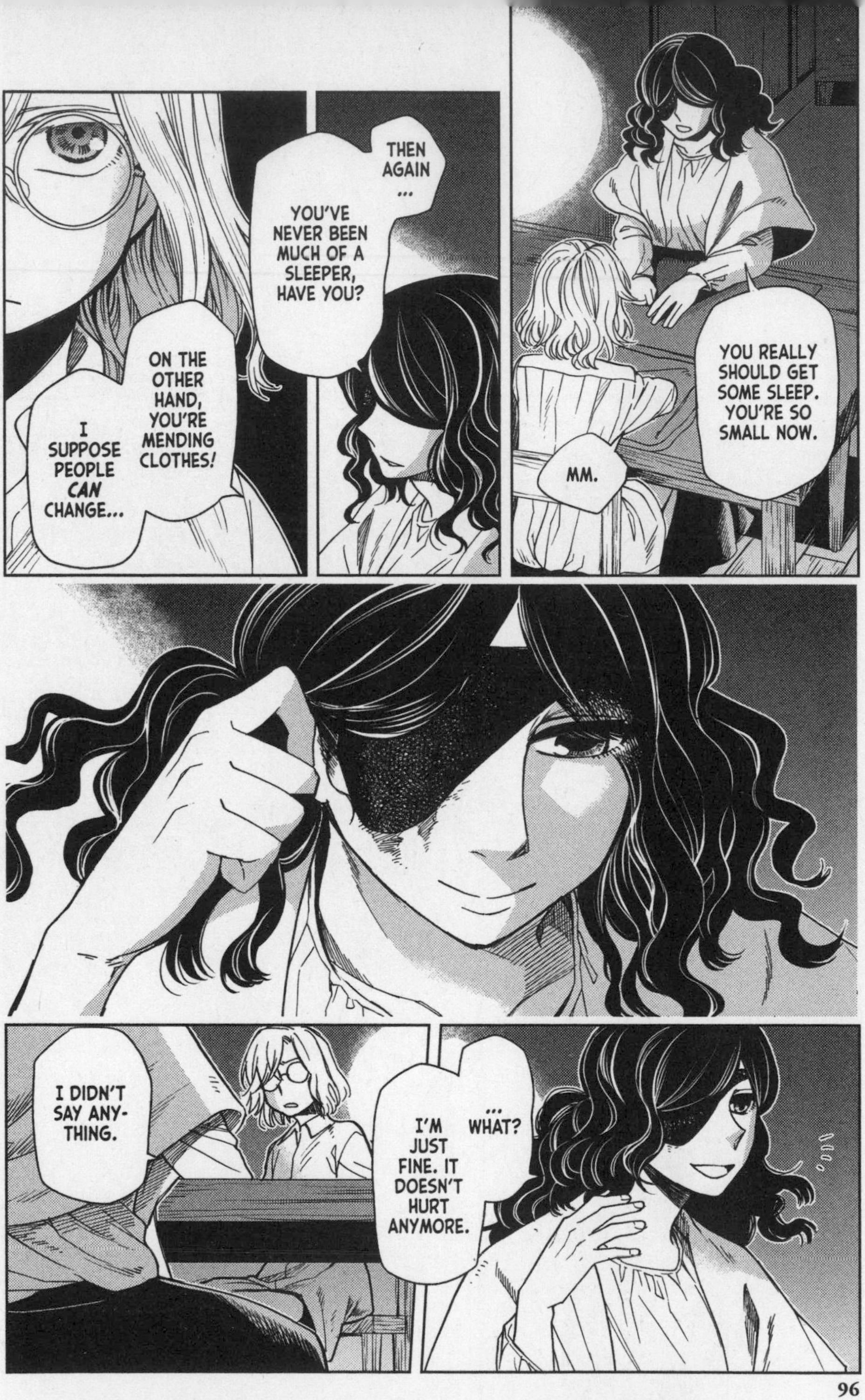
YOU REALLY SHOULD GET SOME SLEEP. YOU'RE SO SMALL NOW.
MM.
THEN AGAIN ...
YOU'VE NEVER BEEN MUCH OF A SLEEPER, HAVE YOU?
ON THE OTHER HAND, YOU'RE MENDING CLOTHES!
I SUPPOSE PEOPLE *CAN* CHANGE...
... WHAT?
I'M JUST FINE. IT DOESN'T HURT ANYMORE.
I DIDN'T SAY ANY-THING.

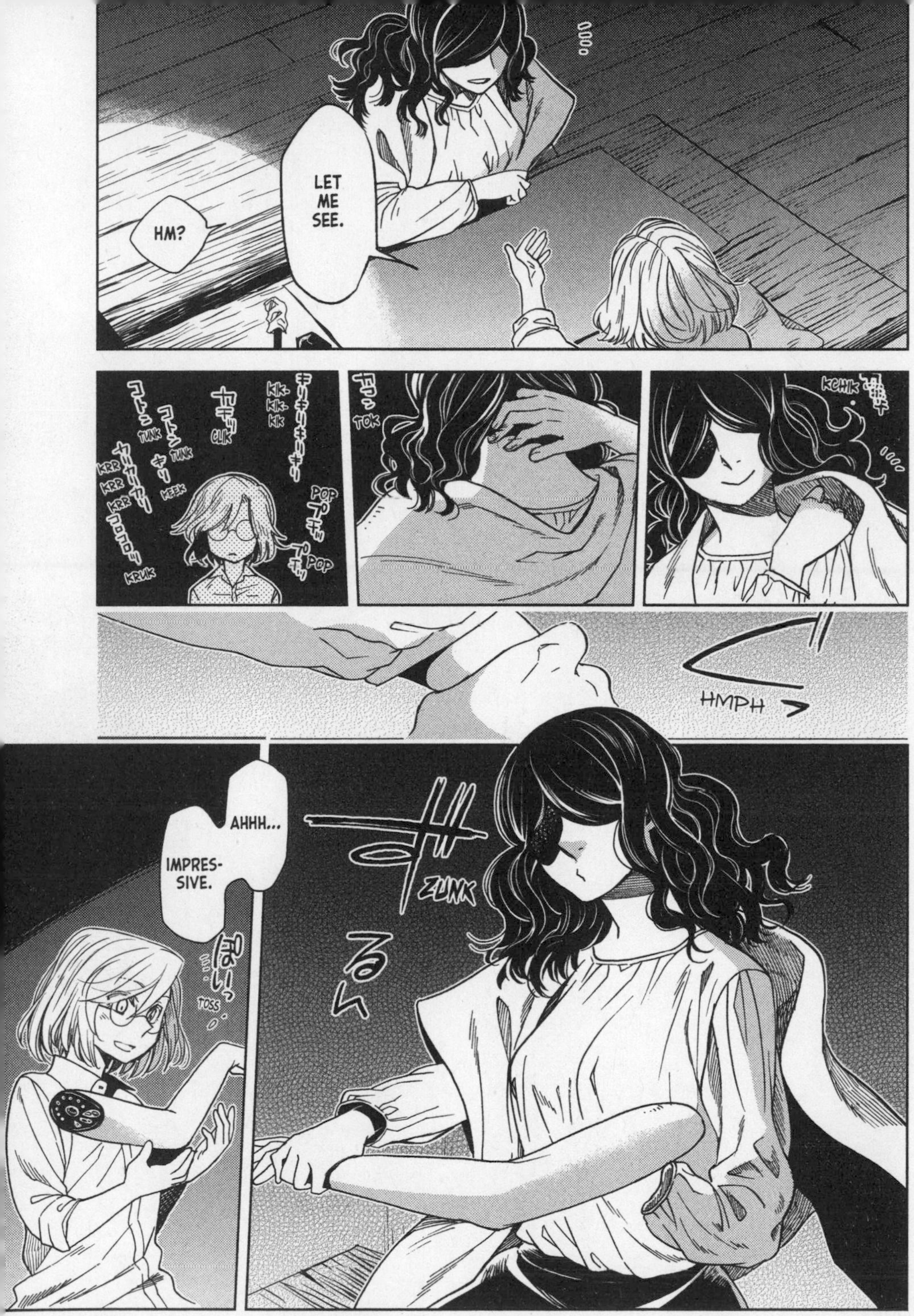
LET ME SEE.
HM?
KCHIK
TOK
KK- KK- KK
CLIK
TUNK
TUNK
KEEK
POP
POP
KRR KRR KRR
KRUK
HMPH
ZUNK
AHHH... IMPRES- SIVE.
TOSS

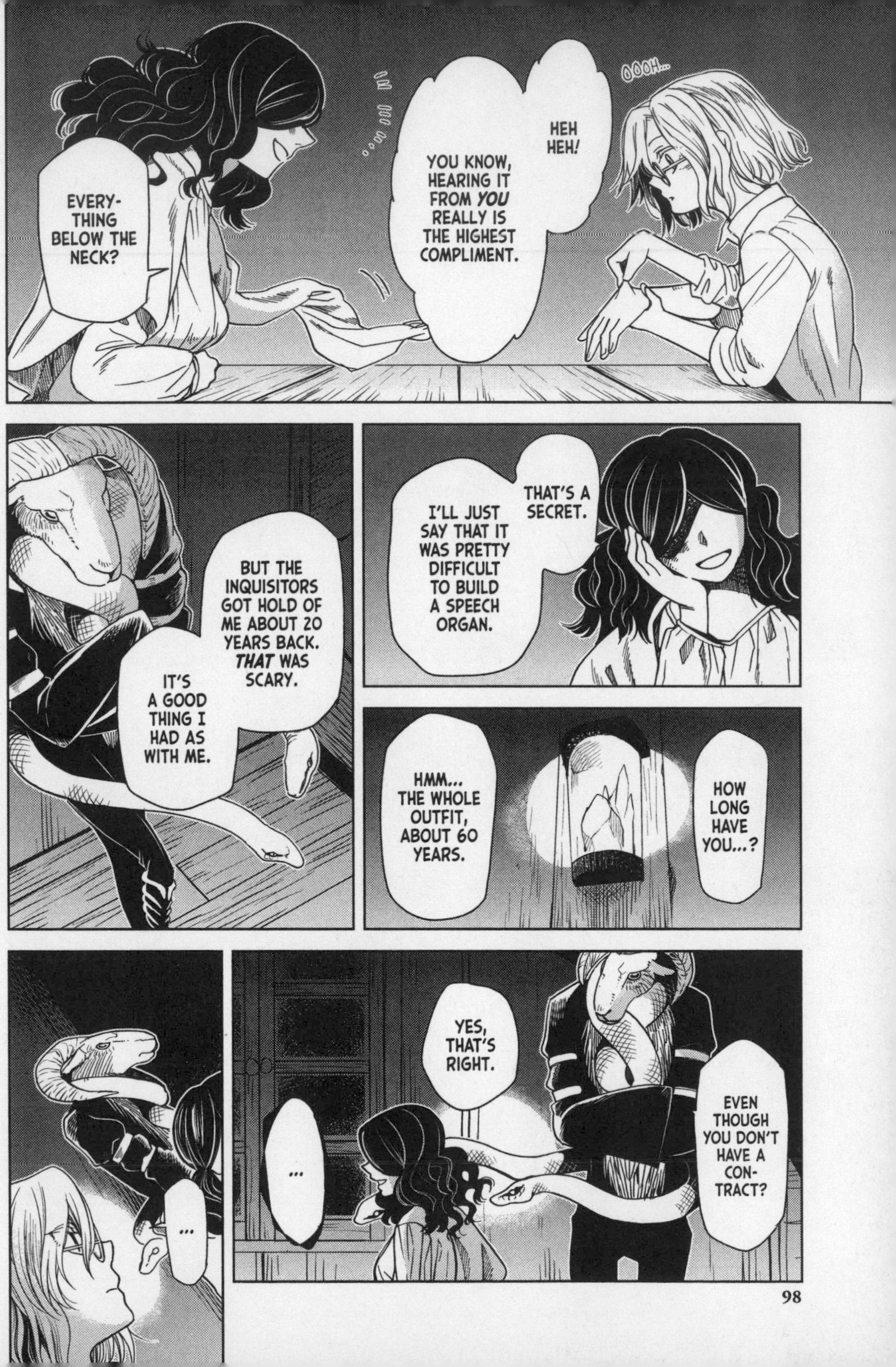
OOOH...
HEH HEH!
YOU KNOW, HEARING IT FROM *YOU* REALLY IS THE HIGHEST COMPLIMENT.
EVERY-THING BELOW THE NECK?
THAT'S A SECRET.
I'LL JUST SAY THAT IT WAS PRETTY DIFFICULT TO BUILD A SPEECH ORGAN.
HOW LONG HAVE YOU...?
HMM... THE WHOLE OUTFIT, ABOUT 60 YEARS.
BUT THE INQUISITORS GOT HOLD OF ME ABOUT 20 YEARS BACK. *THAT* WAS SCARY.
IT'S A GOOD THING I HAD AS WITH ME.
EVEN THOUGH YOU DON'T HAVE A CON-TRACT?
YES, THAT'S RIGHT.
...
...

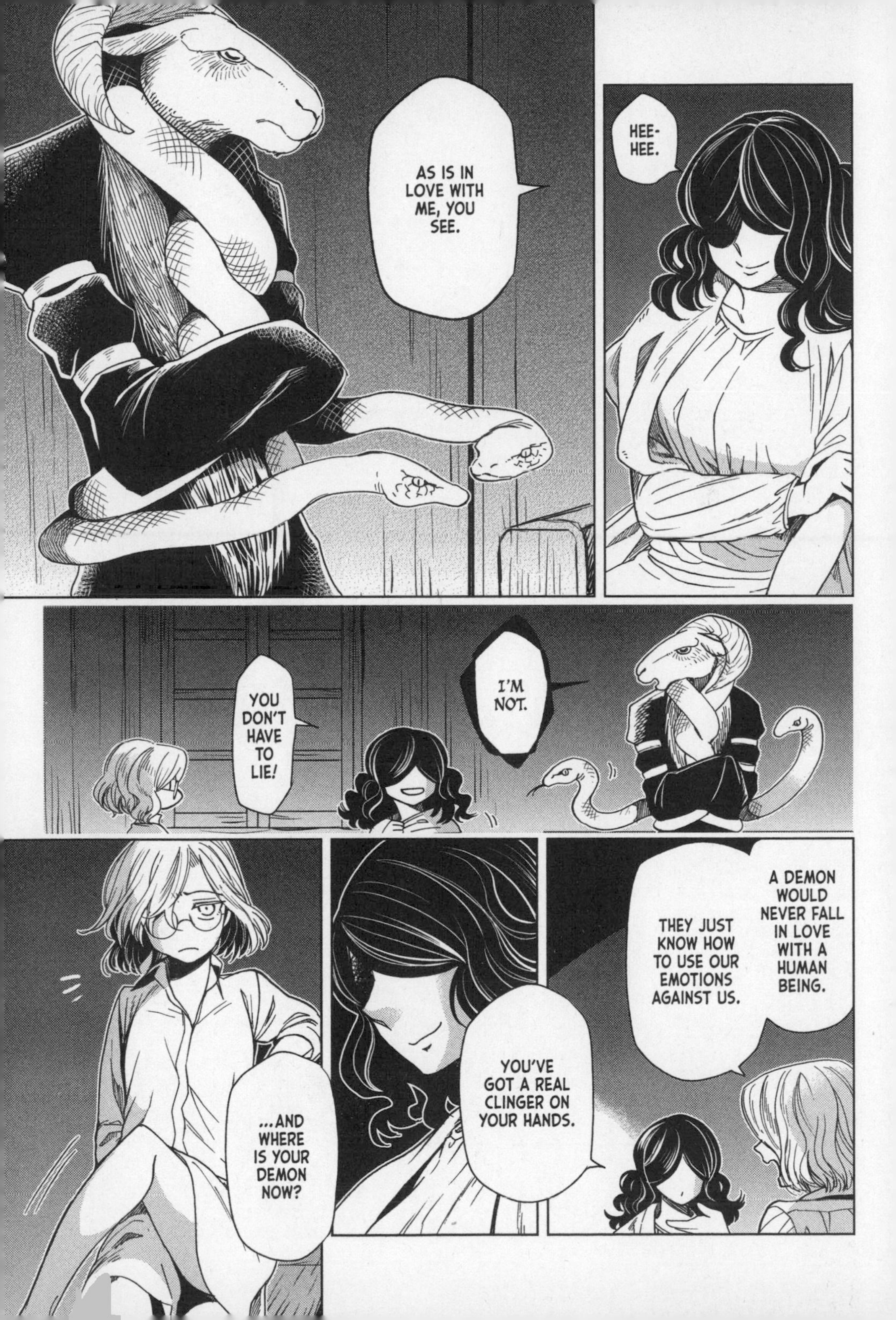
HEE-HEE.
AS IS IN LOVE WITH ME, YOU SEE.
I'M NOT.
YOU DON'T HAVE TO LIE!
A DEMON WOULD NEVER FALL IN LOVE WITH A HUMAN BEING.
THEY JUST KNOW HOW TO USE OUR EMOTIONS AGAINST US.
YOU'VE GOT A REAL CLINGER ON YOUR HANDS.
...AND WHERE IS YOUR DEMON NOW?

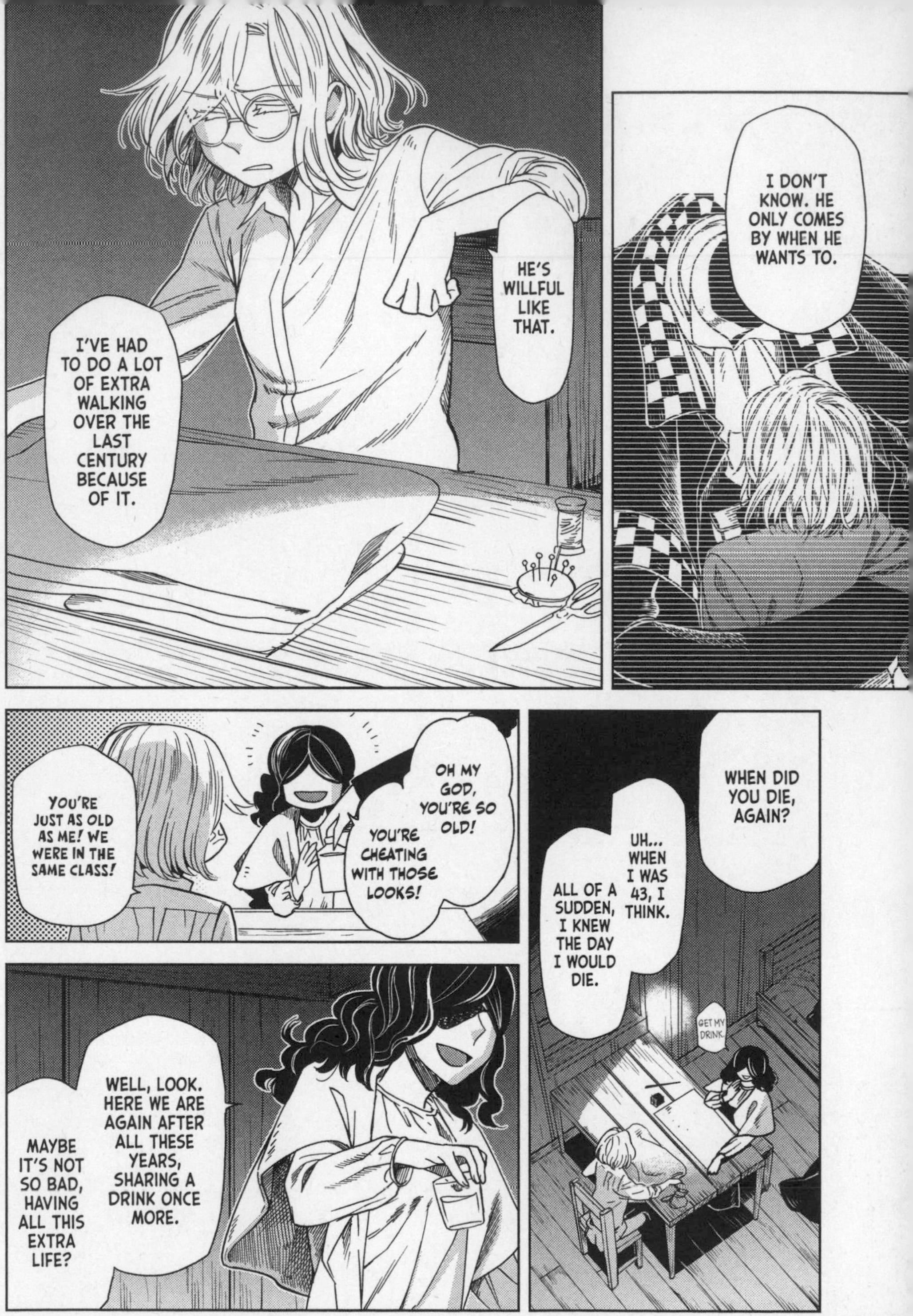
I DON'T KNOW. HE ONLY COMES BY WHEN HE WANTS TO.
HE'S WILLFUL LIKE THAT.
I'VE HAD TO DO A LOT OF EXTRA WALKING OVER THE LAST CENTURY BECAUSE OF IT.
WHEN DID YOU DIE, AGAIN?
UH... WHEN I WAS 43, I THINK.
ALL OF A SUDDEN, I KNEW THE DAY I WOULD DIE.
GET MY DRINK.
OH MY GOD, YOU'RE SO OLD!
YOU'RE CHEATING WITH THOSE LOOKS!
YOU'RE JUST AS OLD AS ME! WE WERE IN THE SAME CLASS!
WELL, LOOK. HERE WE ARE AGAIN AFTER ALL THESE YEARS, SHARING A DRINK ONCE MORE.
MAYBE IT'S NOT SO BAD, HAVING ALL THIS EXTRA LIFE?

I COULDN'T DISAGREE MORE.

URP

THIS IS... TEA, ISN'T IT?

YOU KNOW YOU CAN'T HANDLE YOUR LIQUOR.

KLATTER

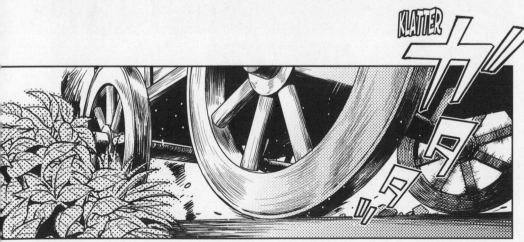

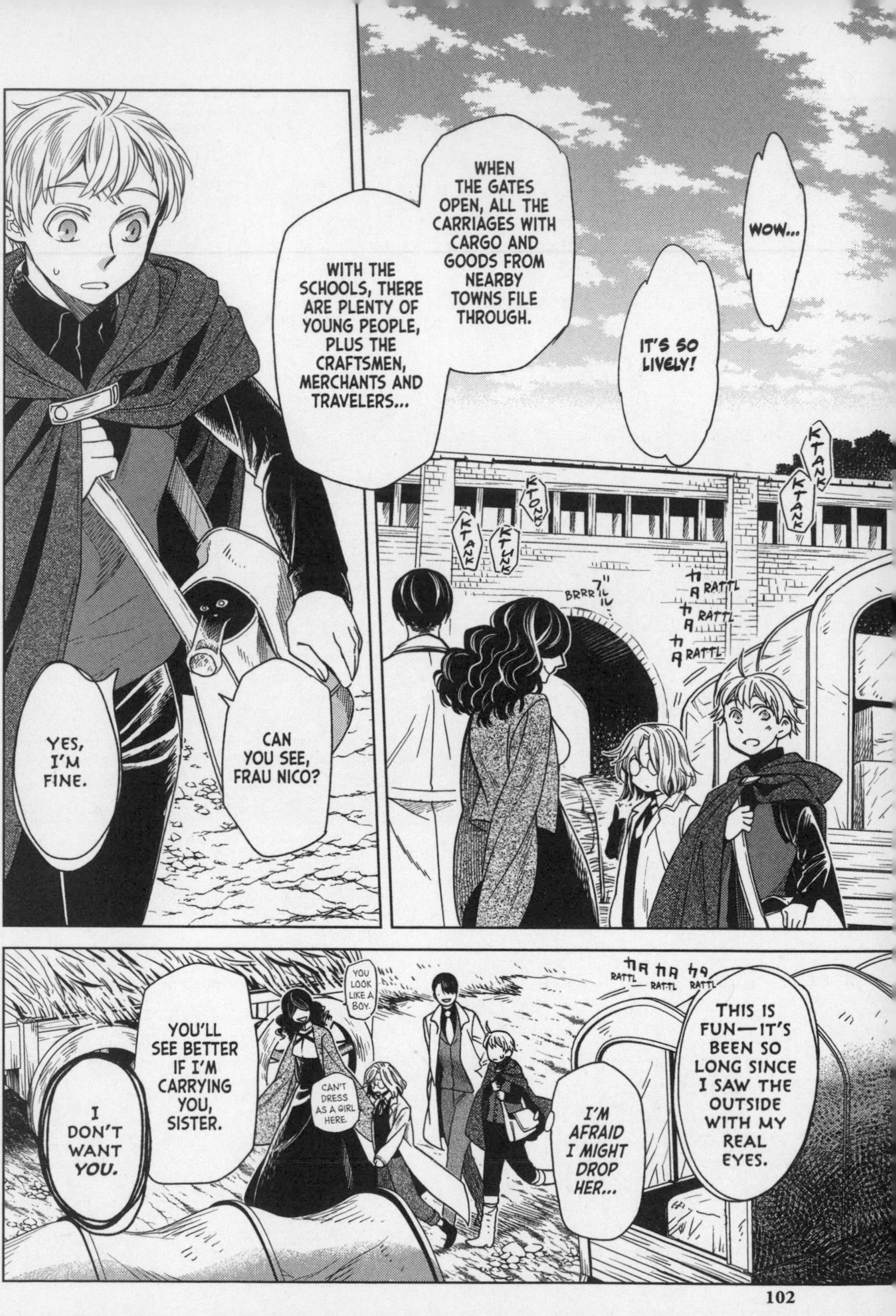

WOW...
IT'S SO LIVELY!
WHEN THE GATES OPEN, ALL THE CARRIAGES WITH CARGO AND GOODS FROM NEARBY TOWNS FILE THROUGH.
WITH THE SCHOOLS, THERE ARE PLENTY OF YOUNG PEOPLE, PLUS THE CRAFTSMEN, MERCHANTS AND TRAVELERS...
KTANK
KTANK
KTONK
KTUNK
KTANK
BRRR
RATTL
RATTL
RATTL
CAN YOU SEE, FRAU NICO?
YES, I'M FINE.
RATTL RATTL RATTL
THIS IS FUN—IT'S BEEN SO LONG SINCE I SAW THE OUTSIDE WITH MY REAL EYES.
I'M AFRAID I MIGHT DROP HER...
YOU LOOK LIKE A BOY.
CAN'T DRESS AS A GIRL HERE.
YOU'LL SEE BETTER IF I'M CARRYING YOU, SISTER.
I DON'T WANT *YOU.*

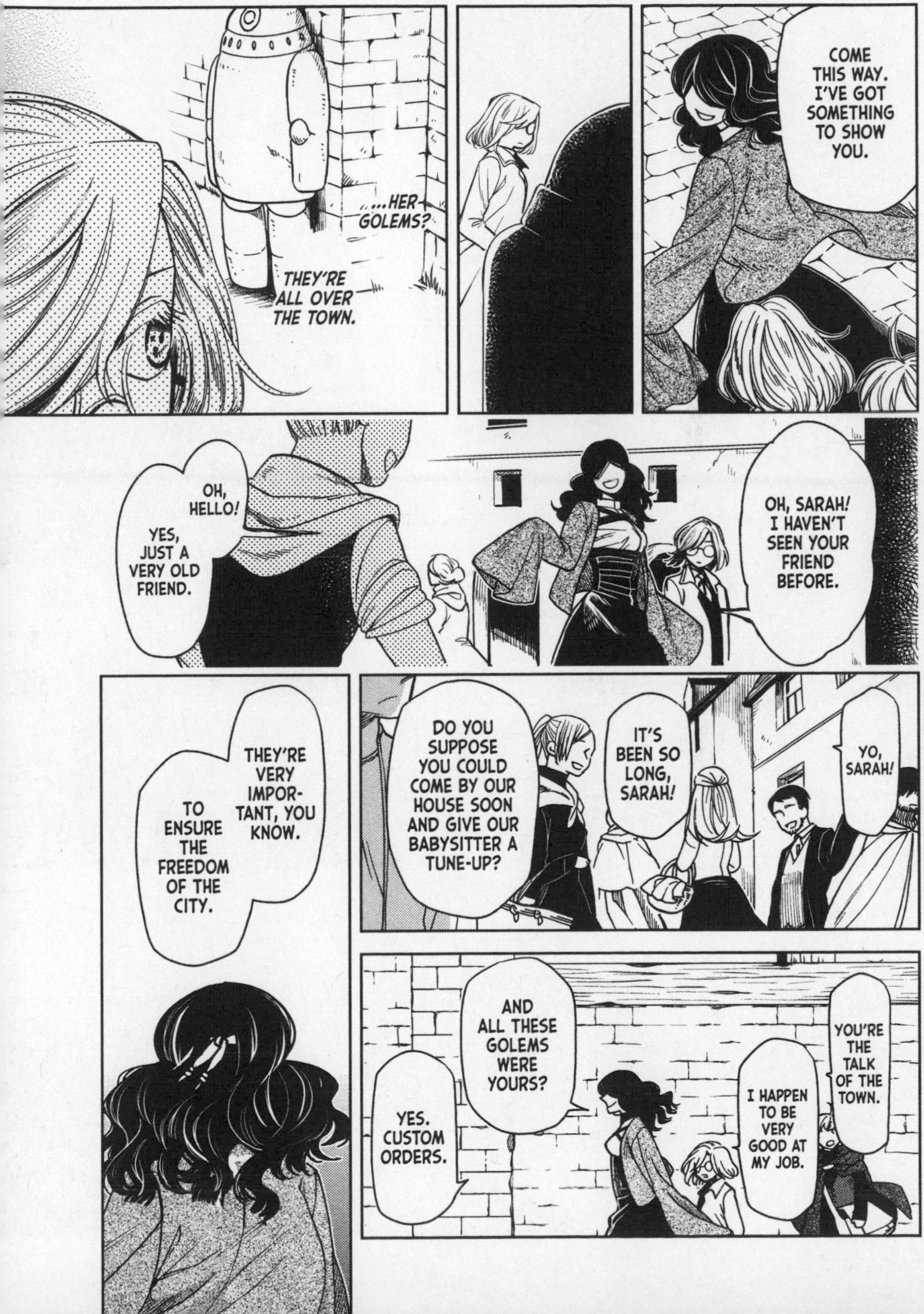
COME THIS WAY. I'VE GOT SOMETHING TO SHOW YOU.
...HER GOLEMS?
THEY'RE ALL OVER THE TOWN.
OH, SARAH! I HAVEN'T SEEN YOUR FRIEND BEFORE.
OH, HELLO!
YES, JUST A VERY OLD FRIEND.
YO, SARAH!
IT'S BEEN SO LONG, SARAH!
DO YOU SUPPOSE YOU COULD COME BY OUR HOUSE SOON AND GIVE OUR BABYSITTER A TUNE-UP?
YOU'RE THE TALK OF THE TOWN.
I HAPPEN TO BE VERY GOOD AT MY JOB.
AND ALL THESE GOLEMS WERE YOURS?
YES. CUSTOM ORDERS.
THEY'RE VERY IMPOR-TANT, YOU KNOW.
TO ENSURE THE FREEDOM OF THE CITY.

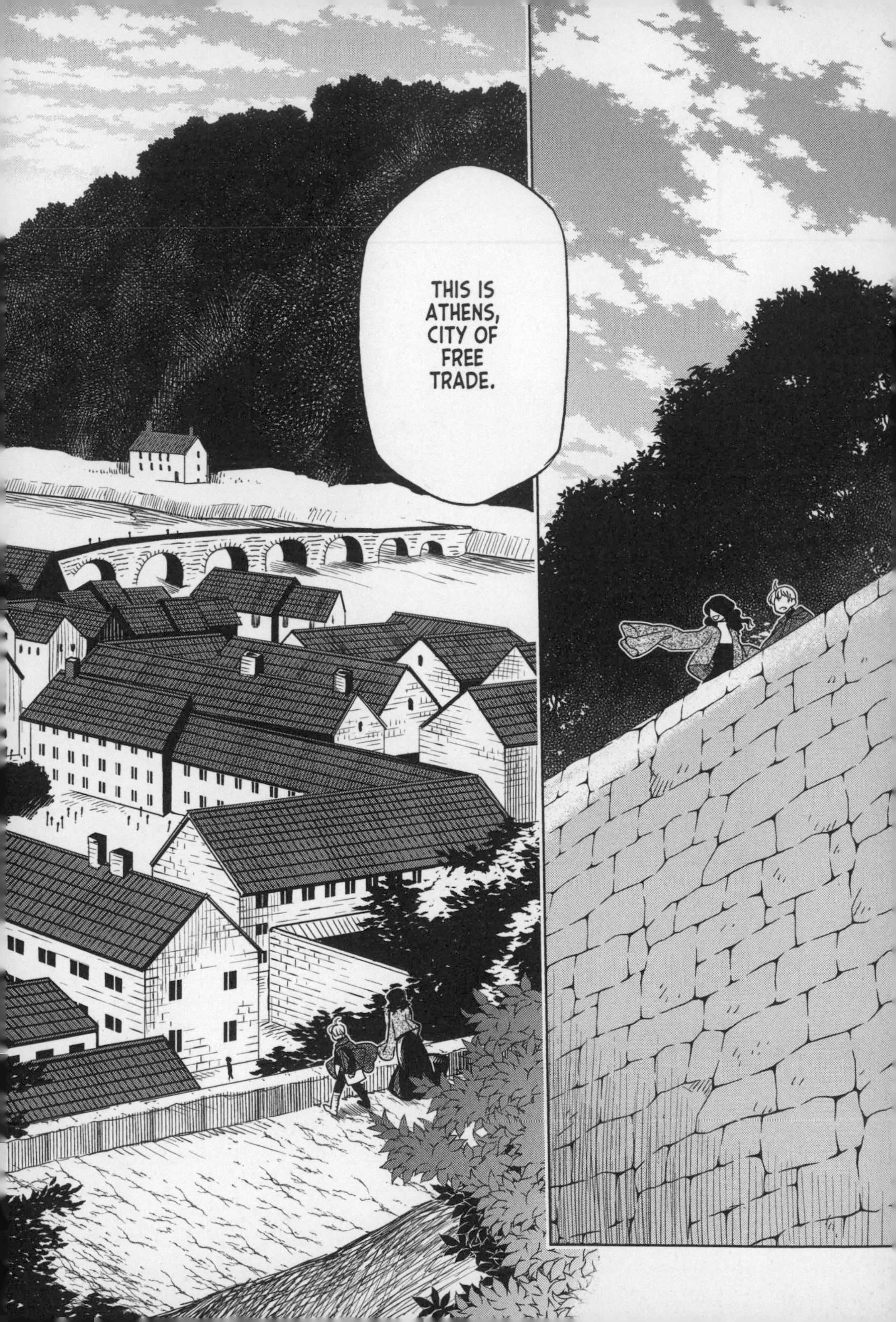
THIS IS ATHENS, CITY OF FREE TRADE.

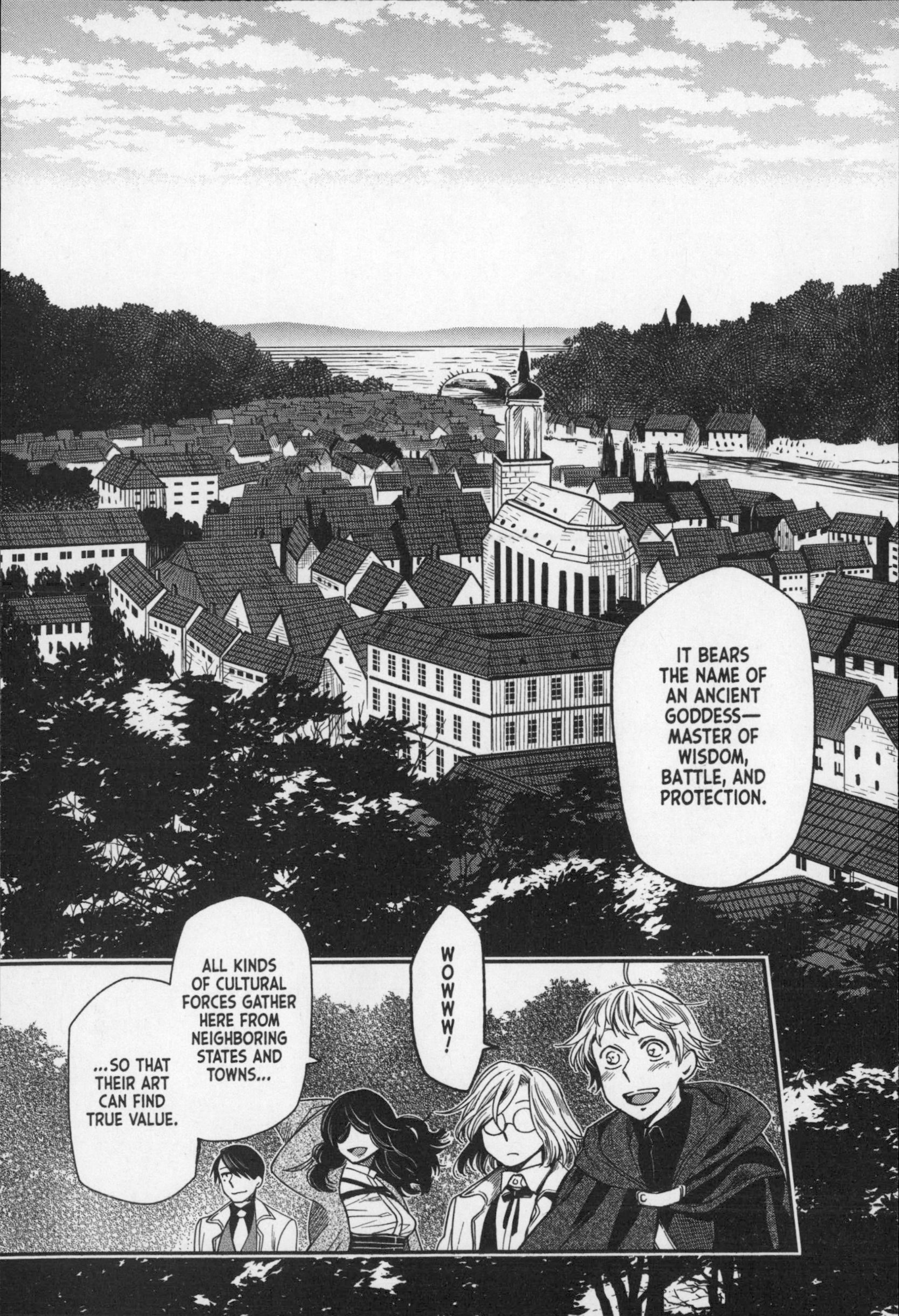
IT BEARS THE NAME OF AN ANCIENT GODDESS—MASTER OF WISDOM, BATTLE, AND PROTECTION.
WOWWW!
ALL KINDS OF CULTURAL FORCES GATHER HERE FROM NEIGHBORING STATES AND TOWNS...
...SO THAT THEIR ART CAN FIND TRUE VALUE.

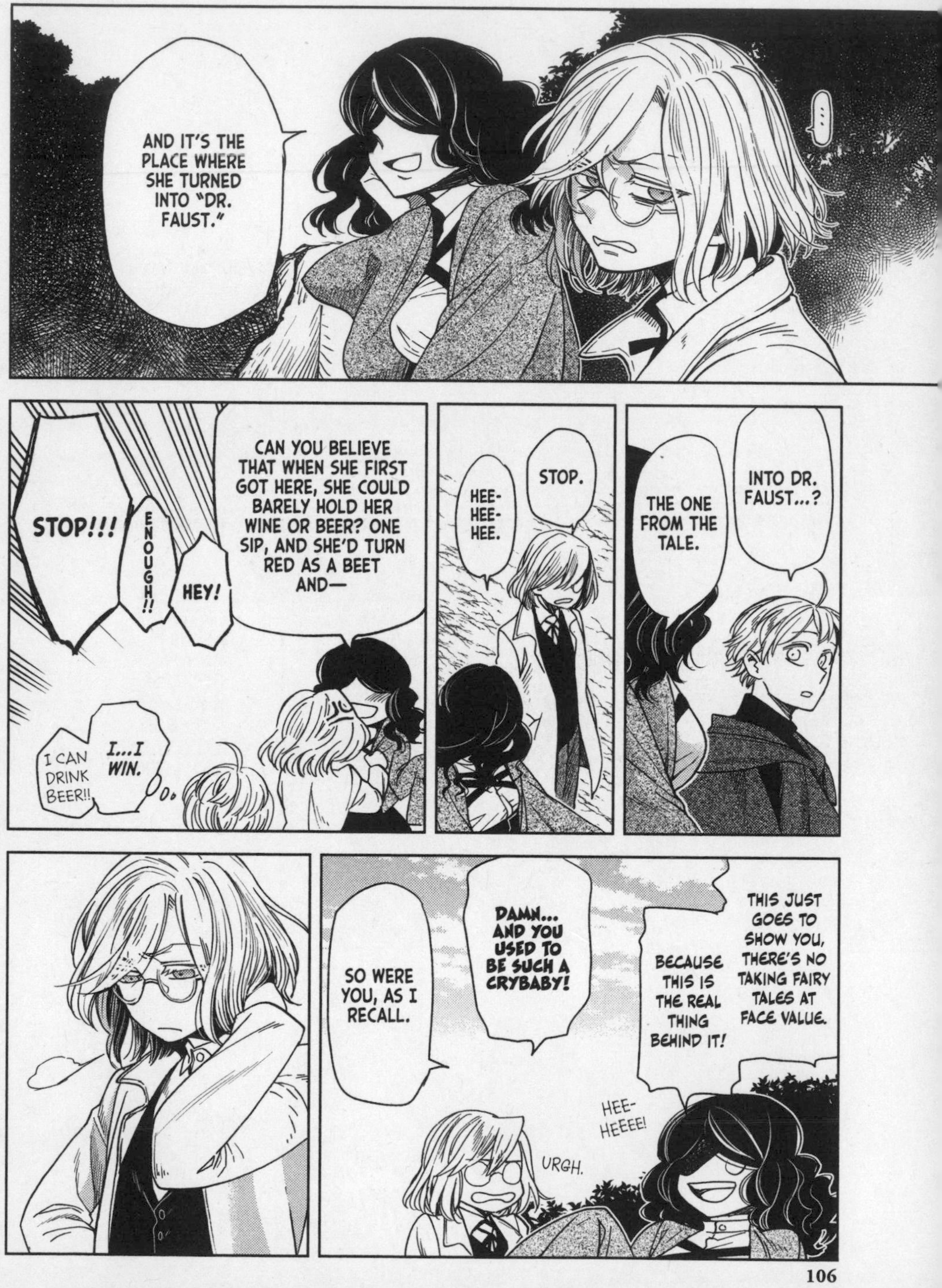
...
AND IT'S THE PLACE WHERE SHE TURNED INTO "DR. FAUST."
INTO DR. FAUST...?
THE ONE FROM THE TALE.
STOP.
HEE-HEE-HEE.
CAN YOU BELIEVE THAT WHEN SHE FIRST GOT HERE, SHE COULD BARELY HOLD HER WINE OR BEER? ONE SIP, AND SHE'D TURN RED AS A BEET AND—
HEY!
ENOUGH!!
STOP!!!
I...I WIN.
I CAN DRINK BEER!!
THIS JUST GOES TO SHOW YOU, THERE'S NO TAKING FAIRY TALES AT FACE VALUE.
BECAUSE THIS IS THE REAL THING BEHIND IT!
DAMN... AND YOU USED TO BE SUCH A CRYBABY!
SO WERE YOU, AS I RECALL.
HEE-HEEEE!
URGH.

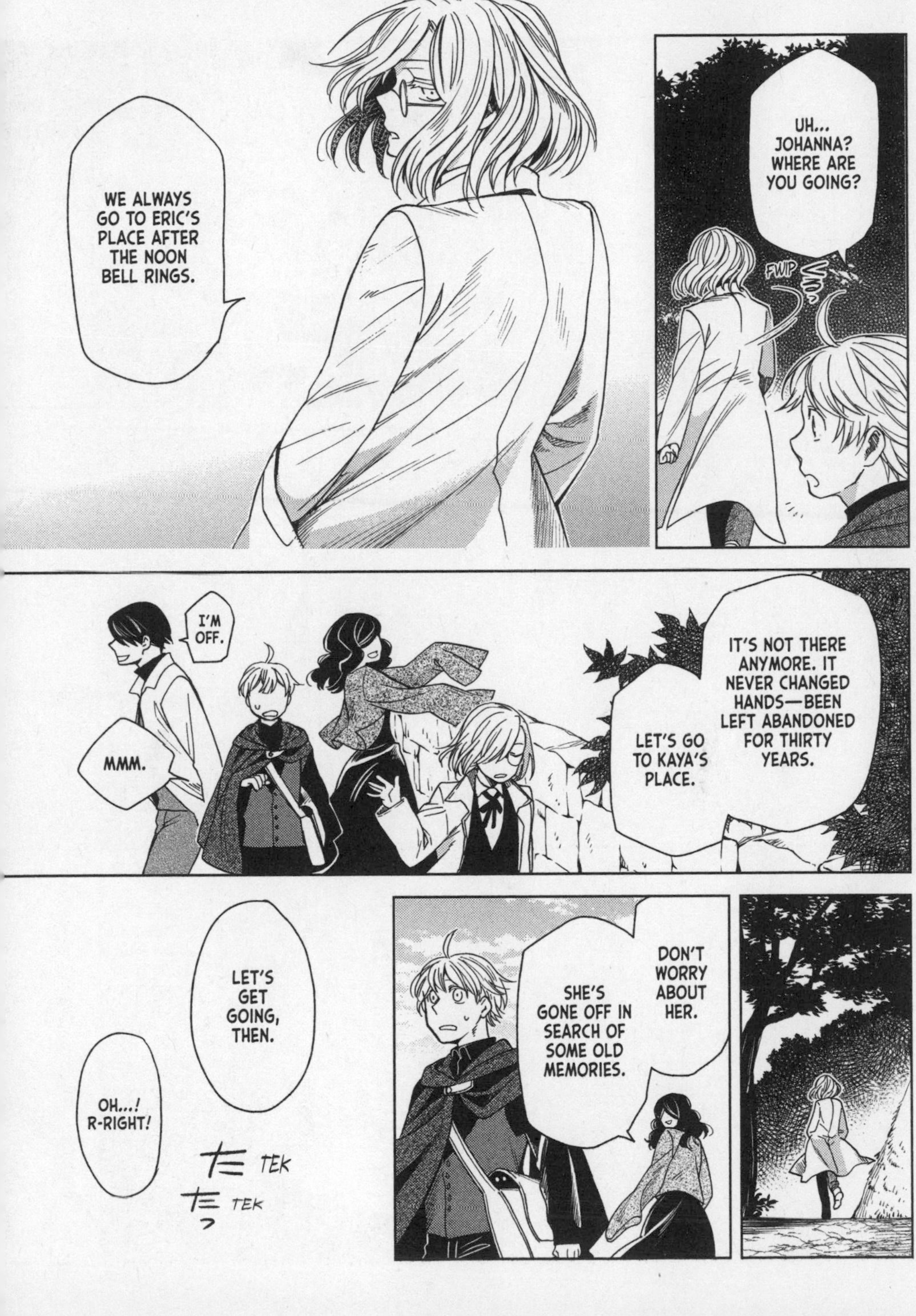
UH... JOHANNA? WHERE ARE YOU GOING?
FWIP
WE ALWAYS GO TO ERIC'S PLACE AFTER THE NOON BELL RINGS.
IT'S NOT THERE ANYMORE. IT NEVER CHANGED HANDS—BEEN LEFT ABANDONED FOR THIRTY YEARS.
LET'S GO TO KAYA'S PLACE.
I'M OFF.
MMM.
DON'T WORRY ABOUT HER.
SHE'S GONE OFF IN SEARCH OF SOME OLD MEMORIES.
LET'S GET GOING, THEN.
OH...! R-RIGHT!
TEK
TEK

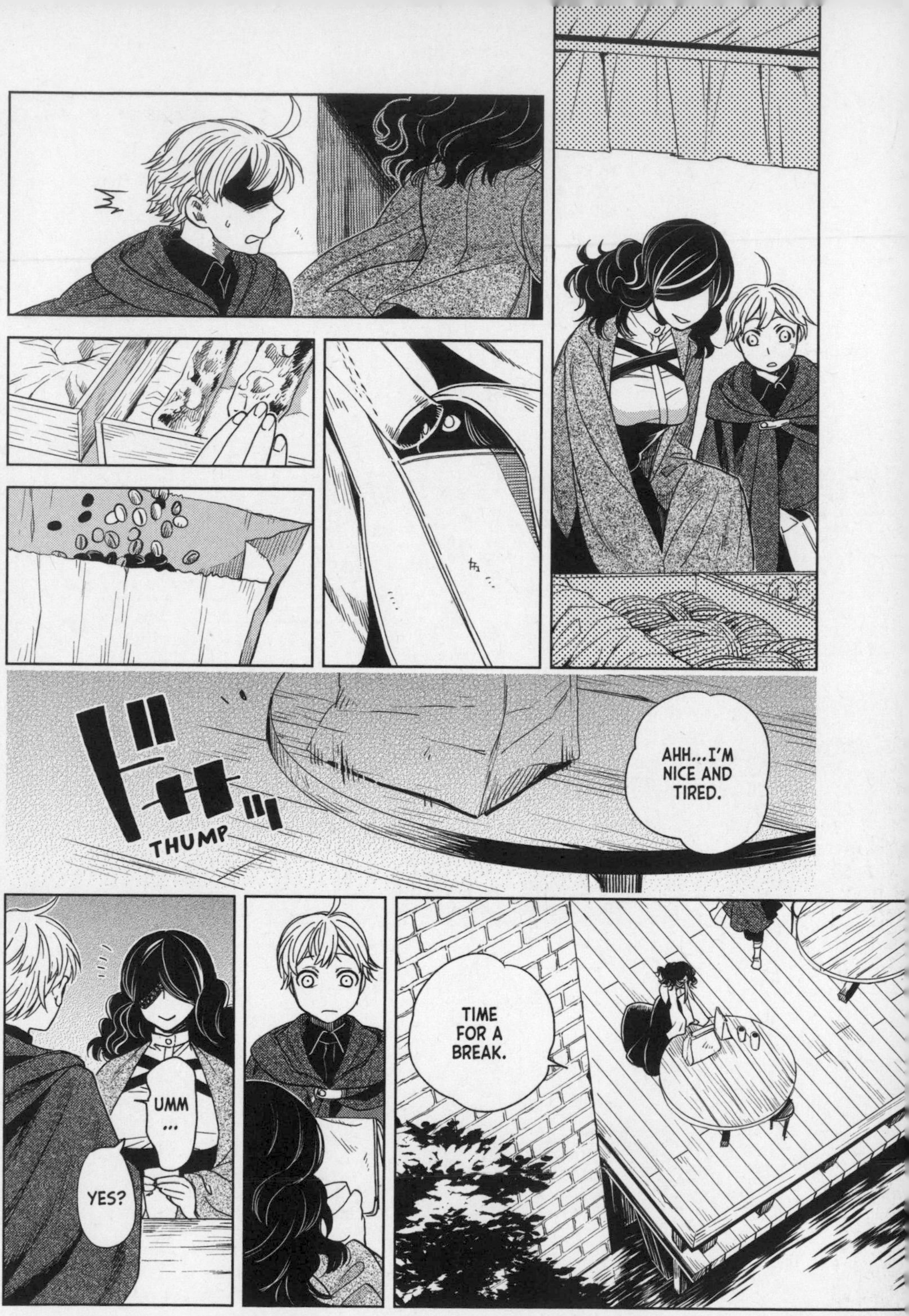
THUMP
AHH...I'M NICE AND TIRED.
TIME FOR A BREAK.
UMM ...
YES?

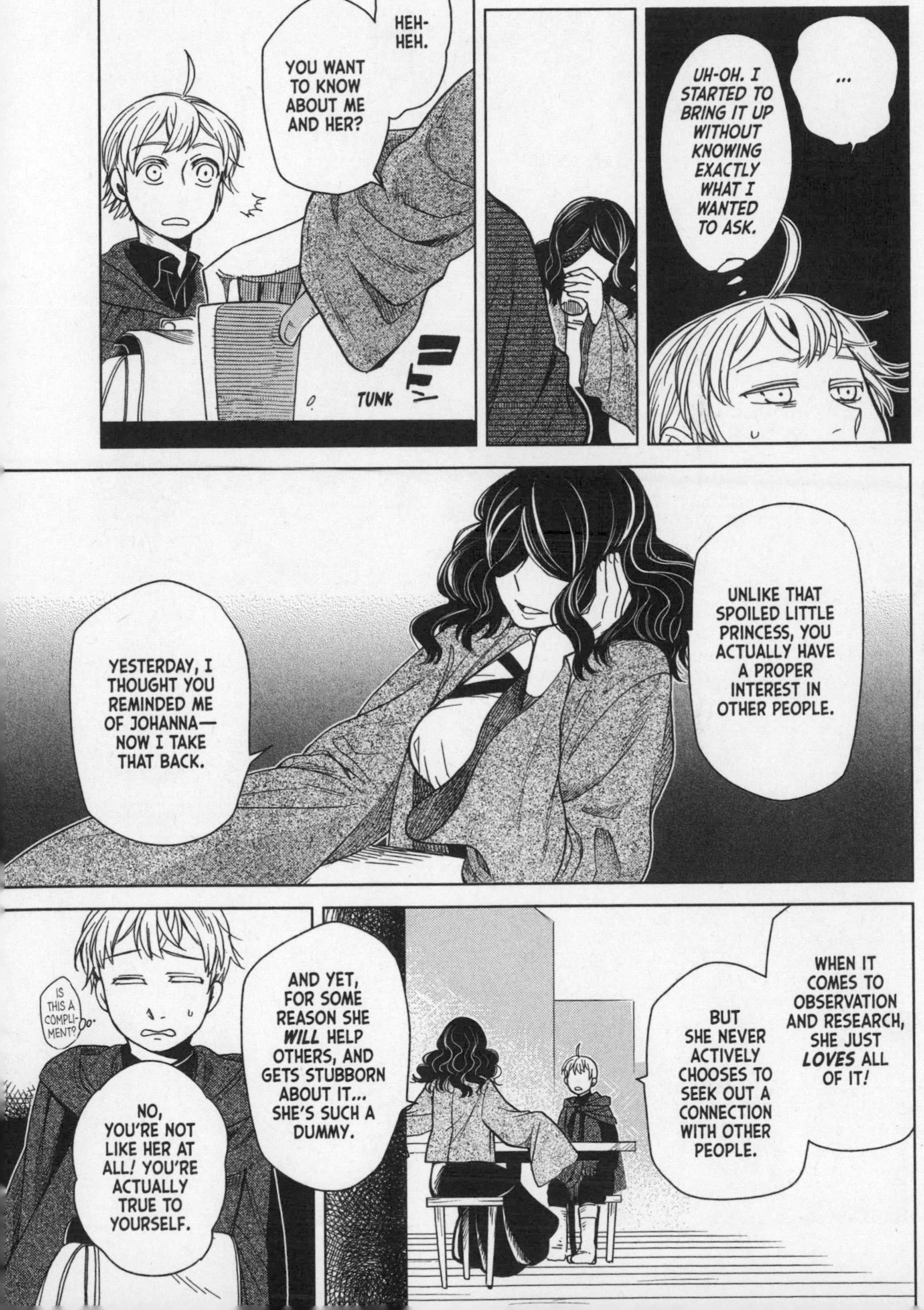
...
UH-OH. I STARTED TO BRING IT UP WITHOUT KNOWING EXACTLY WHAT I WANTED TO ASK.
HEH-HEH.
YOU WANT TO KNOW ABOUT ME AND HER?
TUNK
UNLIKE THAT SPOILED LITTLE PRINCESS, YOU ACTUALLY HAVE A PROPER INTEREST IN OTHER PEOPLE.
YESTERDAY, I THOUGHT YOU REMINDED ME OF JOHANNA— NOW I TAKE THAT BACK.
WHEN IT COMES TO OBSERVATION AND RESEARCH, SHE JUST *LOVES* ALL OF IT!
BUT SHE NEVER ACTIVELY CHOOSES TO SEEK OUT A CONNECTION WITH OTHER PEOPLE.
AND YET, FOR SOME REASON SHE *WILL* HELP OTHERS, AND GETS STUBBORN ABOUT IT... SHE'S SUCH A DUMMY.
IS THIS A COMPLIMENT?
NO, YOU'RE NOT LIKE HER AT ALL! YOU'RE ACTUALLY TRUE TO YOURSELF.

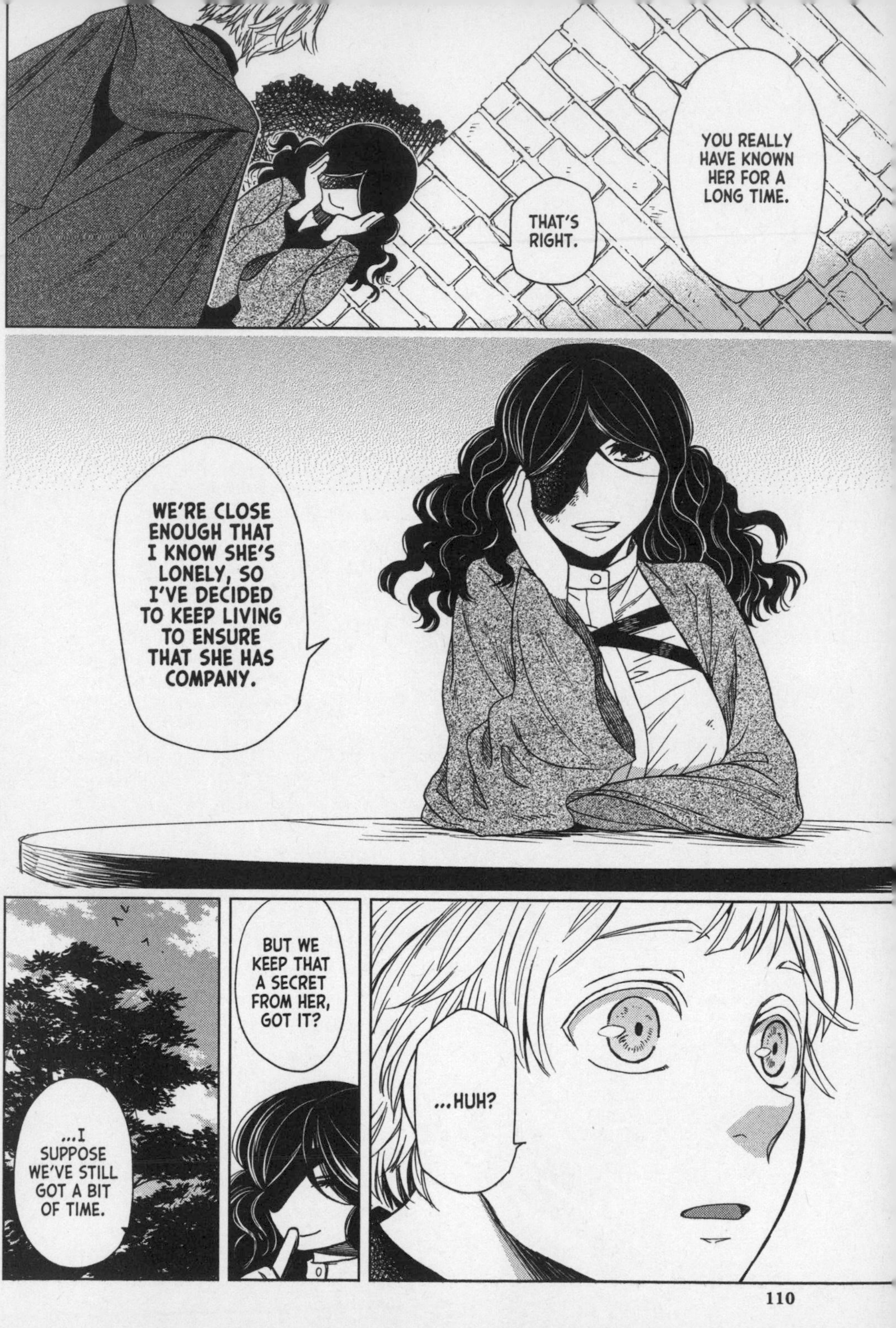
YOU REALLY HAVE KNOWN HER FOR A LONG TIME.
THAT'S RIGHT.
WE'RE CLOSE ENOUGH THAT I KNOW SHE'S LONELY, SO I'VE DECIDED TO KEEP LIVING TO ENSURE THAT SHE HAS COMPANY.
...HUH?
BUT WE KEEP THAT A SECRET FROM HER, GOT IT?
...I SUPPOSE WE'VE STILL GOT A BIT OF TIME.

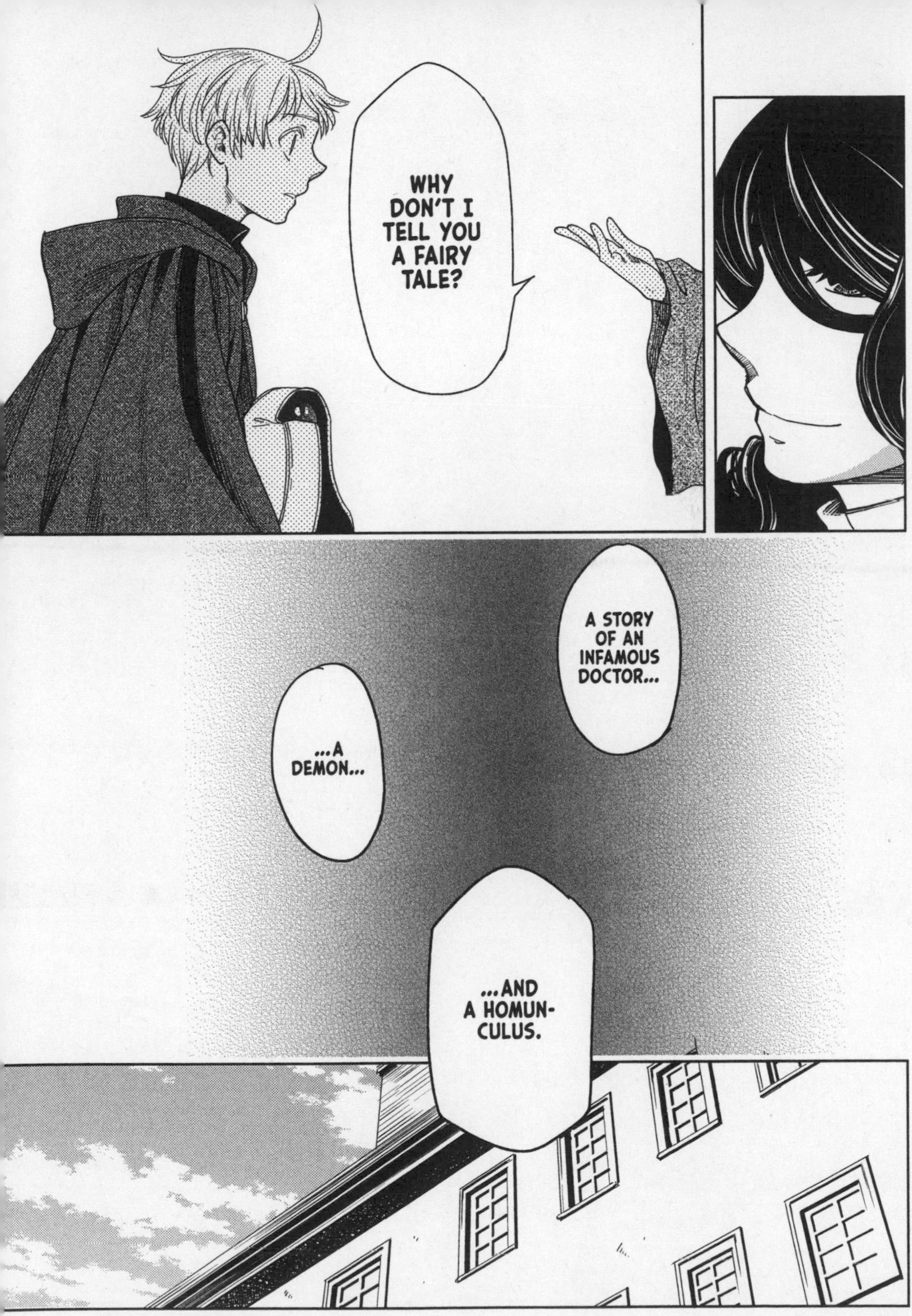
WHY DON'T I TELL YOU A FAIRY TALE?
A STORY OF AN INFAMOUS DOCTOR...
...A DEMON...
...AND A HOMUN-CULUS.

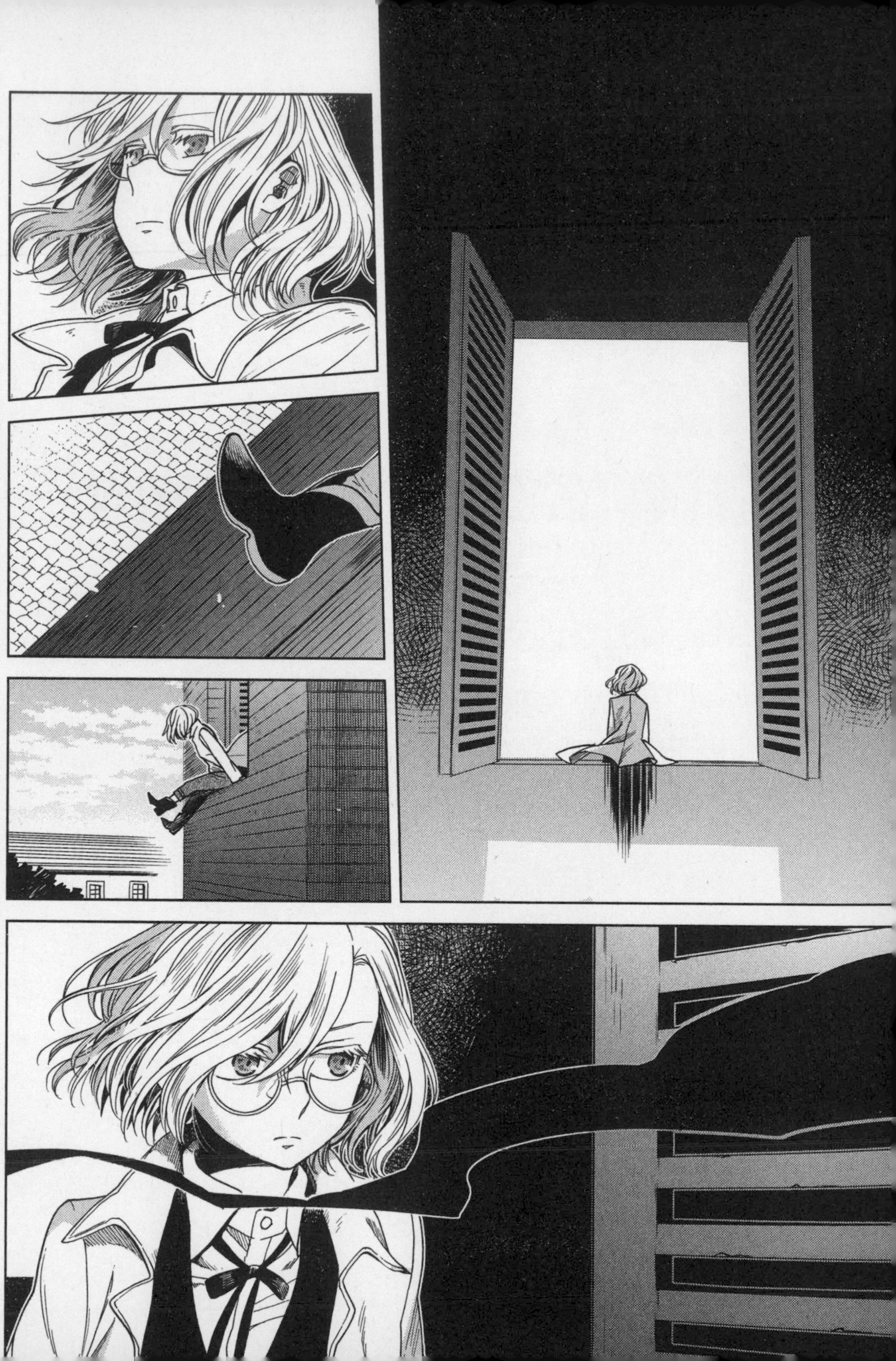

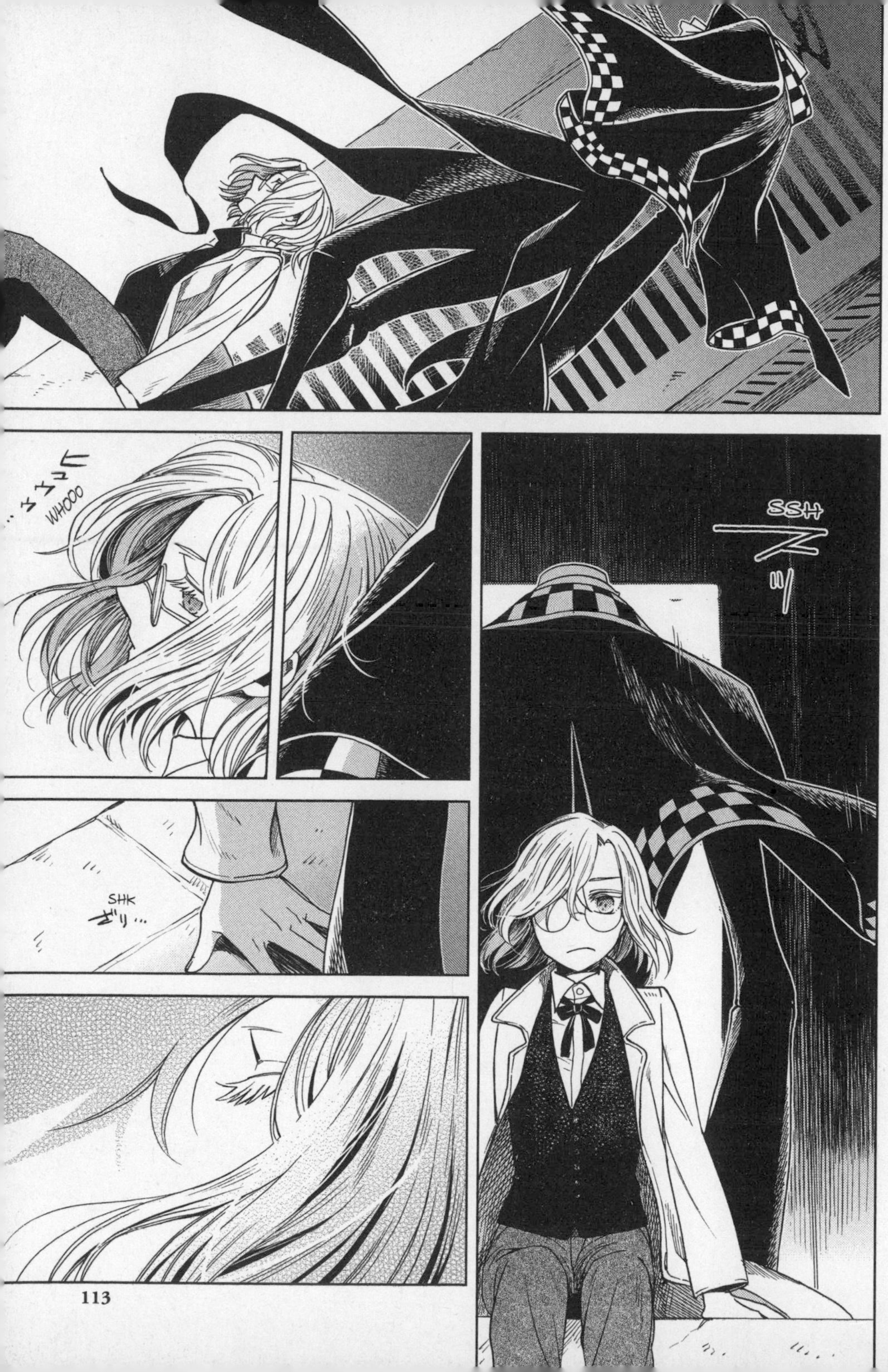
SSH
WHOOO
SHK

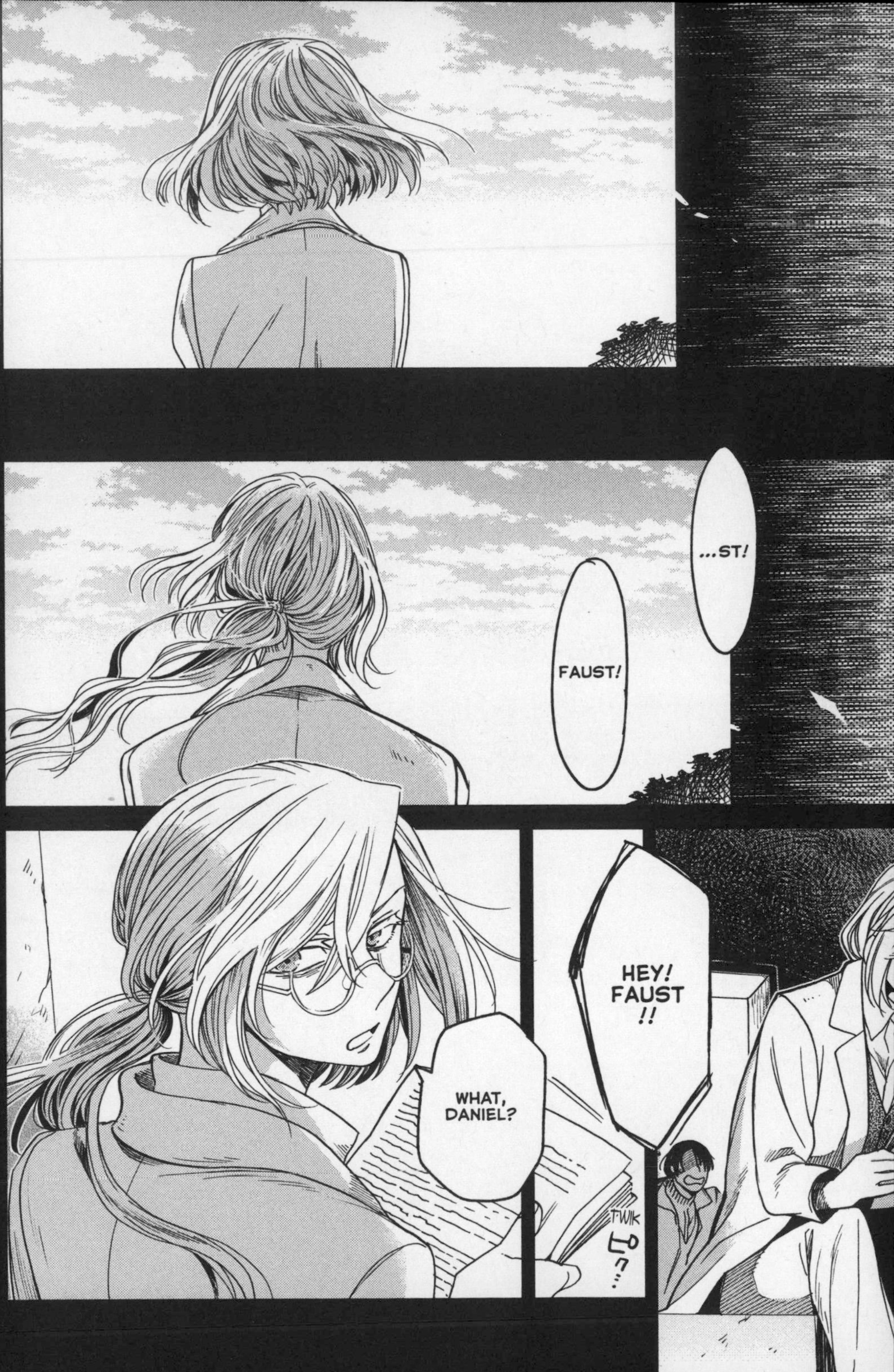
...ST!
FAUST!
HEY! FAUST!!
T-WIK ピク...
WHAT, DANIEL?

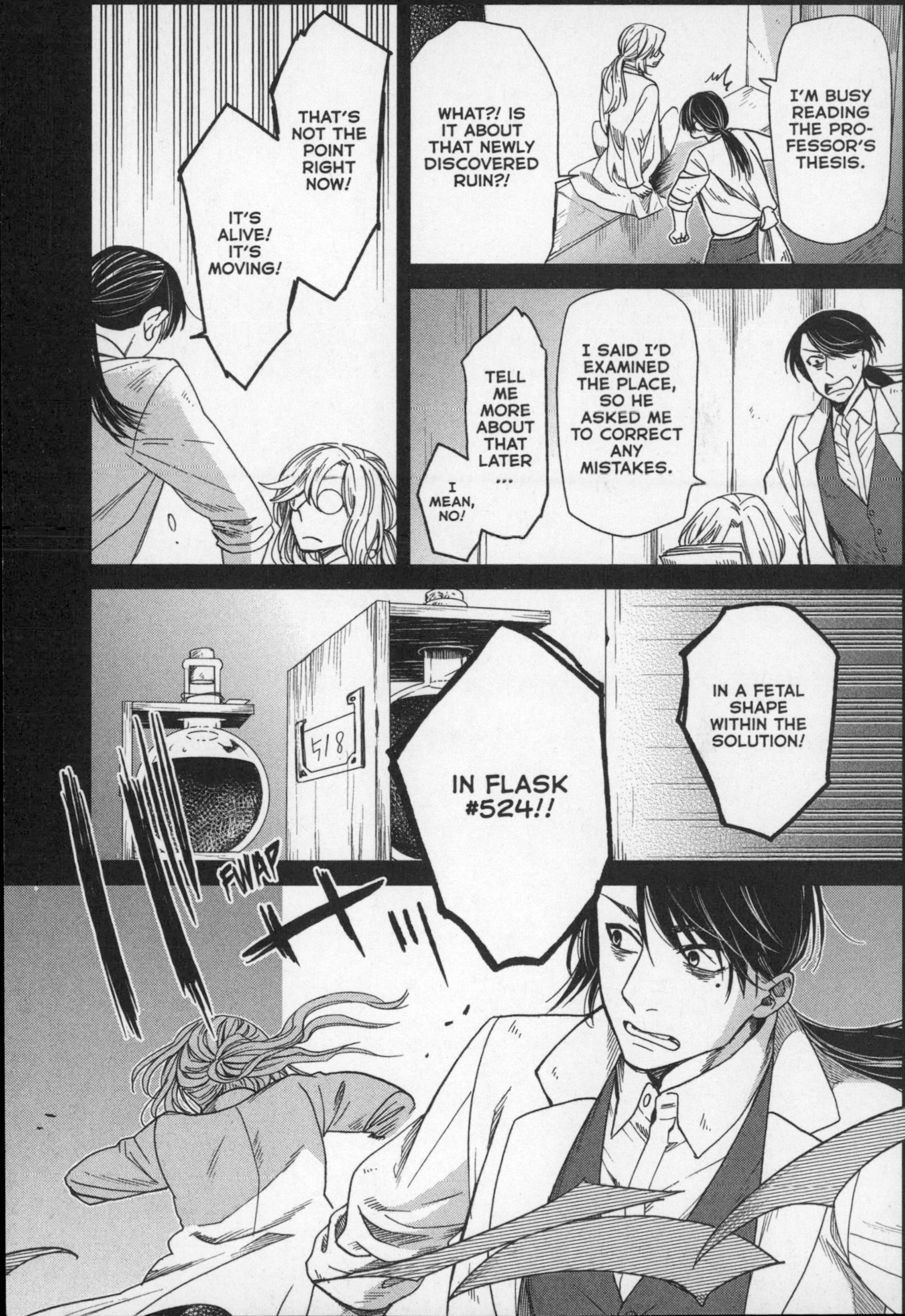
I'M BUSY READING THE PRO-FESSOR'S THESIS.
WHAT?! IS IT ABOUT THAT NEWLY DISCOVERED RUIN?!
I SAID I'D EXAMINED THE PLACE, SO HE ASKED ME TO CORRECT ANY MISTAKES.
TELL ME MORE ABOUT THAT LATER...
I MEAN, NO!
THAT'S NOT THE POINT RIGHT NOW!
IT'S ALIVE! IT'S MOVING!
IN A FETAL SHAPE WITHIN THE SOLUTION!
IN FLASK #524!!
518
FWAP

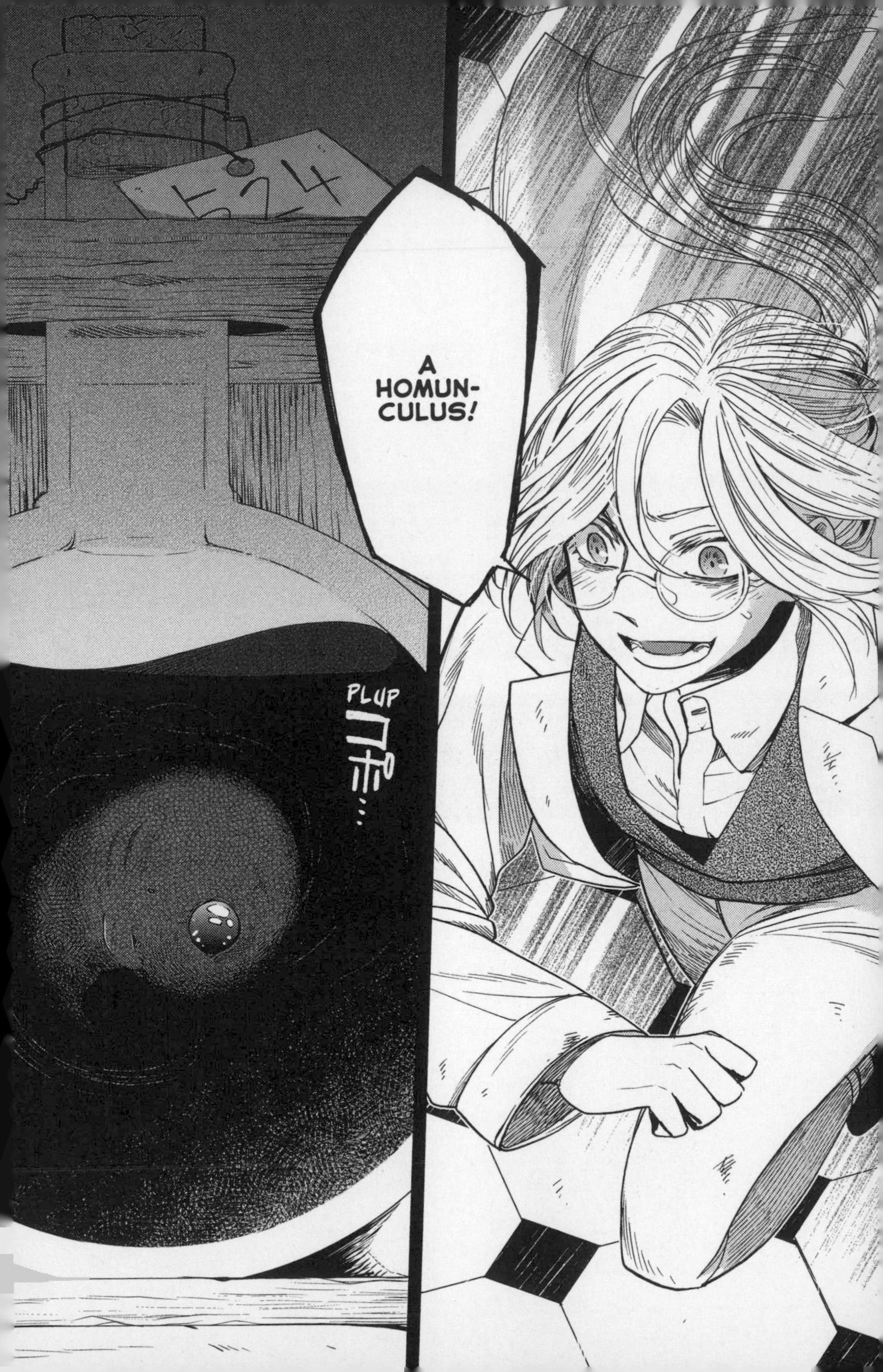
A HOMUN-
CULUS!
PLUP
コポ…

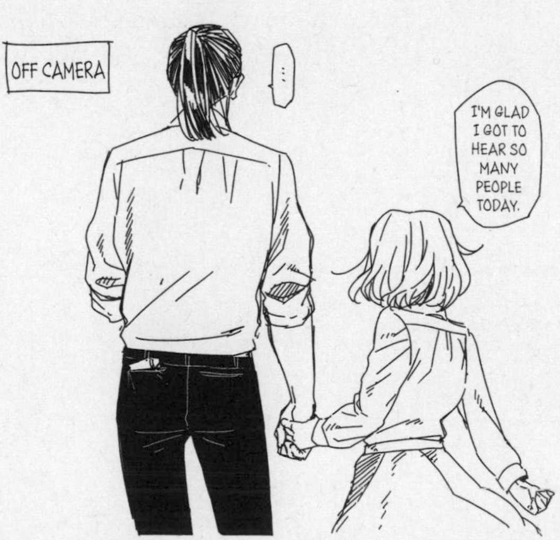
OFF CAMERA
I'M GLAD I GOT TO HEAR SO MANY PEOPLE TODAY.
...

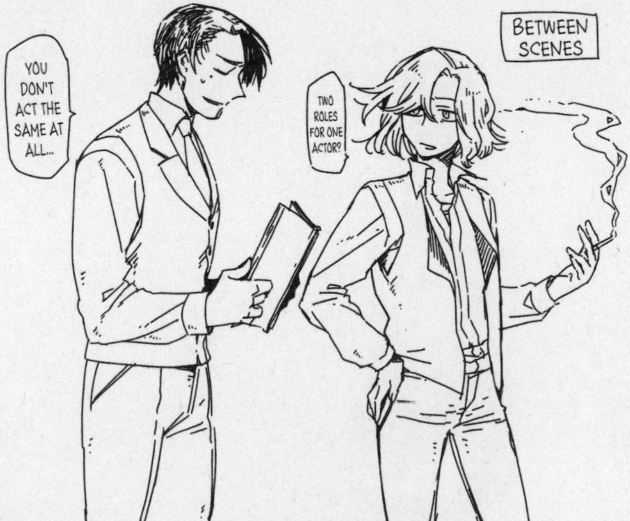
BETWEEN SCENES
TWO ROLES FOR ONE ACTOR?
YOU DON'T ACT THE SAME AT ALL...

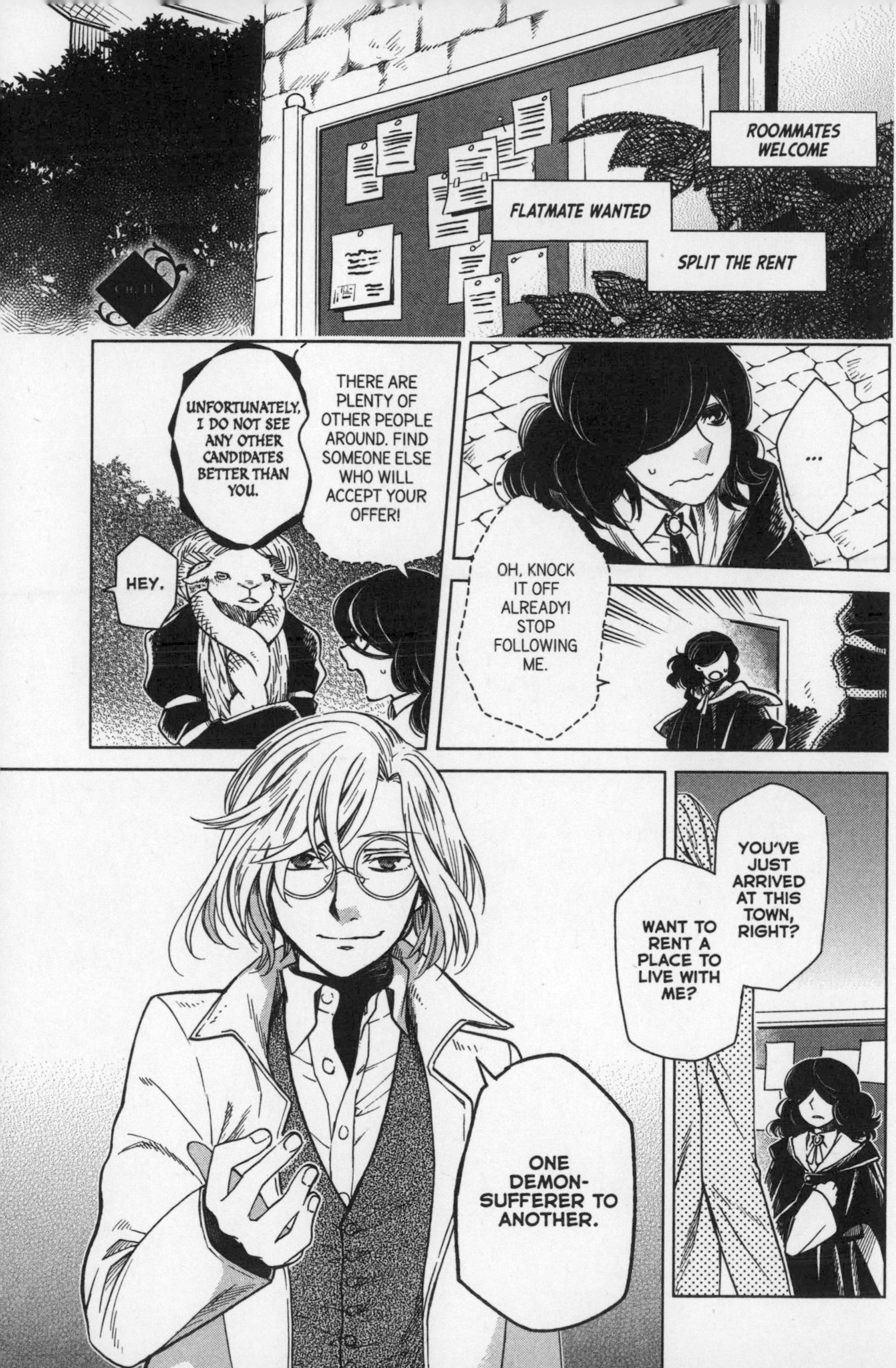
ROOMMATES WELCOME
FLATMATE WANTED
SPLIT THE RENT
...
OH, KNOCK IT OFF ALREADY! STOP FOLLOWING ME.
THERE ARE PLENTY OF OTHER PEOPLE AROUND. FIND SOMEONE ELSE WHO WILL ACCEPT YOUR OFFER!
UNFORTUNATELY, I DO NOT SEE ANY OTHER CANDIDATES BETTER THAN YOU.
HEY.
YOU'VE JUST ARRIVED AT THIS TOWN, RIGHT?
WANT TO RENT A PLACE TO LIVE WITH ME?
ONE DEMON-SUFFERER TO ANOTHER.

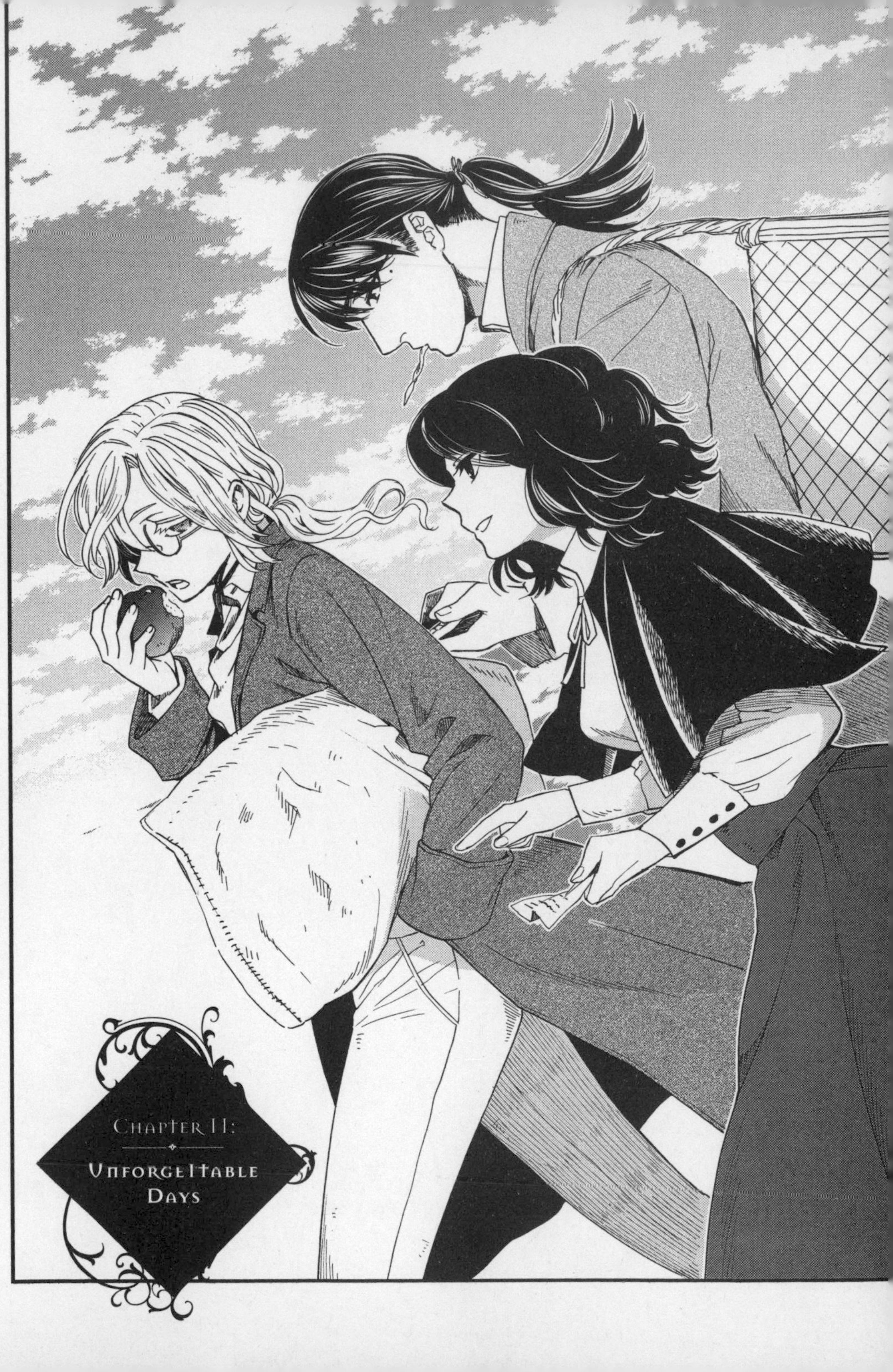
Chapter 11:
Unforgettable Days

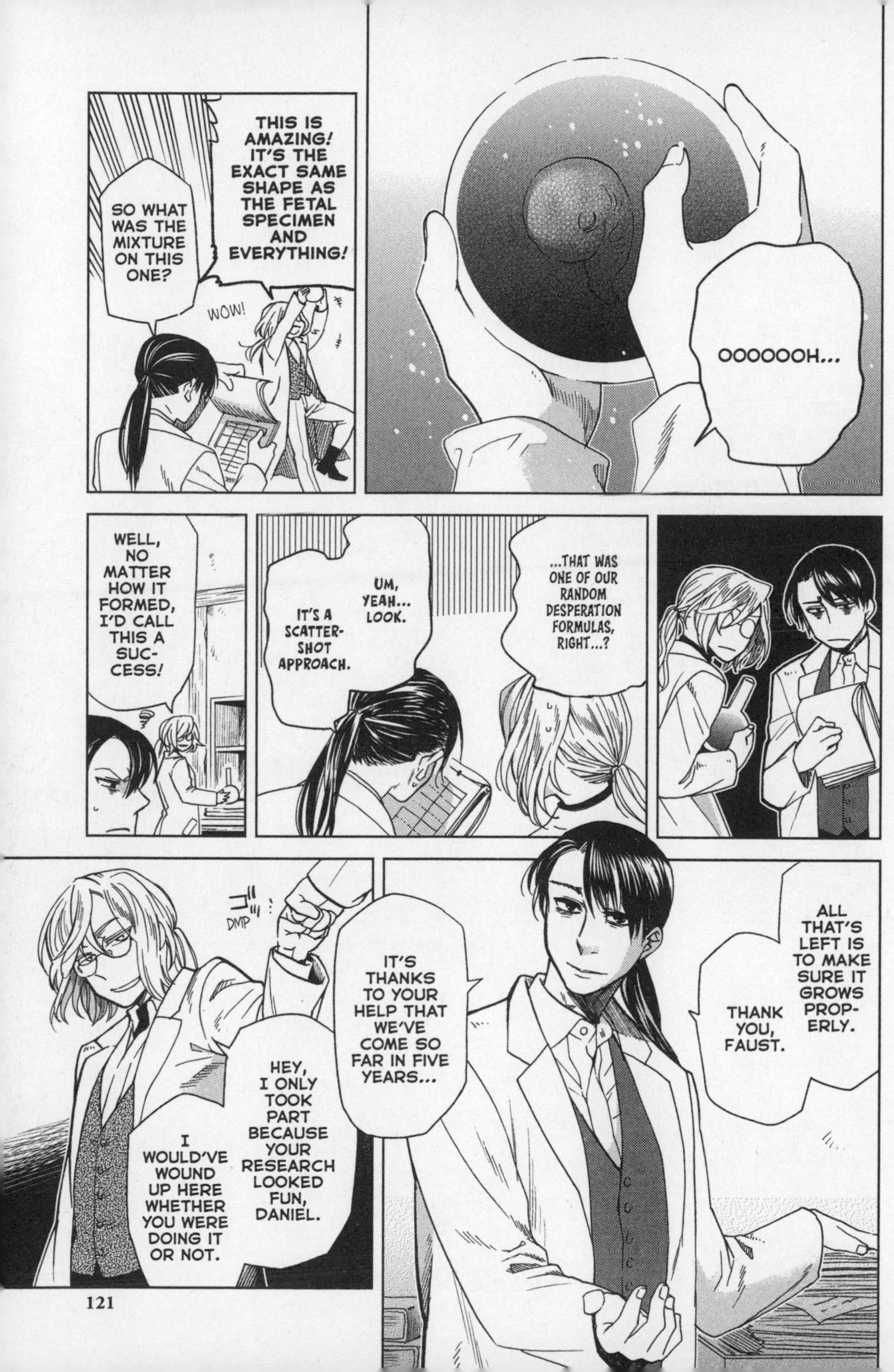
OOOOOOH...
THIS IS AMAZING! IT'S THE EXACT SAME SHAPE AS THE FETAL SPECIMEN AND EVERYTHING!
SO WHAT WAS THE MIXTURE ON THIS ONE?
WOW!
...THAT WAS ONE OF OUR RANDOM DESPERATION FORMULAS, RIGHT...?
UM, YEAH... LOOK.
IT'S A SCATTER-SHOT APPROACH.
WELL, NO MATTER HOW IT FORMED, I'D CALL THIS A SUC-CESS!
ALL THAT'S LEFT IS TO MAKE SURE IT GROWS PROPER-LY.
THANK YOU, FAUST.
IT'S THANKS TO YOUR HELP THAT WE'VE COME SO FAR IN FIVE YEARS...
DMP
HEY, I ONLY TOOK PART BECAUSE YOUR RESEARCH LOOKED FUN, DANIEL.
I WOULD'VE WOUND UP HERE WHETHER YOU WERE DOING IT OR NOT.

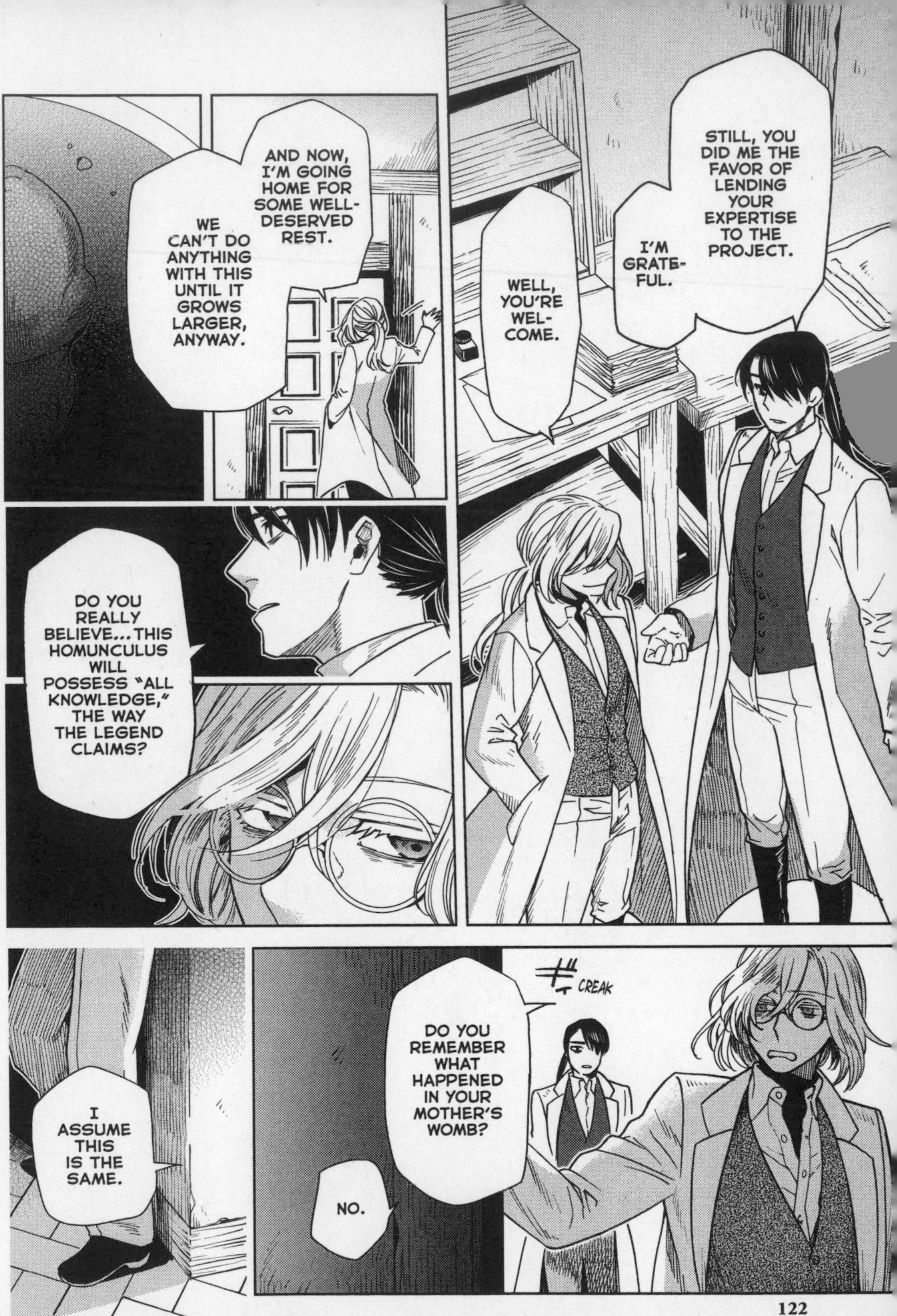
STILL, YOU DID ME THE FAVOR OF LENDING YOUR EXPERTISE TO THE PROJECT.
I'M GRATE-FUL.
WELL, YOU'RE WEL-COME.
AND NOW, I'M GOING HOME FOR SOME WELL-DESERVED REST.
WE CAN'T DO ANYTHING WITH THIS UNTIL IT GROWS LARGER, ANYWAY.
DO YOU REALLY BELIEVE... THIS HOMUNCULUS WILL POSSESS "ALL KNOWLEDGE," THE WAY THE LEGEND CLAIMS?
CREAK
DO YOU REMEMBER WHAT HAPPENED IN YOUR MOTHER'S WOMB?
NO.
I ASSUME THIS IS THE SAME.

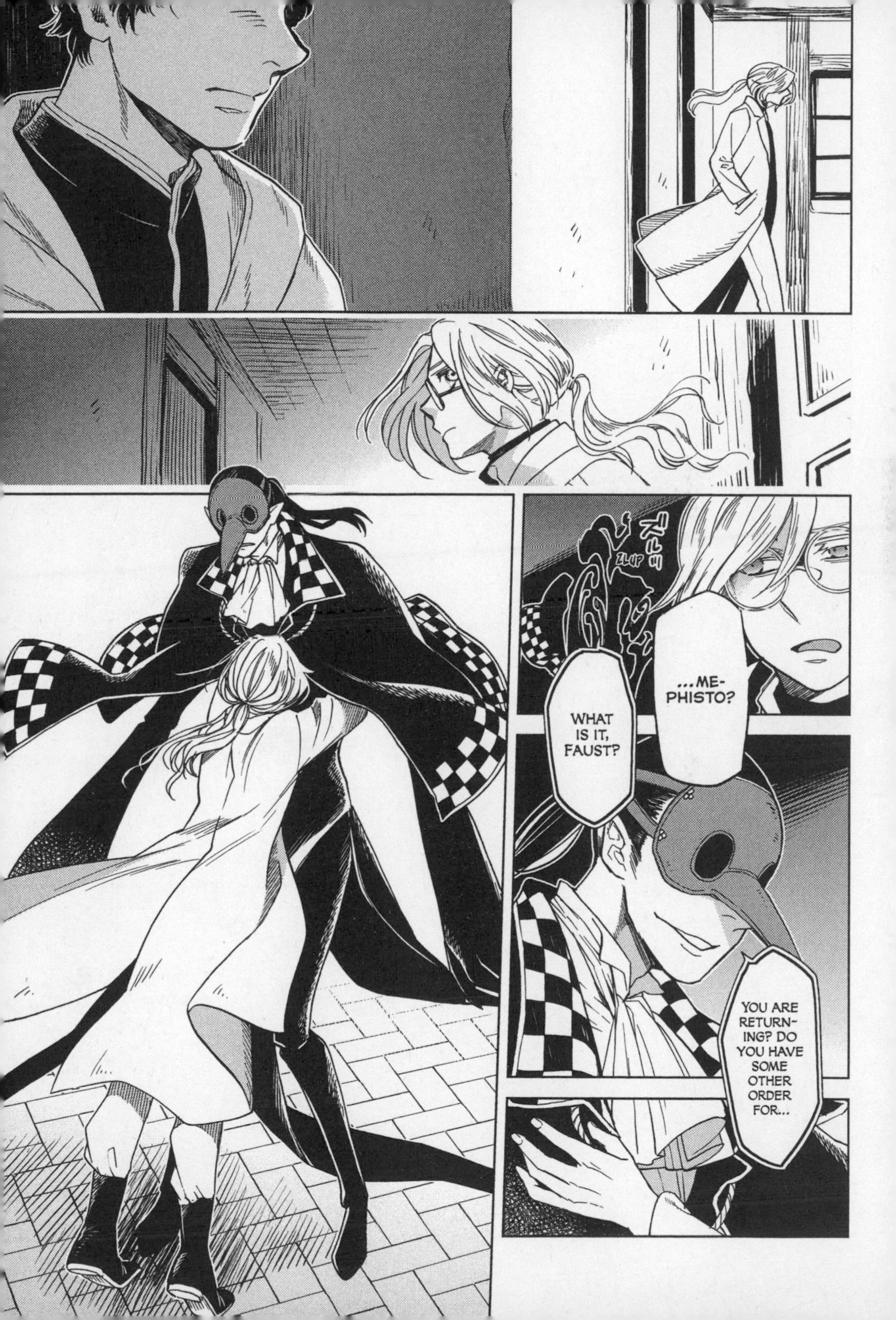
ZLIP
...ME-PHISTO?
WHAT IS IT, FAUST?
YOU ARE RETURN-ING? DO YOU HAVE SOME OTHER ORDER FOR...

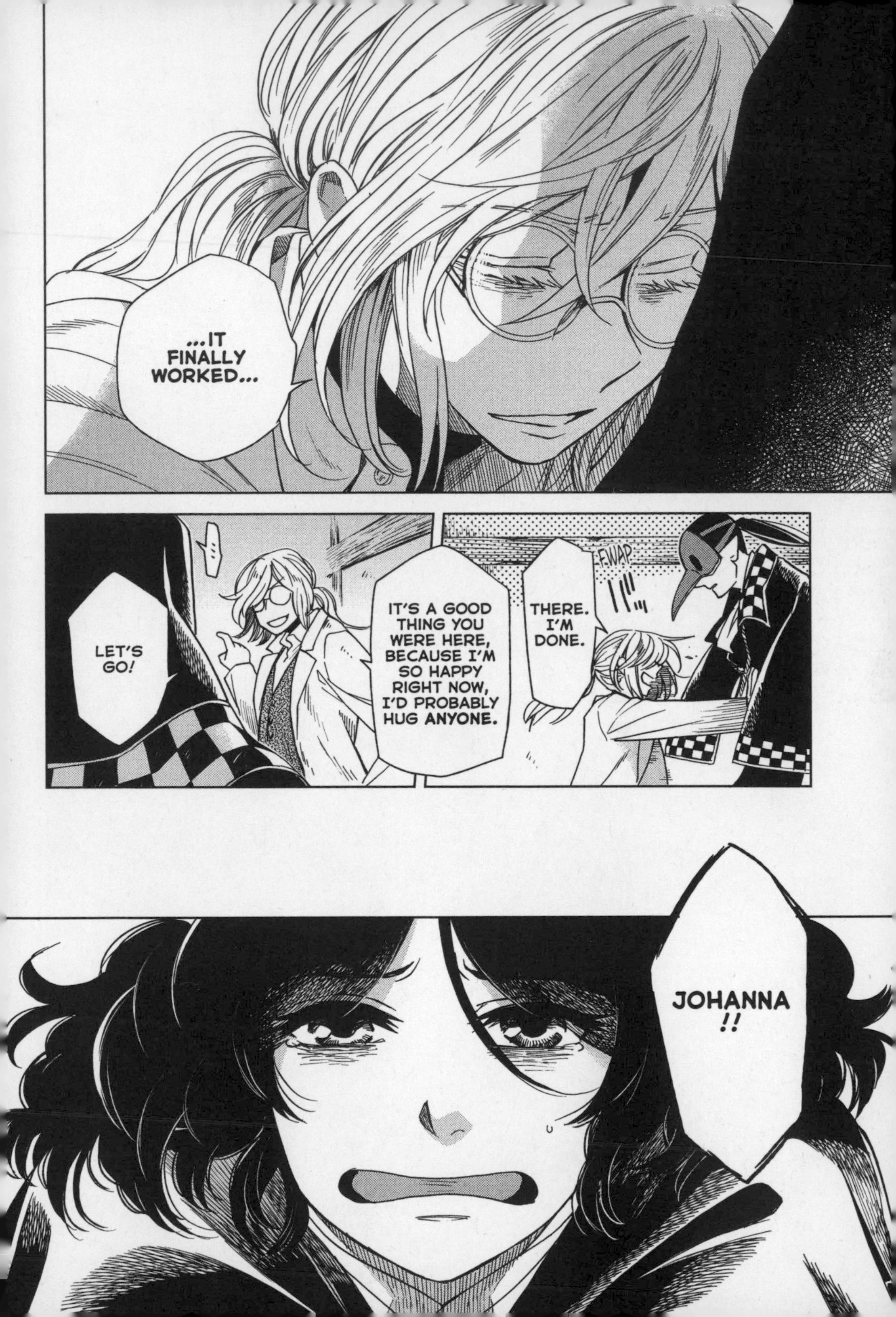
...IT FINALLY WORKED...
FWAP
THERE. I'M DONE.
IT'S A GOOD THING YOU WERE HERE, BECAUSE I'M SO HAPPY RIGHT NOW, I'D PROBABLY HUG ANYONE.
LET'S GO!
JOHANNA !!

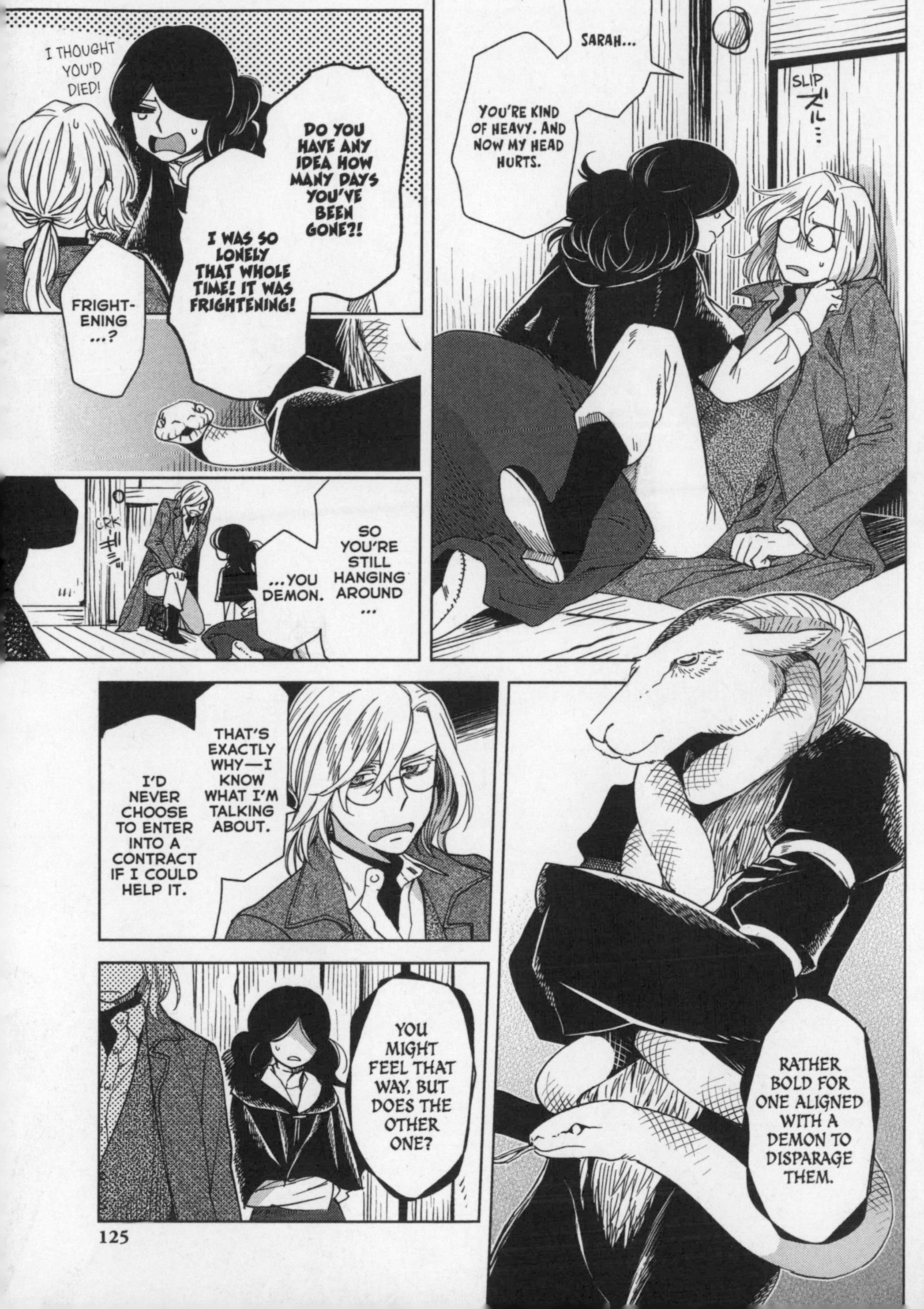
SARAH...
YOU'RE KIND OF HEAVY. AND NOW MY HEAD HURTS.
SLIP ズル…
DO YOU HAVE ANY IDEA HOW MANY DAYS YOU'VE BEEN GONE?!
I THOUGHT YOU'D DIED!
I WAS SO LONELY THAT WHOLE TIME! IT WAS FRIGHTENING!
FRIGHT-ENING ...?
SO YOU'RE STILL HANGING AROUND ...
...YOU DEMON.
CRK ギ…
RATHER BOLD FOR ONE ALIGNED WITH A DEMON TO DISPARAGE THEM.
THAT'S EXACTLY WHY—I KNOW WHAT I'M TALKING ABOUT.
I'D NEVER CHOOSE TO ENTER INTO A CONTRACT IF I COULD HELP IT.
YOU MIGHT FEEL THAT WAY, BUT DOES THE OTHER ONE?

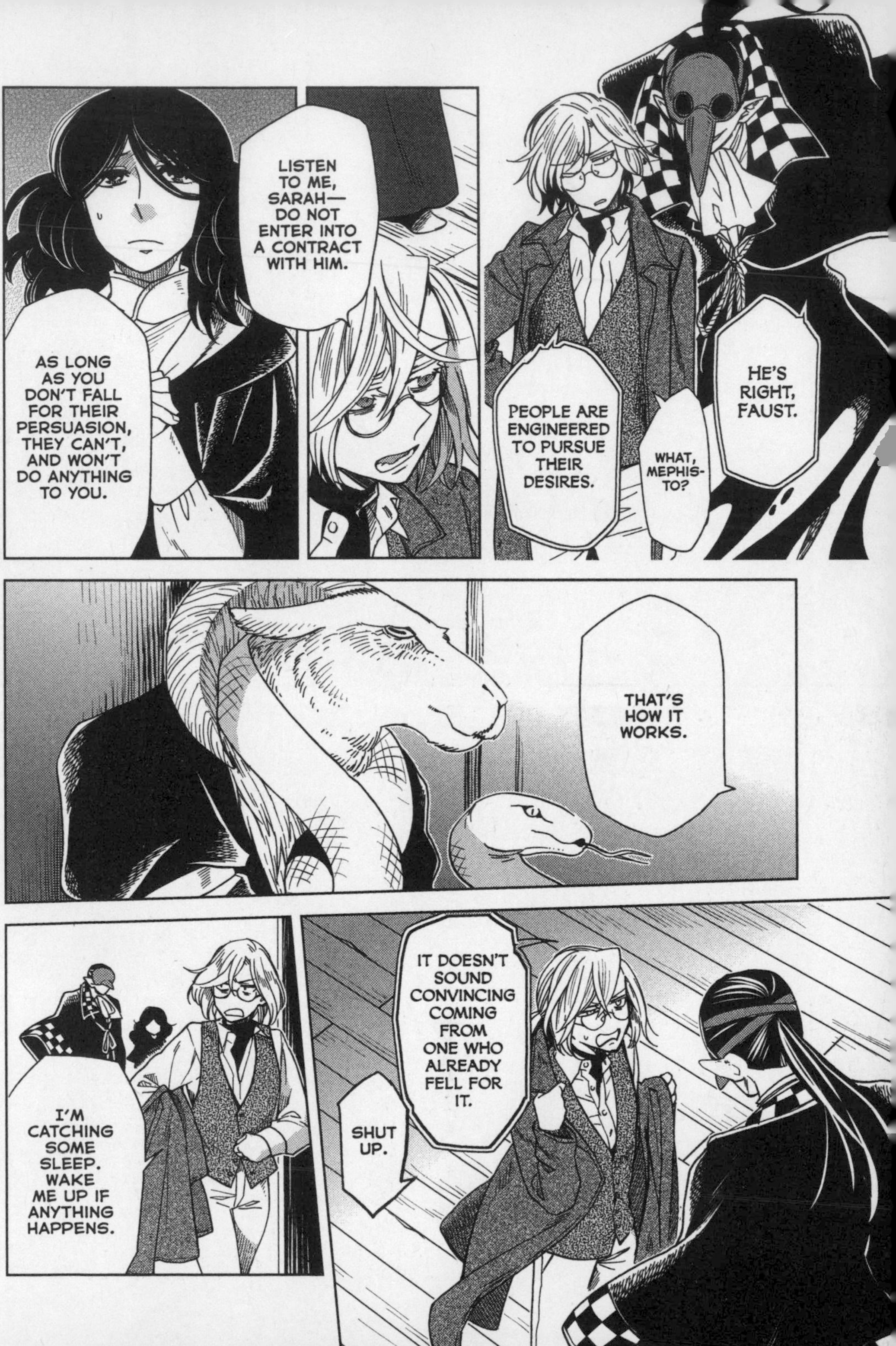
HE'S RIGHT, FAUST.
WHAT, MEPHISTO?
PEOPLE ARE ENGINEERED TO PURSUE THEIR DESIRES.
LISTEN TO ME, SARAH—DO NOT ENTER INTO A CONTRACT WITH HIM.
AS LONG AS YOU DON'T FALL FOR THEIR PERSUASION, THEY CAN'T, AND WON'T DO ANYTHING TO YOU.
THAT'S HOW IT WORKS.
IT DOESN'T SOUND CONVINCING COMING FROM ONE WHO ALREADY FELL FOR IT.
SHUT UP.
I'M CATCHING SOME SLEEP. WAKE ME UP IF ANYTHING HAPPENS.

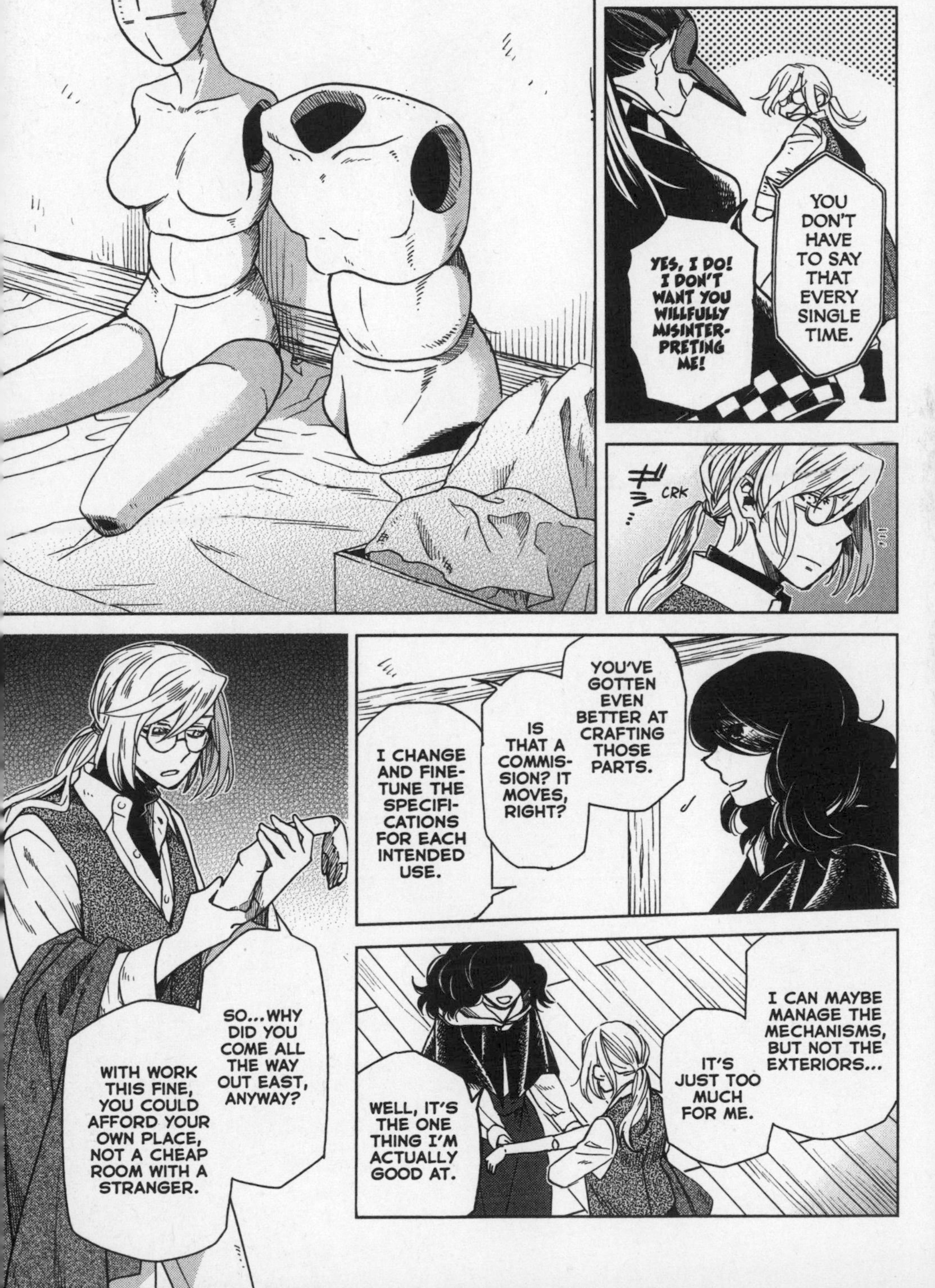
YOU DON'T HAVE TO SAY THAT EVERY SINGLE TIME.
YES, I DO! I DON'T WANT YOU WILLFULLY MISINTERPRETING ME!
CRK
YOU'VE GOTTEN EVEN BETTER AT CRAFTING THOSE PARTS.
IS THAT A COMMISSION? IT MOVES, RIGHT?
I CHANGE AND FINE-TUNE THE SPECIFICATIONS FOR EACH INTENDED USE.
I CAN MAYBE MANAGE THE MECHANISMS, BUT NOT THE EXTERIORS...
IT'S JUST TOO MUCH FOR ME.
WELL, IT'S THE ONE THING I'M ACTUALLY GOOD AT.
SO...WHY DID YOU COME ALL THE WAY OUT EAST, ANYWAY?
WITH WORK THIS FINE, YOU COULD AFFORD YOUR OWN PLACE, NOT A CHEAP ROOM WITH A STRANGER.

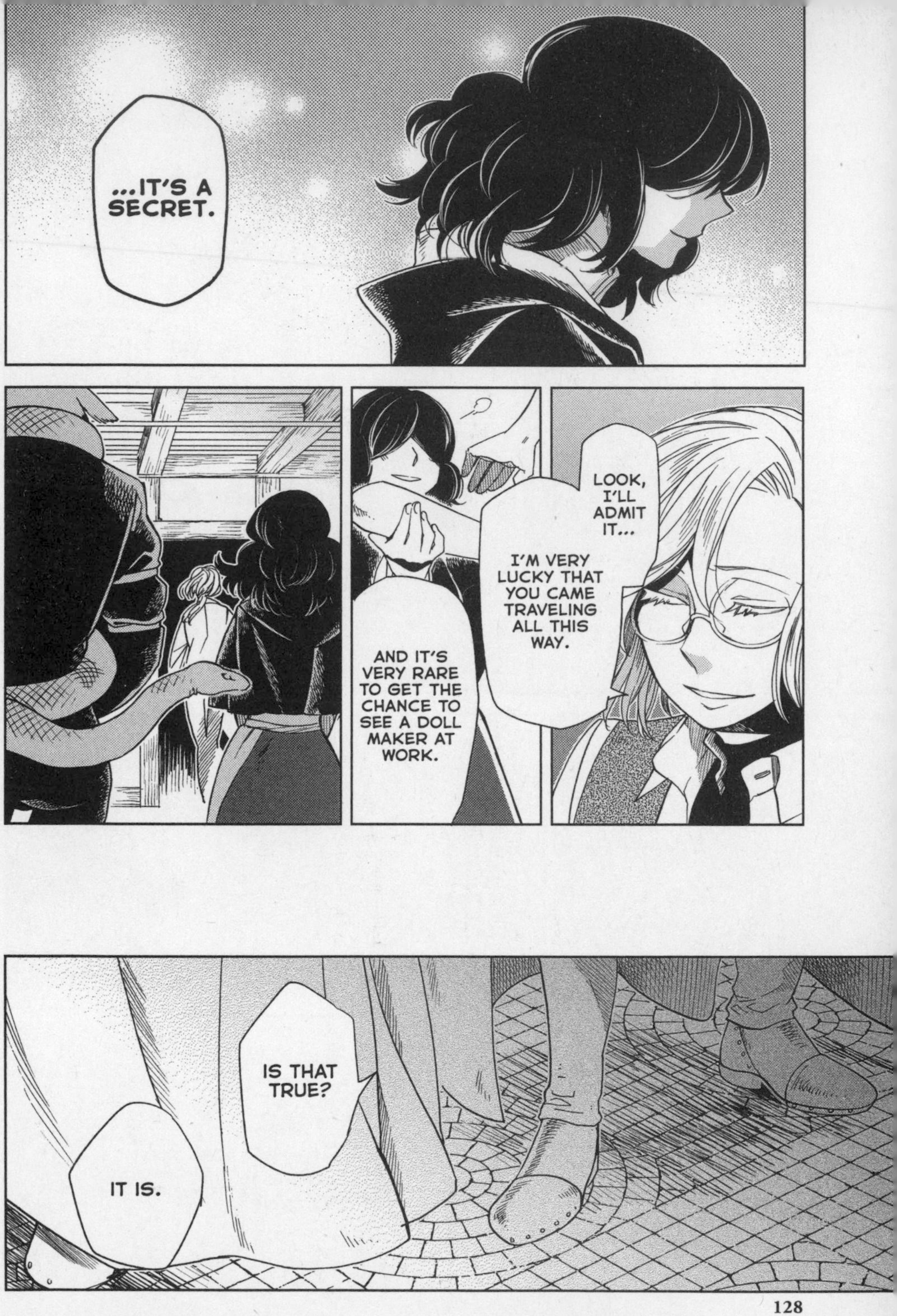
...IT'S A SECRET.
LOOK, I'LL ADMIT IT...
I'M VERY LUCKY THAT YOU CAME TRAVELING ALL THIS WAY.
AND IT'S VERY RARE TO GET THE CHANCE TO SEE A DOLL MAKER AT WORK.
IS THAT TRUE?
IT IS.

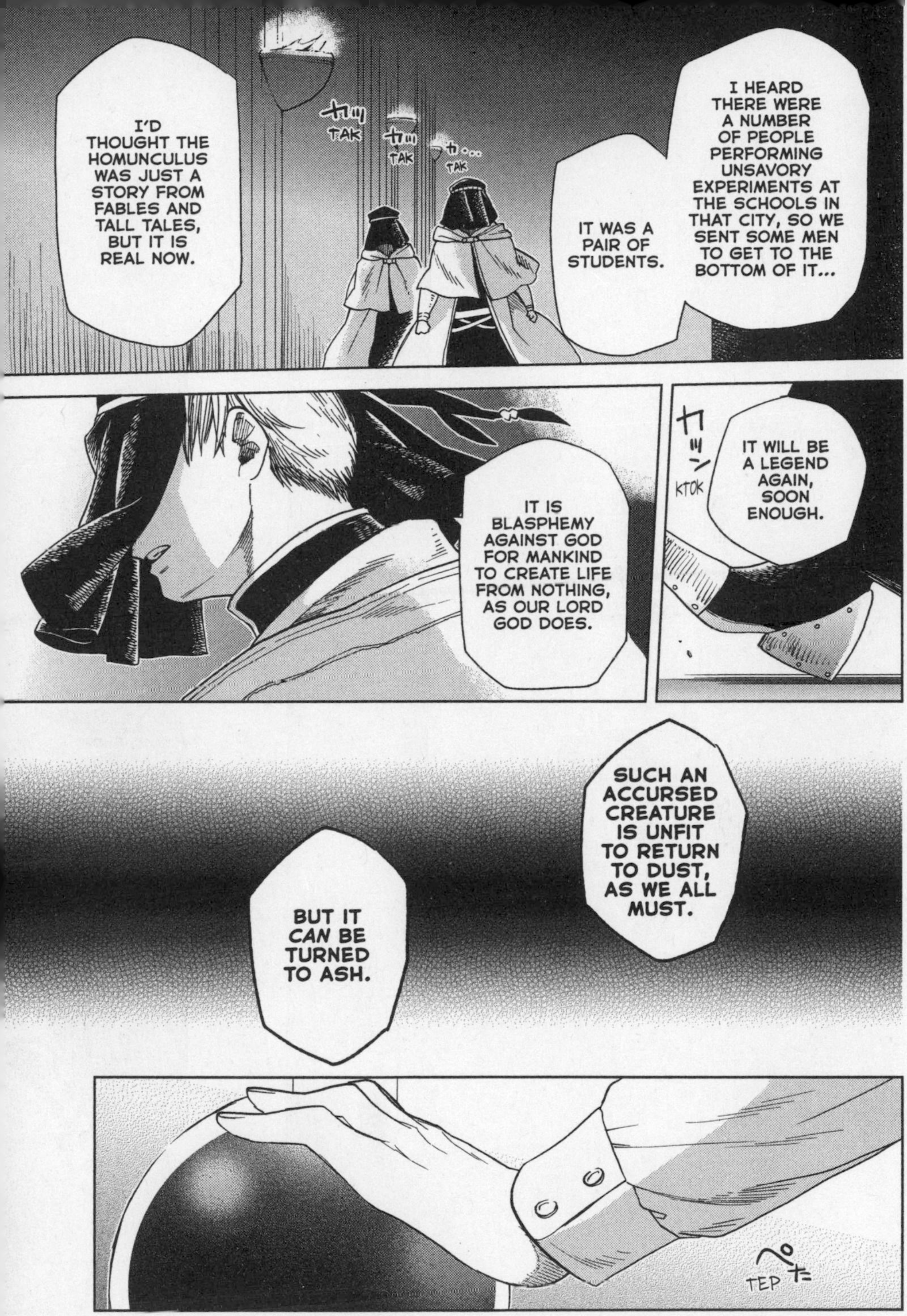
I HEARD THERE WERE A NUMBER OF PEOPLE PERFORMING UNSAVORY EXPERIMENTS AT THE SCHOOLS IN THAT CITY, SO WE SENT SOME MEN TO GET TO THE BOTTOM OF IT...
IT WAS A PAIR OF STUDENTS.
TAK
TAK
TAK
I'D THOUGHT THE HOMUNCULUS WAS JUST A STORY FROM FABLES AND TALL TALES, BUT IT IS REAL NOW.
KTOK
IT WILL BE A LEGEND AGAIN, SOON ENOUGH.
IT IS BLASPHEMY AGAINST GOD FOR MANKIND TO CREATE LIFE FROM NOTHING, AS OUR LORD GOD DOES.
SUCH AN ACCURSED CREATURE IS UNFIT TO RETURN TO DUST, AS WE ALL MUST.
BUT IT *CAN* BE TURNED TO ASH.
TEP

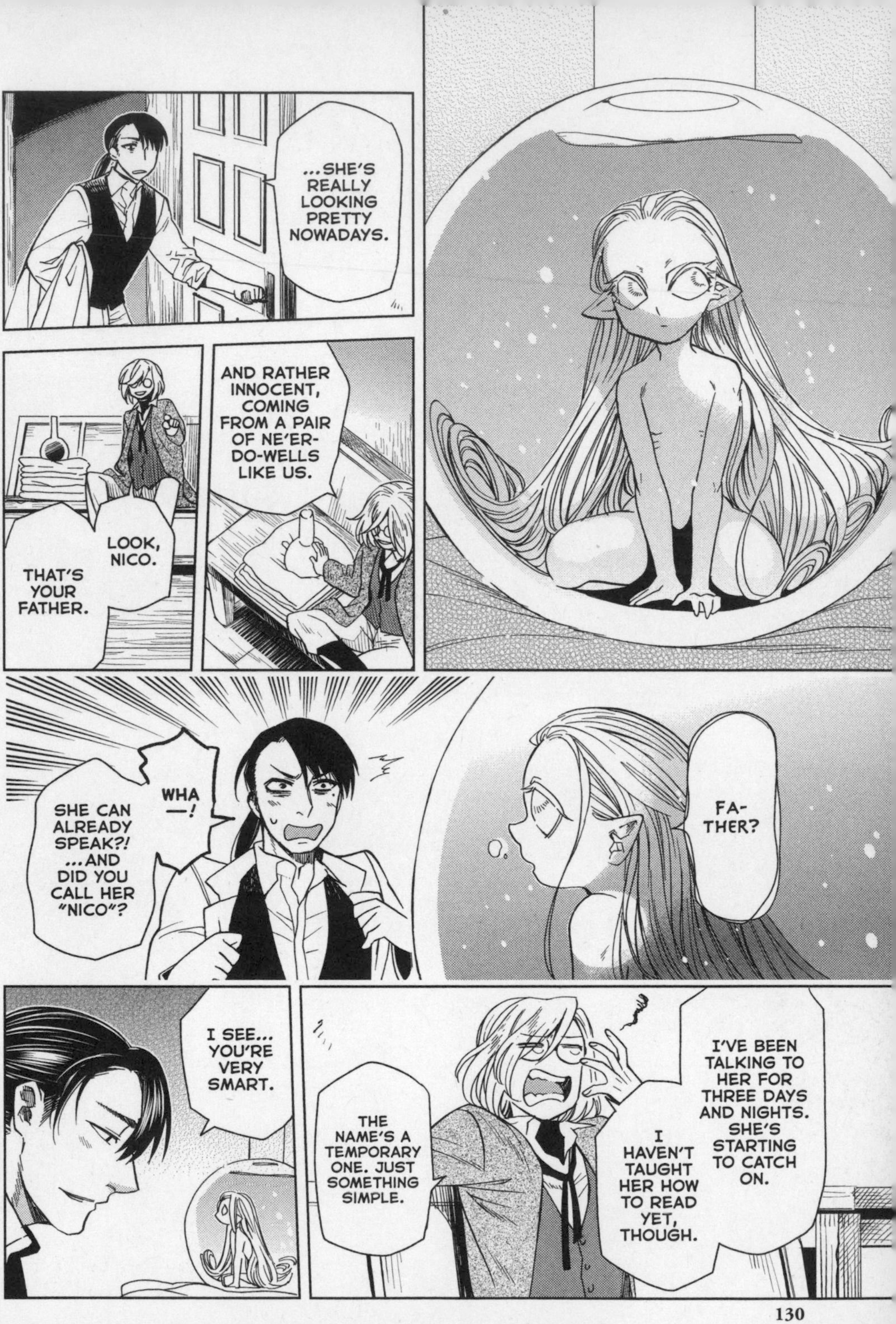
...SHE'S REALLY LOOKING PRETTY NOWADAYS.
AND RATHER INNOCENT, COMING FROM A PAIR OF NE'ER-DO-WELLS LIKE US.
LOOK, NICO.
THAT'S YOUR FATHER.
FA-THER?
WHA—!
SHE CAN ALREADY SPEAK?! ...AND DID YOU CALL HER "NICO"?
I'VE BEEN TALKING TO HER FOR THREE DAYS AND NIGHTS. SHE'S STARTING TO CATCH ON.
I HAVEN'T TAUGHT HER HOW TO READ YET, THOUGH.
THE NAME'S A TEMPORARY ONE. JUST SOMETHING SIMPLE.
I SEE... YOU'RE VERY SMART.

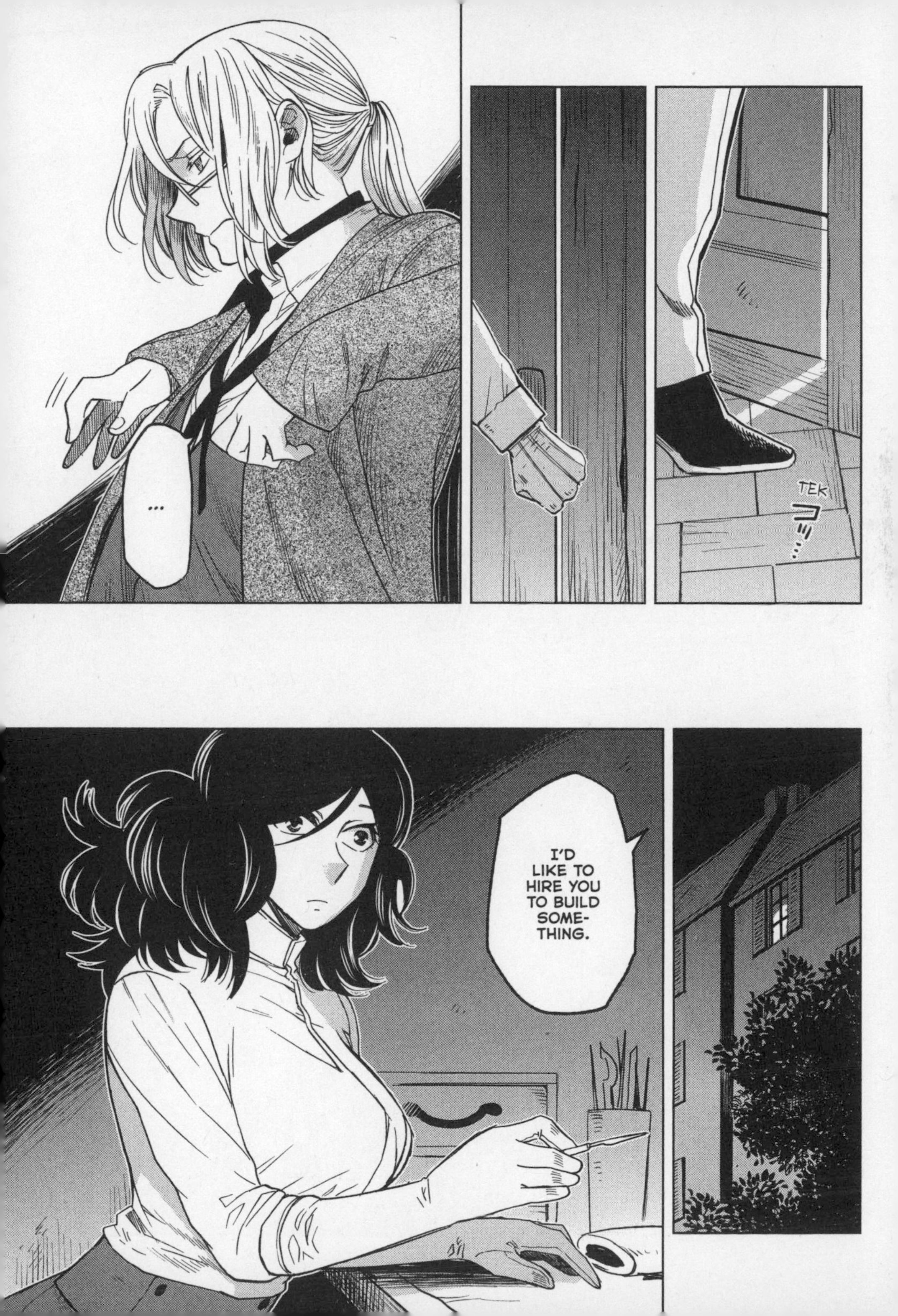
TEK
ゴッ…
...
I'D LIKE TO HIRE YOU TO BUILD SOME-THING.

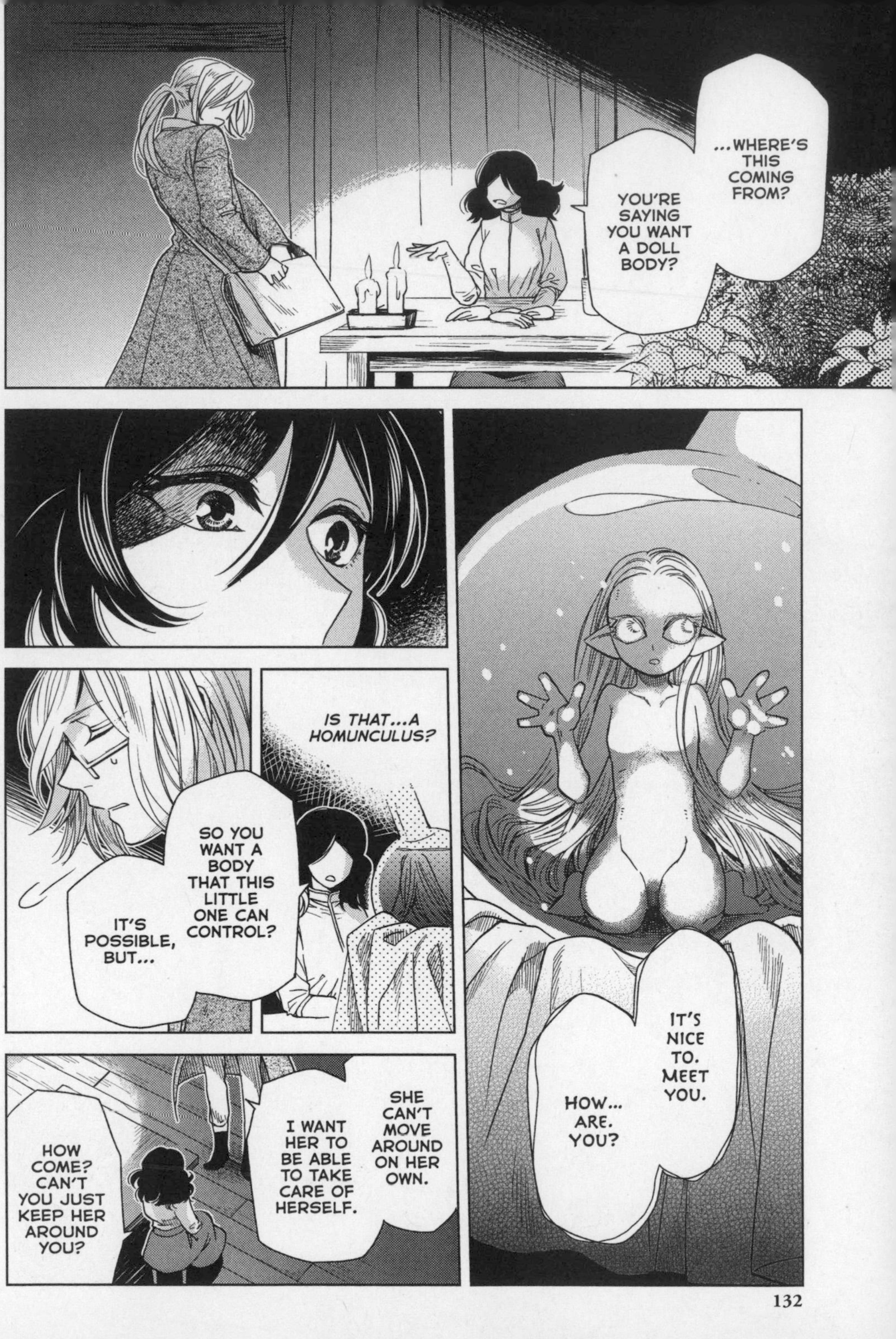
...WHERE'S THIS COMING FROM?
YOU'RE SAYING YOU WANT A DOLL BODY?
IT'S NICE TO. MEET YOU.
HOW... ARE. YOU?
IS THAT...A HOMUNCULUS?
SO YOU WANT A BODY THAT THIS LITTLE ONE CAN CONTROL?
IT'S POSSIBLE, BUT...
SHE CAN'T MOVE AROUND ON HER OWN.
I WANT HER TO BE ABLE TO TAKE CARE OF HERSELF.
HOW COME? CAN'T YOU JUST KEEP HER AROUND YOU?

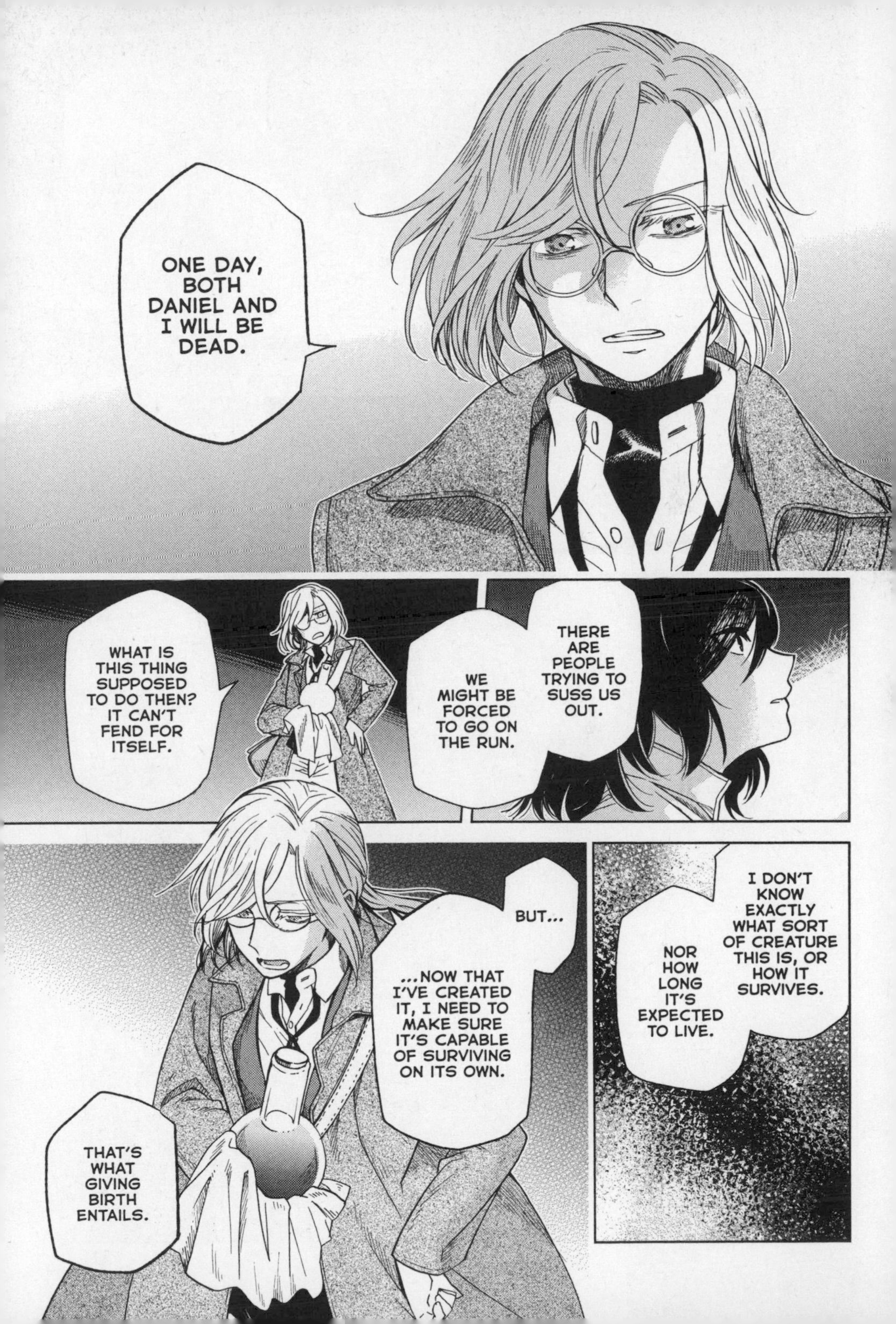
ONE DAY, BOTH DANIEL AND I WILL BE DEAD.
THERE ARE PEOPLE TRYING TO SUSS US OUT.
WE MIGHT BE FORCED TO GO ON THE RUN.
WHAT IS THIS THING SUPPOSED TO DO THEN? IT CAN'T FEND FOR ITSELF.
I DON'T KNOW EXACTLY WHAT SORT OF CREATURE THIS IS, OR HOW IT SURVIVES.
NOR HOW LONG IT'S EXPECTED TO LIVE.
BUT...
...NOW THAT I'VE CREATED IT, I NEED TO MAKE SURE IT'S CAPABLE OF SURVIVING ON ITS OWN.
THAT'S WHAT GIVING BIRTH ENTAILS.

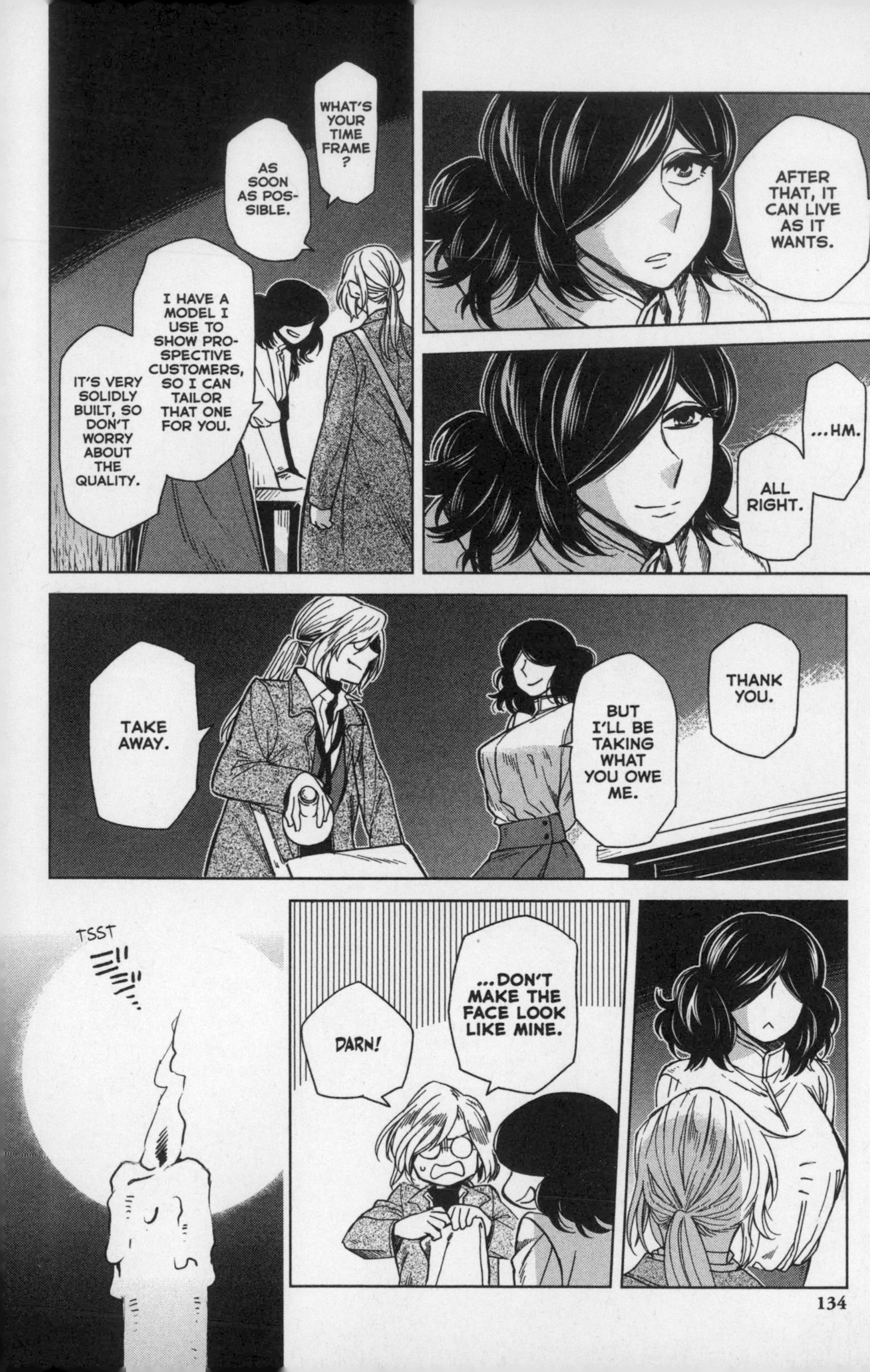
AFTER THAT, IT CAN LIVE AS IT WANTS.
...HM.
ALL RIGHT.
WHAT'S YOUR TIME FRAME?
AS SOON AS POS-SIBLE.
I HAVE A MODEL I USE TO SHOW PRO-SPECTIVE CUSTOMERS, SO I CAN TAILOR THAT ONE FOR YOU.
IT'S VERY SOLIDLY BUILT, SO DON'T WORRY ABOUT THE QUALITY.
THANK YOU.
BUT I'LL BE TAKING WHAT YOU OWE ME.
TAKE AWAY.
...DON'T MAKE THE FACE LOOK LIKE MINE.
DARN!
TSST

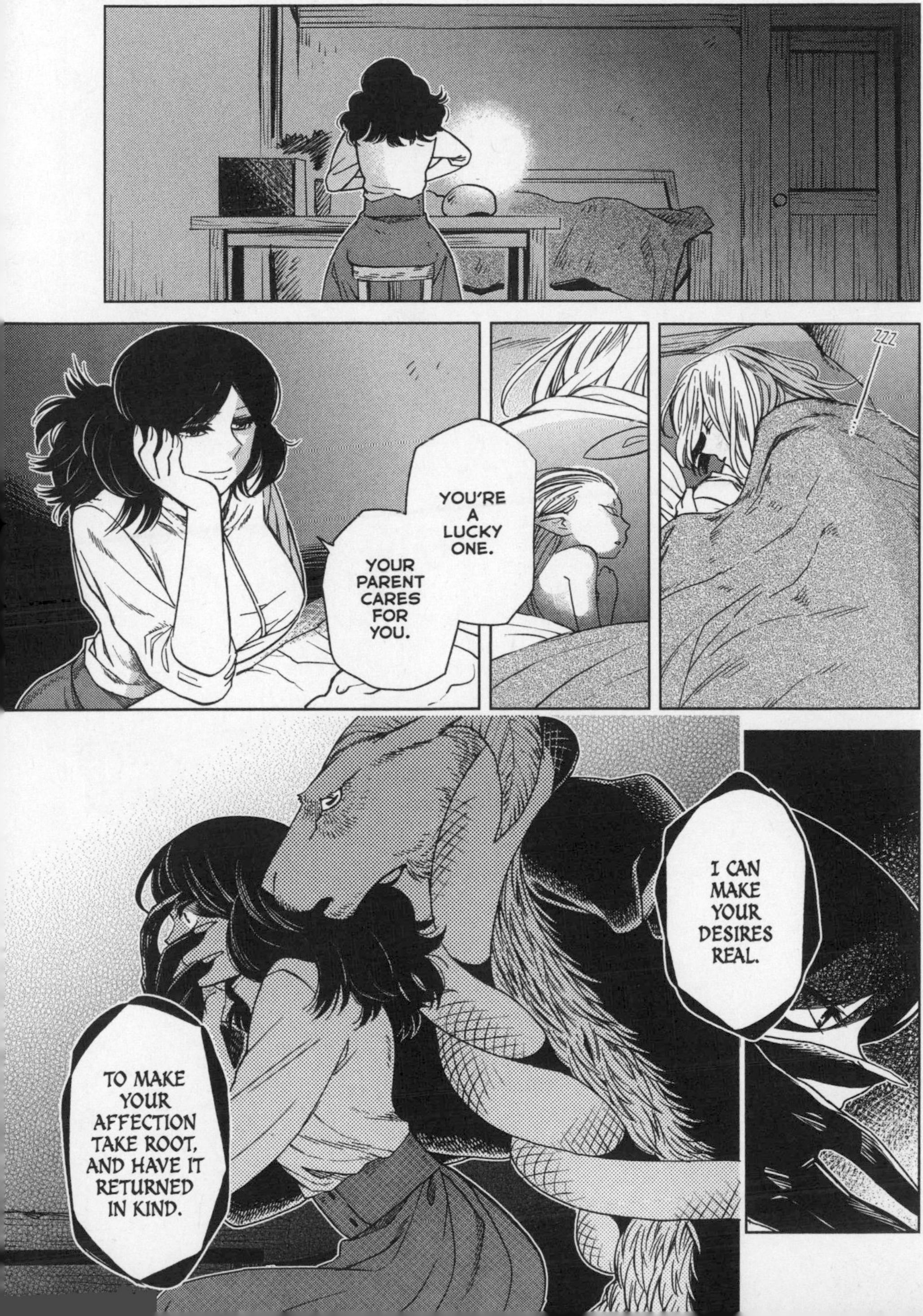
ZZZ
YOU'RE A LUCKY ONE.
YOUR PARENT CARES FOR YOU.
I CAN MAKE YOUR DESIRES REAL.
TO MAKE YOUR AFFECTION TAKE ROOT, AND HAVE IT RETURNED IN KIND.

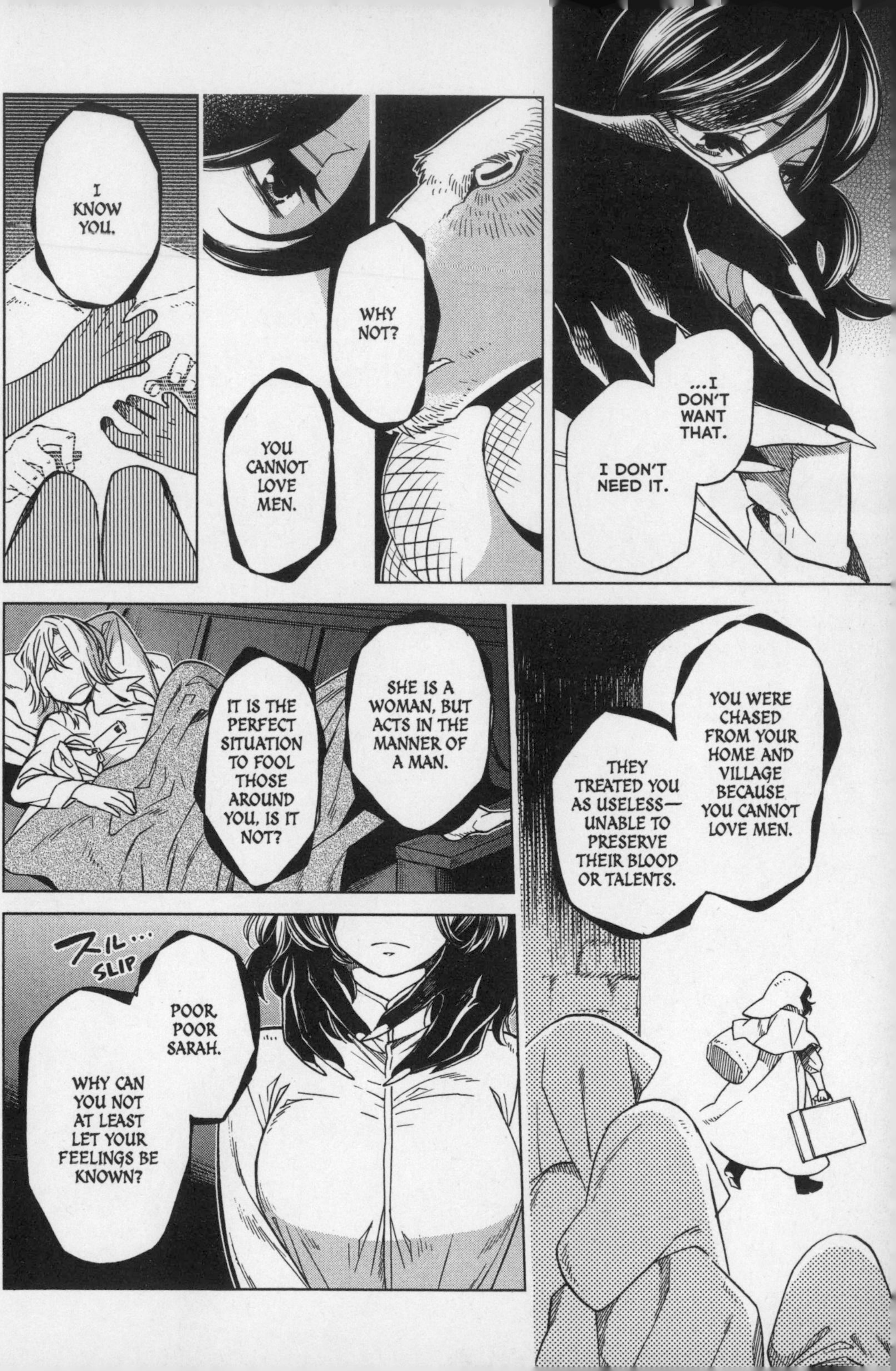
...I DON'T WANT THAT.
I DON'T NEED IT.
WHY NOT?
YOU CANNOT LOVE MEN.
I KNOW YOU.
YOU WERE CHASED FROM YOUR HOME AND VILLAGE BECAUSE YOU CANNOT LOVE MEN.
THEY TREATED YOU AS USELESS— UNABLE TO PRESERVE THEIR BLOOD OR TALENTS.
SHE IS A WOMAN, BUT ACTS IN THE MANNER OF A MAN.
IT IS THE PERFECT SITUATION TO FOOL THOSE AROUND YOU, IS IT NOT?
スル... SLIP
POOR POOR SARAH.
WHY CAN YOU NOT AT LEAST LET YOUR FEELINGS BE KNOWN?

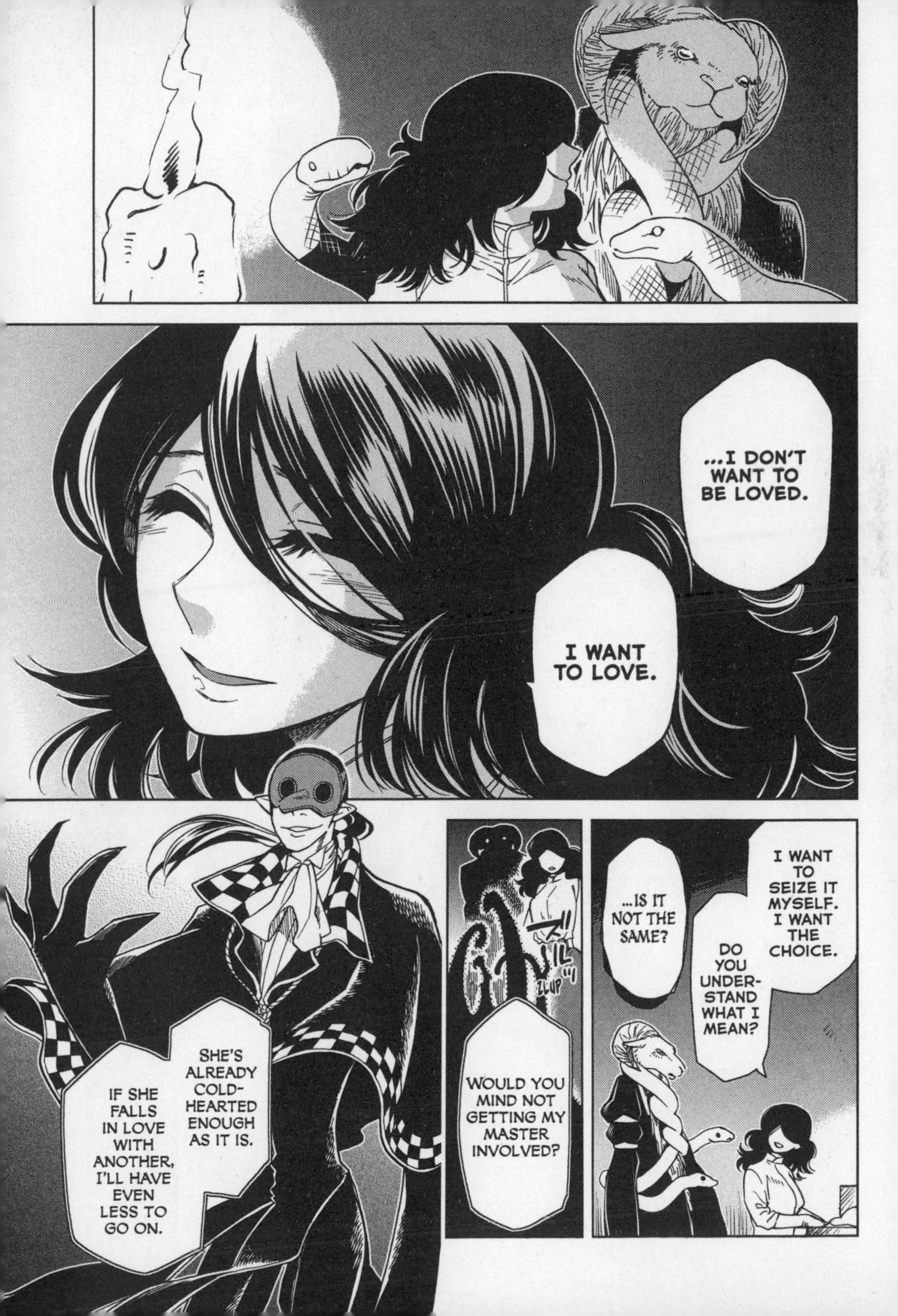

...I DON'T WANT TO BE LOVED.
I WANT TO LOVE.
I WANT TO SEIZE IT MYSELF. I WANT THE CHOICE.
DO YOU UNDERSTAND WHAT I MEAN?
...IS IT NOT THE SAME?
ZLUP
WOULD YOU MIND NOT GETTING MY MASTER INVOLVED?
SHE'S ALREADY COLD-HEARTED ENOUGH AS IT IS.
IF SHE FALLS IN LOVE WITH ANOTHER, I'LL HAVE EVEN LESS TO GO ON.

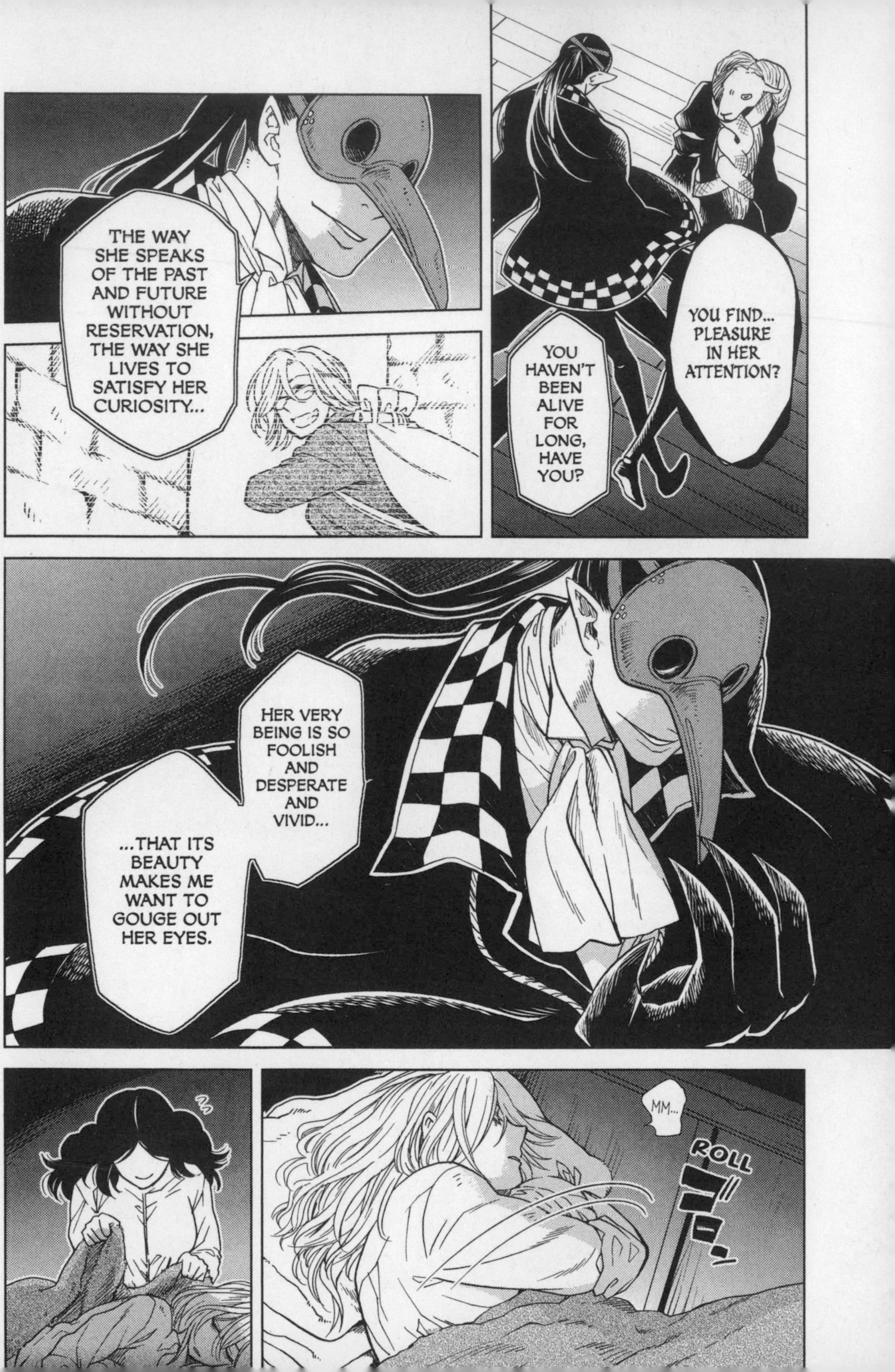
YOU FIND... PLEASURE IN HER ATTENTION?
YOU HAVEN'T BEEN ALIVE FOR LONG, HAVE YOU?
THE WAY SHE SPEAKS OF THE PAST AND FUTURE WITHOUT RESERVATION, THE WAY SHE LIVES TO SATISFY HER CURIOSITY...
HER VERY BEING IS SO FOOLISH AND DESPERATE AND VIVID...
...THAT ITS BEAUTY MAKES ME WANT TO GOUGE OUT HER EYES.
MM...
ROLL

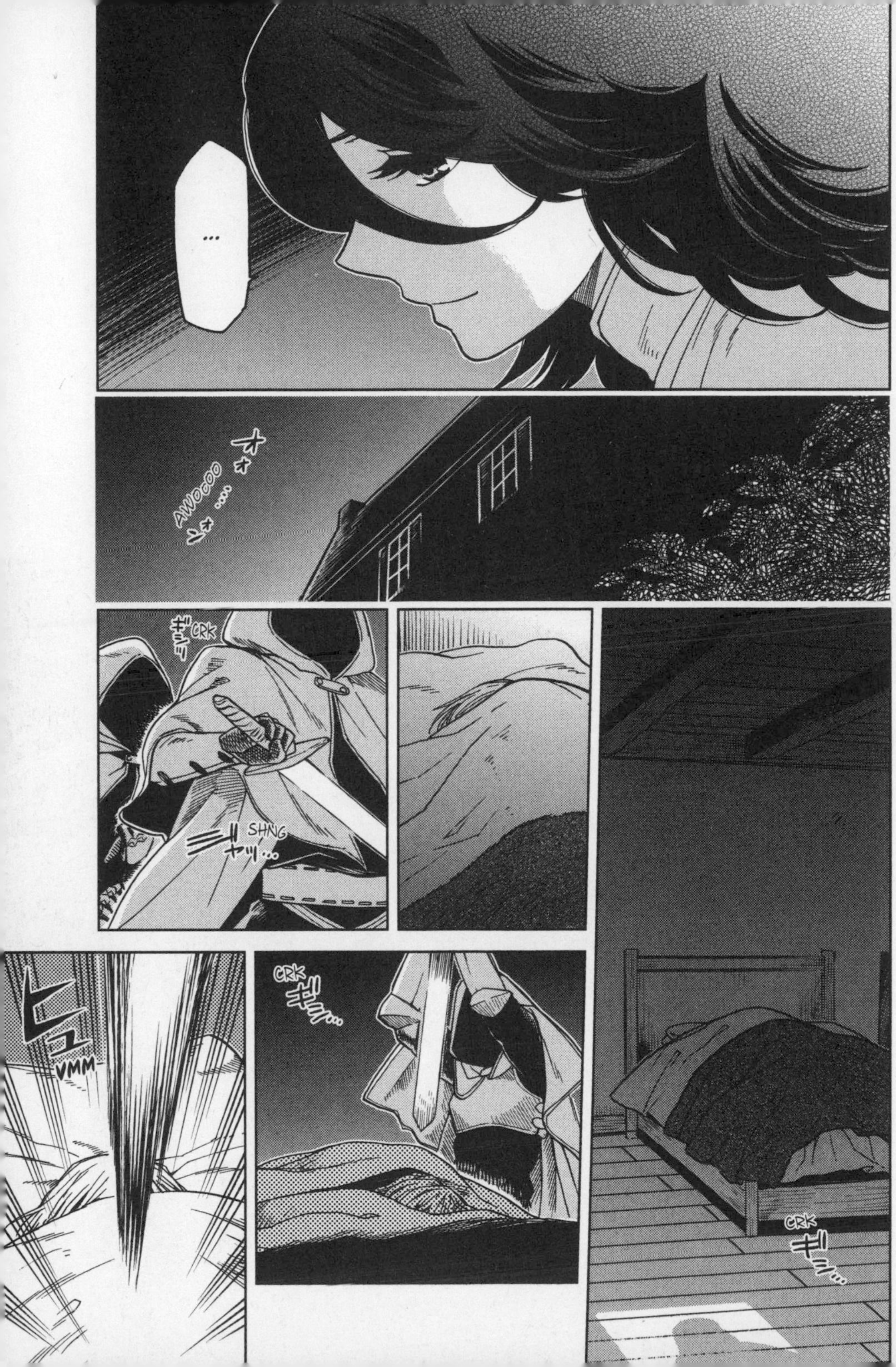
...
オォ……オン
AWOOOO
CRK
ギッ…
CRK
ギッ
SHNG
ジャッ…
CRK
ギシ…
ヒュ
VMM

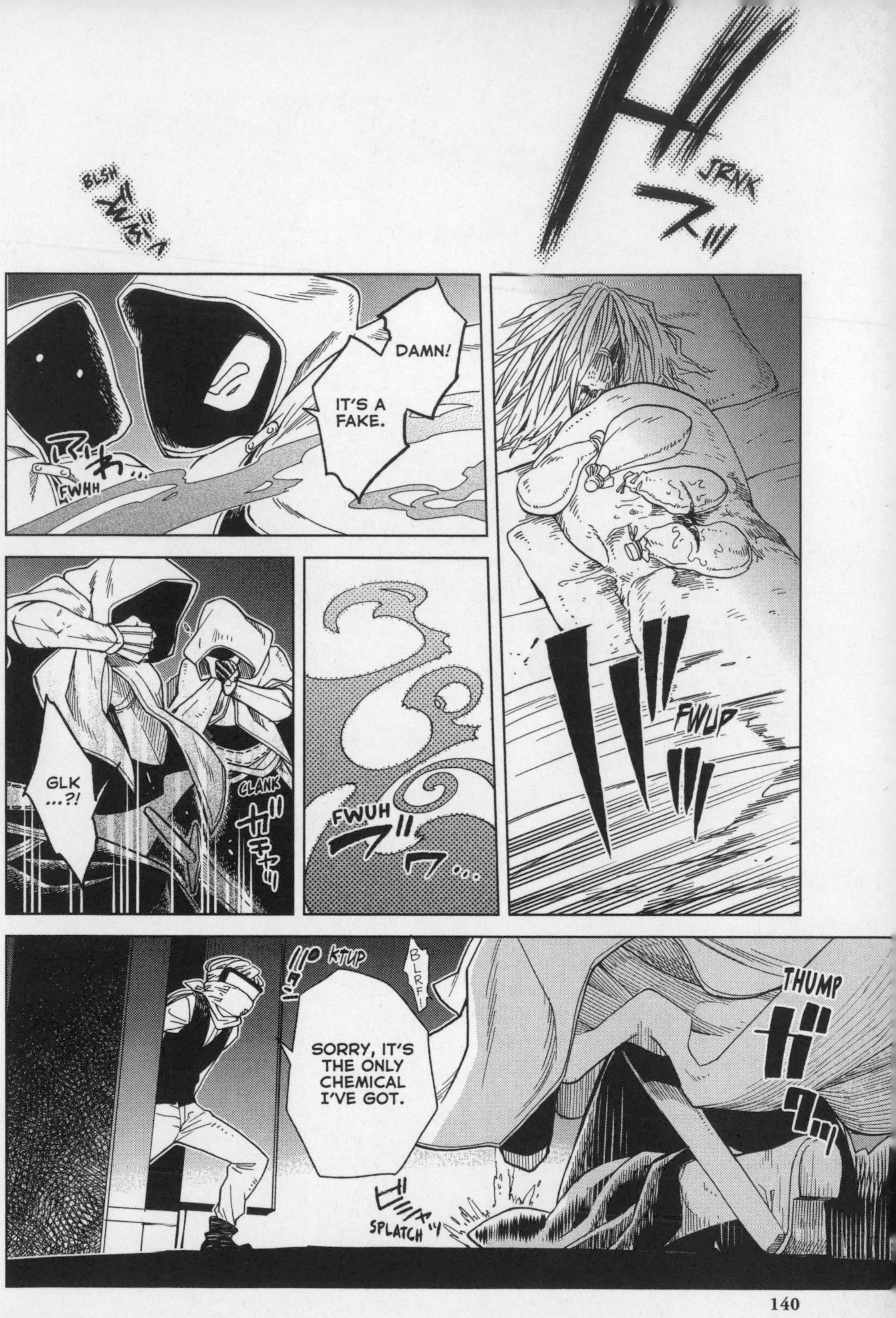
JRNK
BLSH
FWUP
DAMN!
IT'S A FAKE.
FWHH
FWUH
GLK ...?!
CLANK
THUMP
BLRF!
KTUP
SORRY, IT'S THE ONLY CHEMICAL I'VE GOT.
SPLATCH

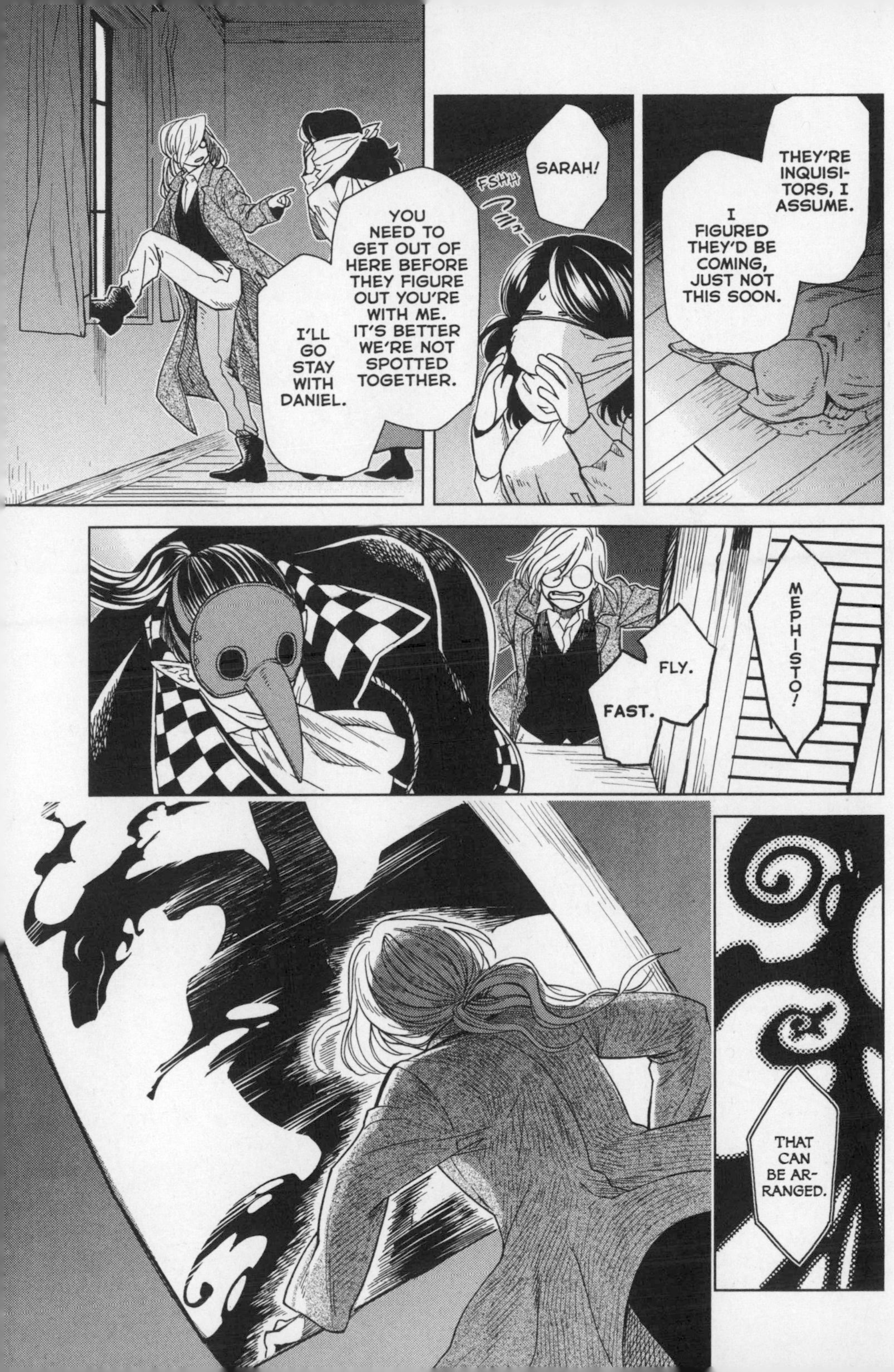
THEY'RE INQUISITORS, I ASSUME.
I FIGURED THEY'D BE COMING, JUST NOT THIS SOON.
SARAH!
FSHH
YOU NEED TO GET OUT OF HERE BEFORE THEY FIGURE OUT YOU'RE WITH ME. IT'S BETTER WE'RE NOT SPOTTED TOGETHER.
I'LL GO STAY WITH DANIEL.
MEPHISTO!
FLY.
FAST.
THAT CAN BE ARRANGED.

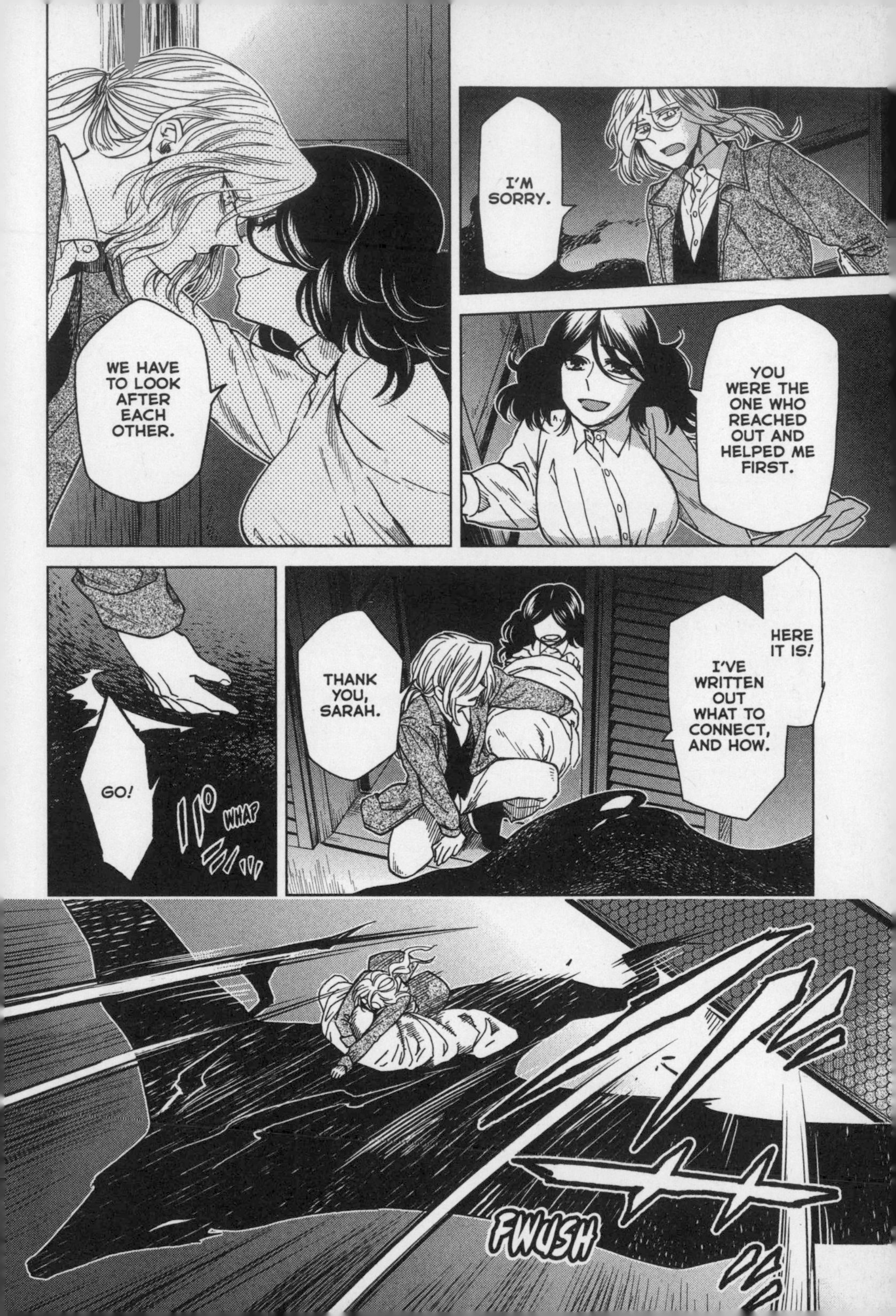
I'M SORRY.
YOU WERE THE ONE WHO REACHED OUT AND HELPED ME FIRST.
WE HAVE TO LOOK AFTER EACH OTHER.
HERE IT IS! I'VE WRITTEN OUT WHAT TO CONNECT, AND HOW.
THANK YOU, SARAH.
GO!
WHAP
FWUSH

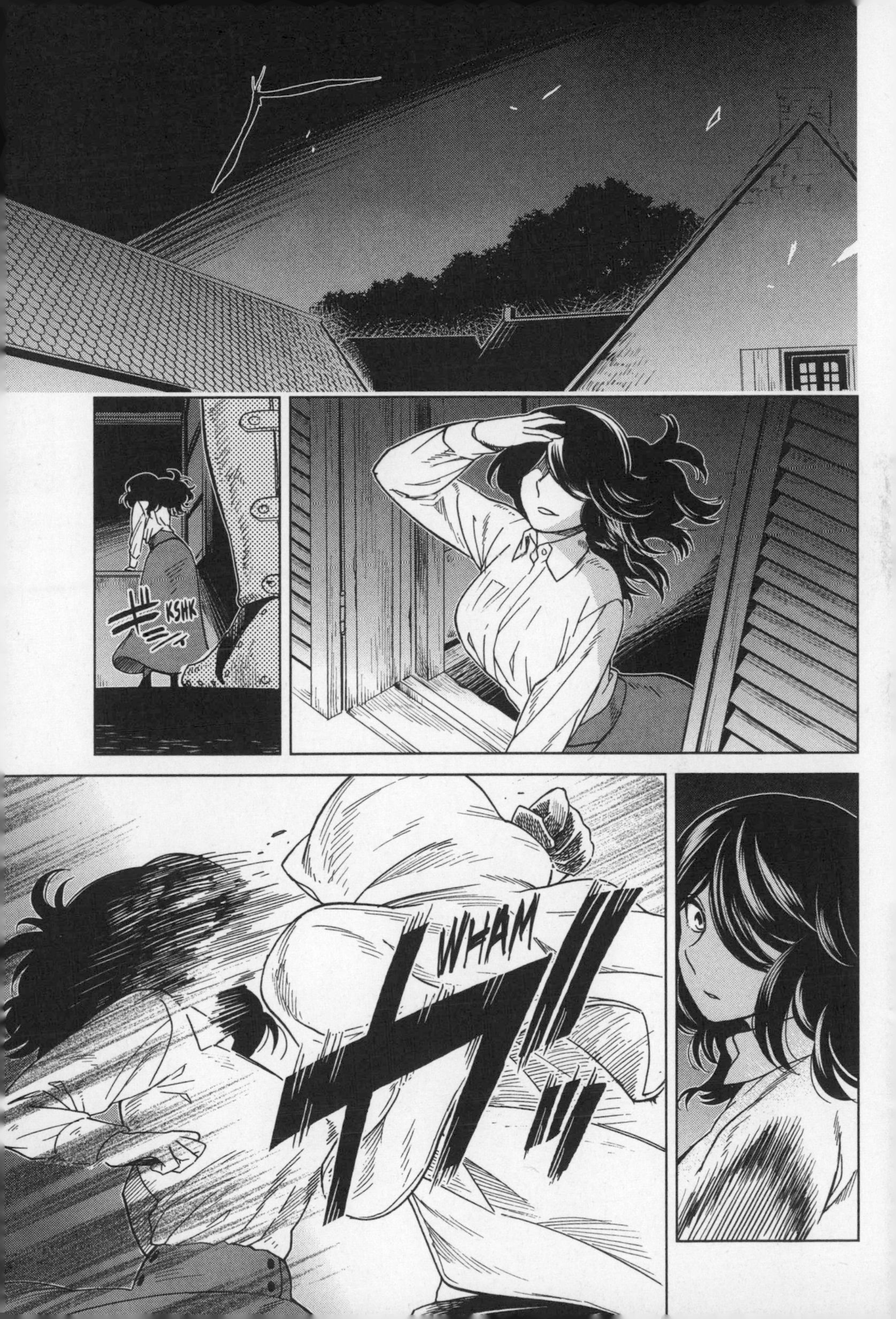
KSHK
WHAM

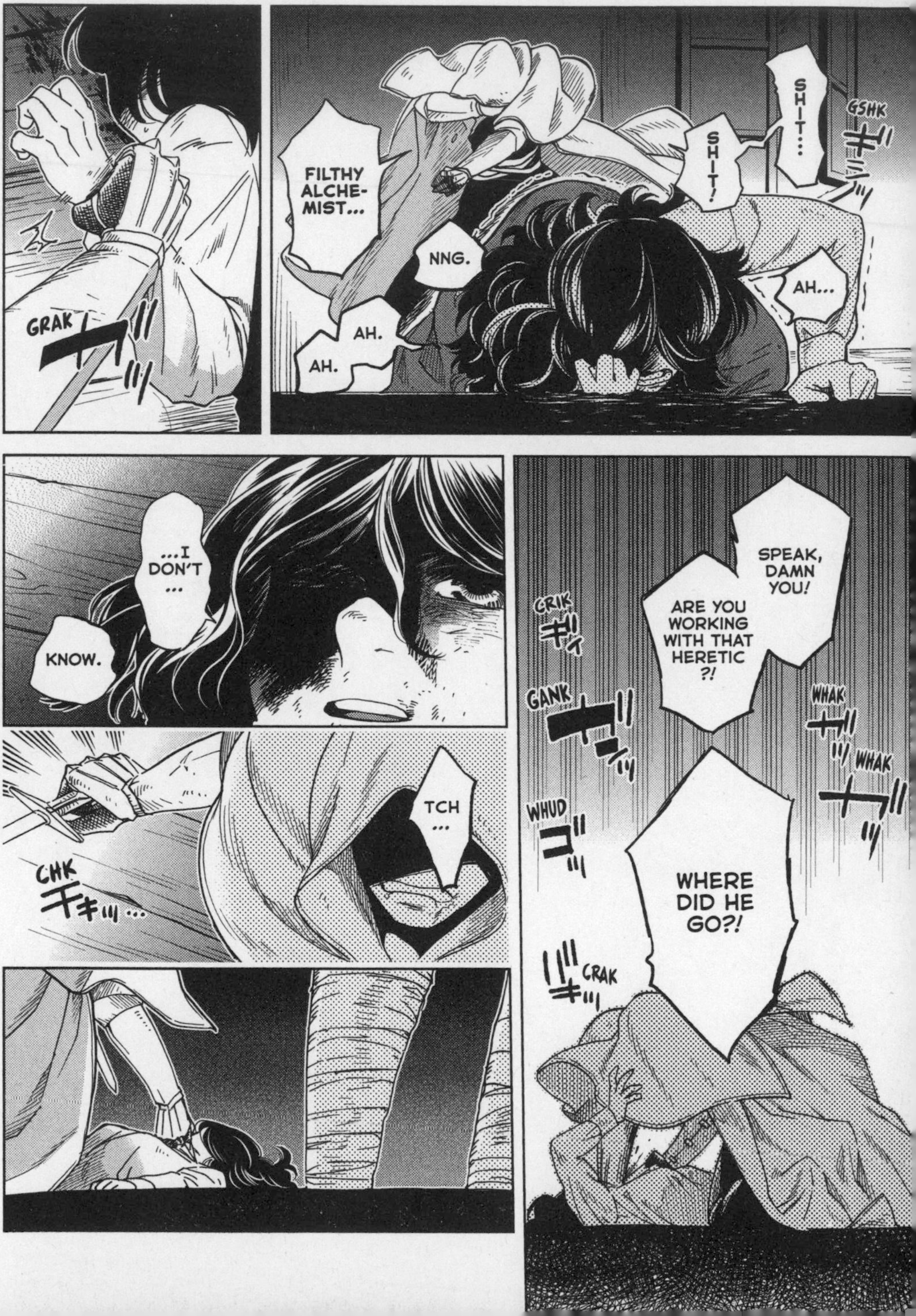
GSHK
SHIT...
SHIT!
FILTHY ALCHEMIST...
AH...
NNG.
AH.
AH.
GRAK
SPEAK, DAMN YOU!
ARE YOU WORKING WITH THAT HERETIC ?!
CRIK
WHAK
WHAK
GANK
WHUD
WHERE DID HE GO?!
CRAK
...I DON'T ...
KNOW.
TCH ...
CHK

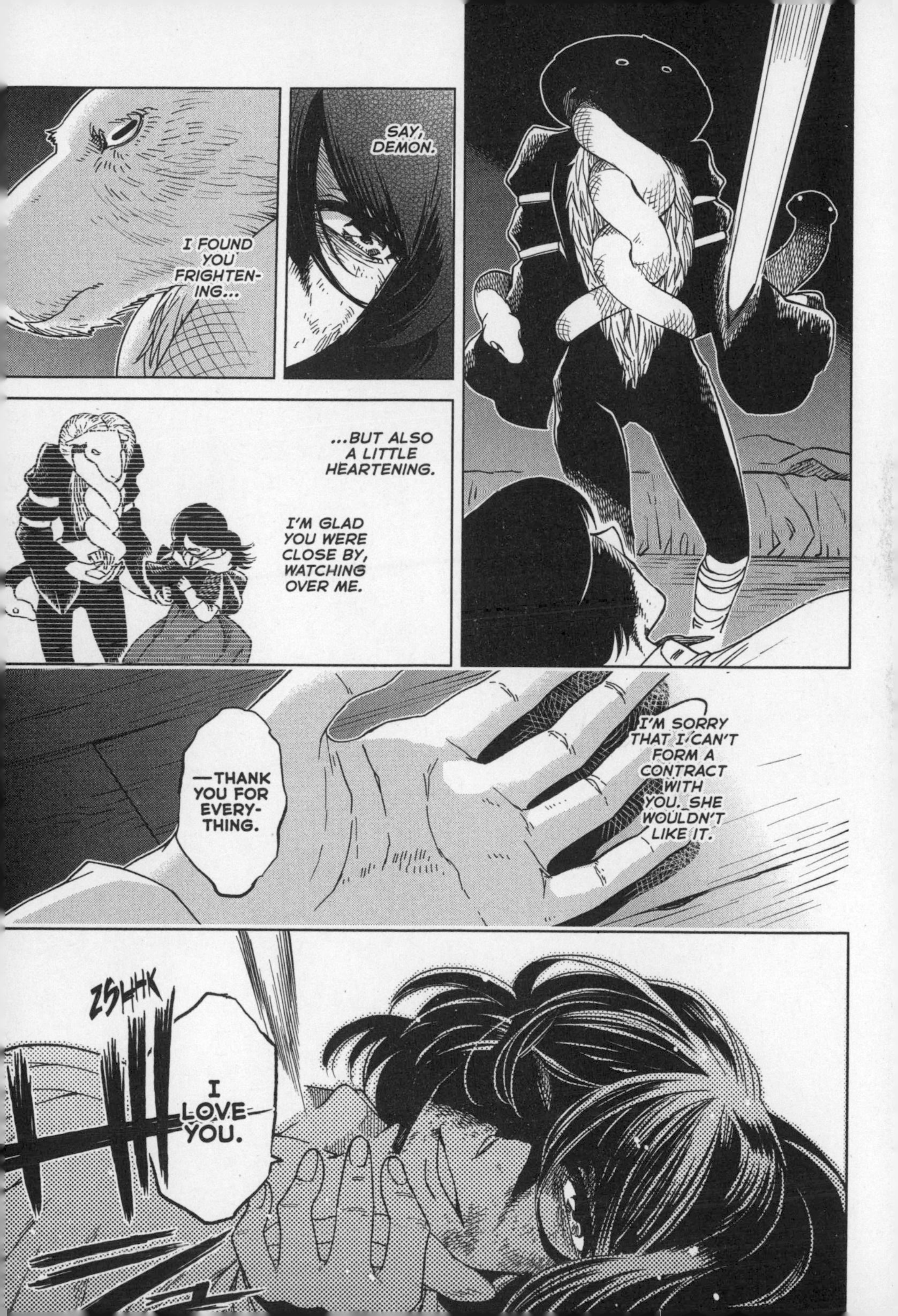
SAY, DEMON.
I FOUND YOU FRIGHTENING...
...BUT ALSO A LITTLE HEARTENING.
I'M GLAD YOU WERE CLOSE BY, WATCHING OVER ME.
I'M SORRY THAT I CAN'T FORM A CONTRACT WITH YOU. SHE WOULDN'T LIKE IT.
—THANK YOU FOR EVERYTHING.
ZSHHK
I LOVE YOU.

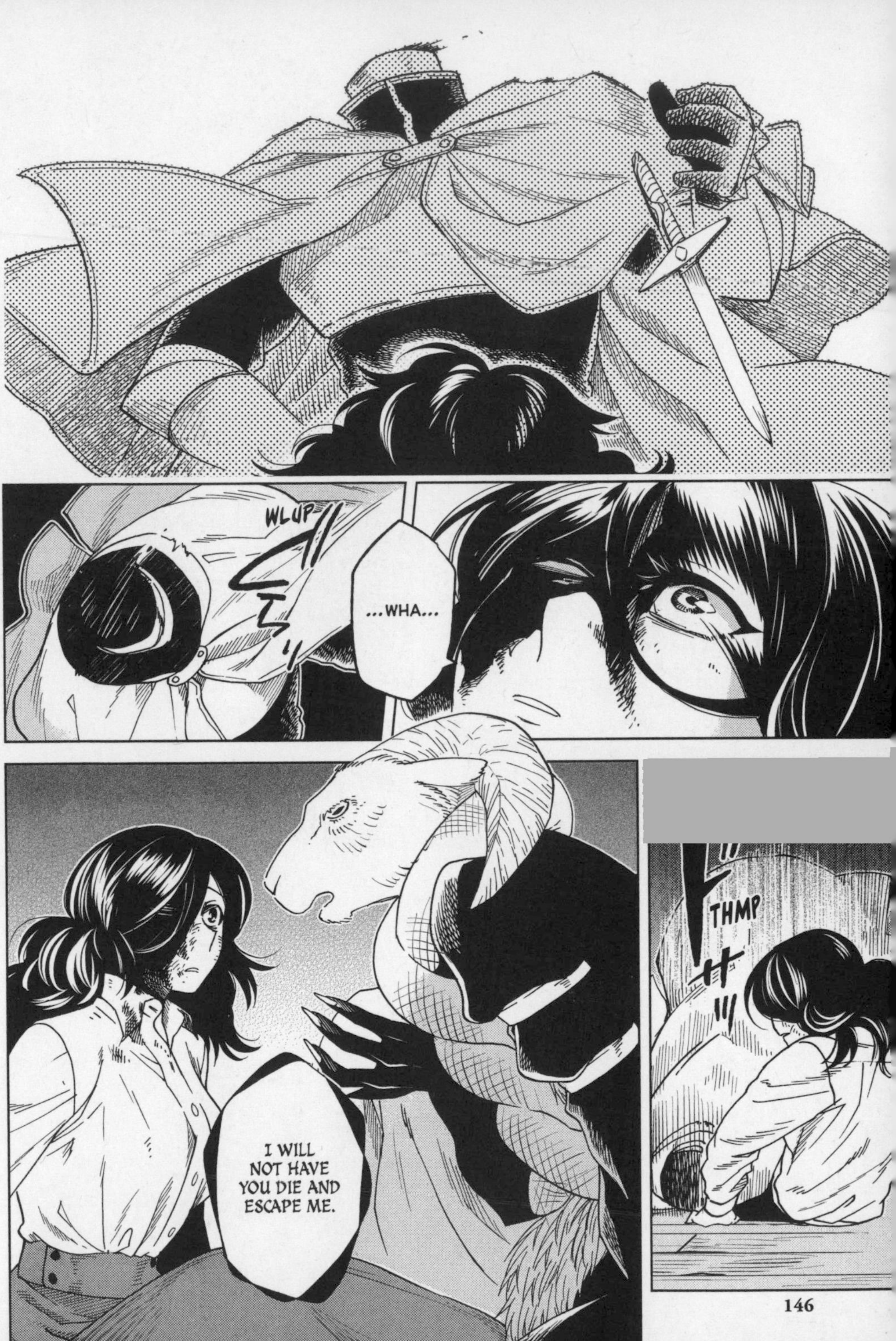
...WHA...
WLUP
THMP
I WILL NOT HAVE YOU DIE AND ESCAPE ME.

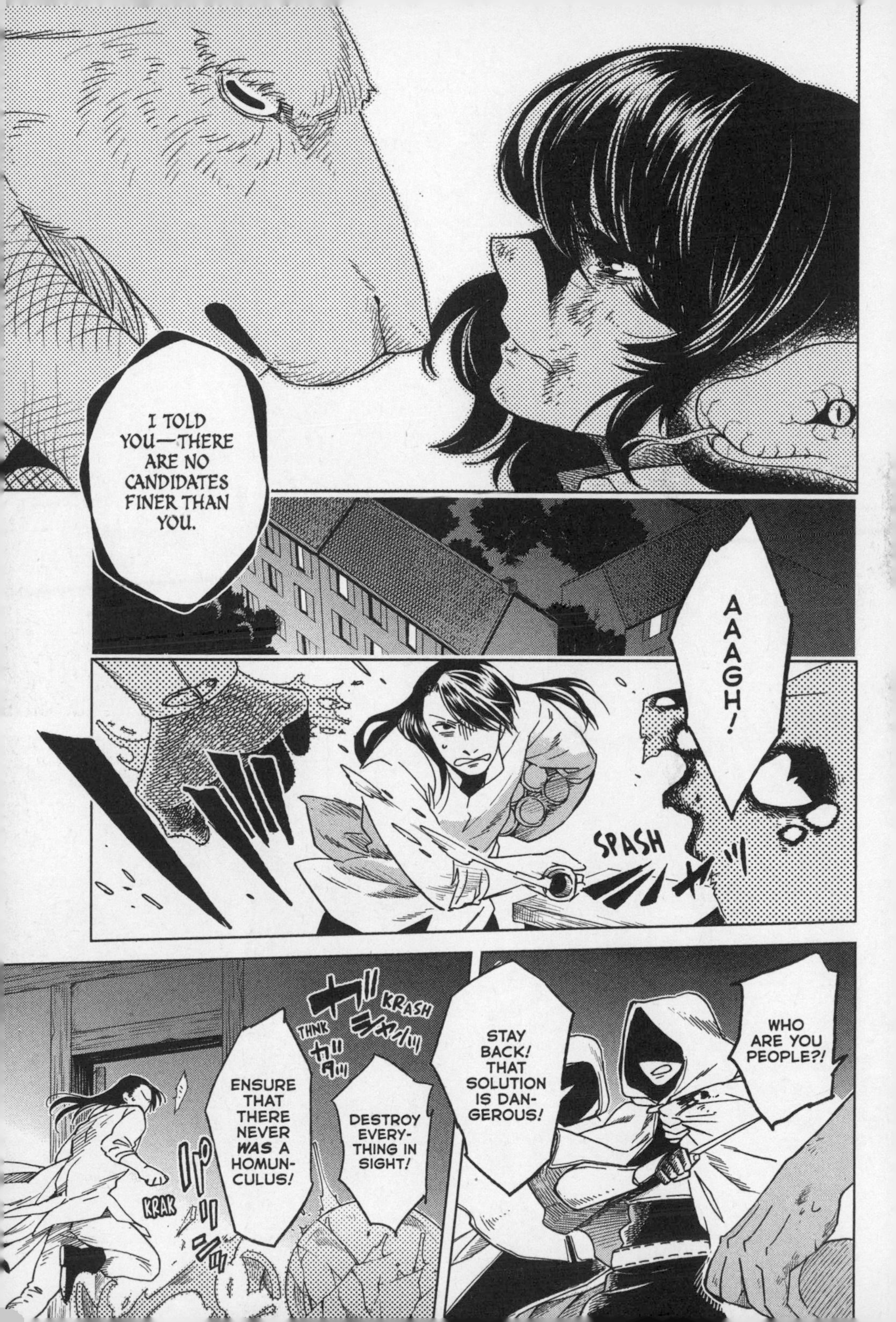
I TOLD YOU—THERE ARE NO CANDIDATES FINER THAN YOU.
AAAGH!
SPASH
WHO ARE YOU PEOPLE?!
STAY BACK! THAT SOLUTION IS DANGEROUS!
KRASH
THNK
DESTROY EVERYTHING IN SIGHT!
ENSURE THAT THERE NEVER *WAS* A HOMUNCULUS!
KRAK

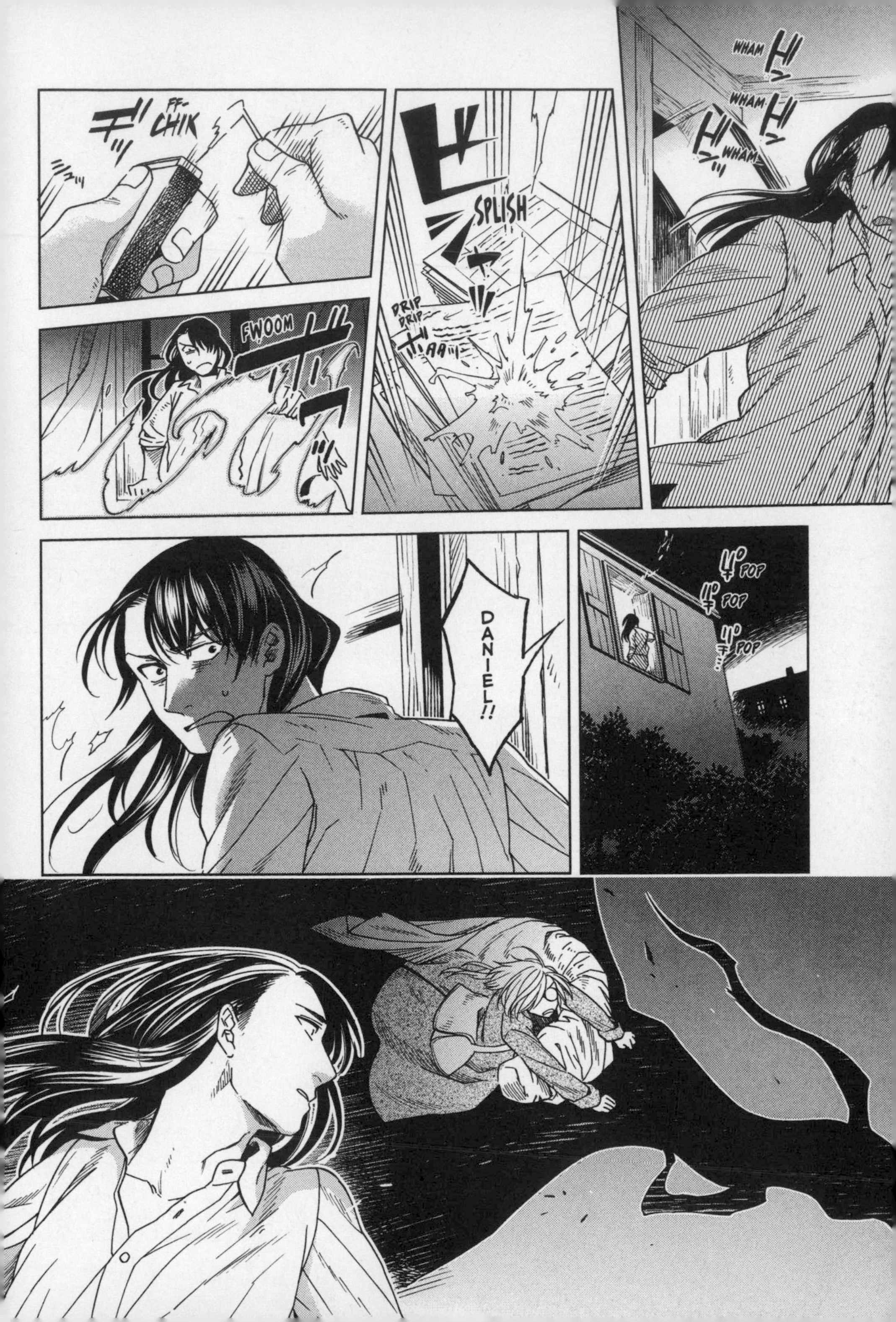
WHAM
WHAM
WHAM
SPLISH
DRIP DRIP
AA
FF-CHIK
FWOOM
POP
POP
POP
DANIEL!!

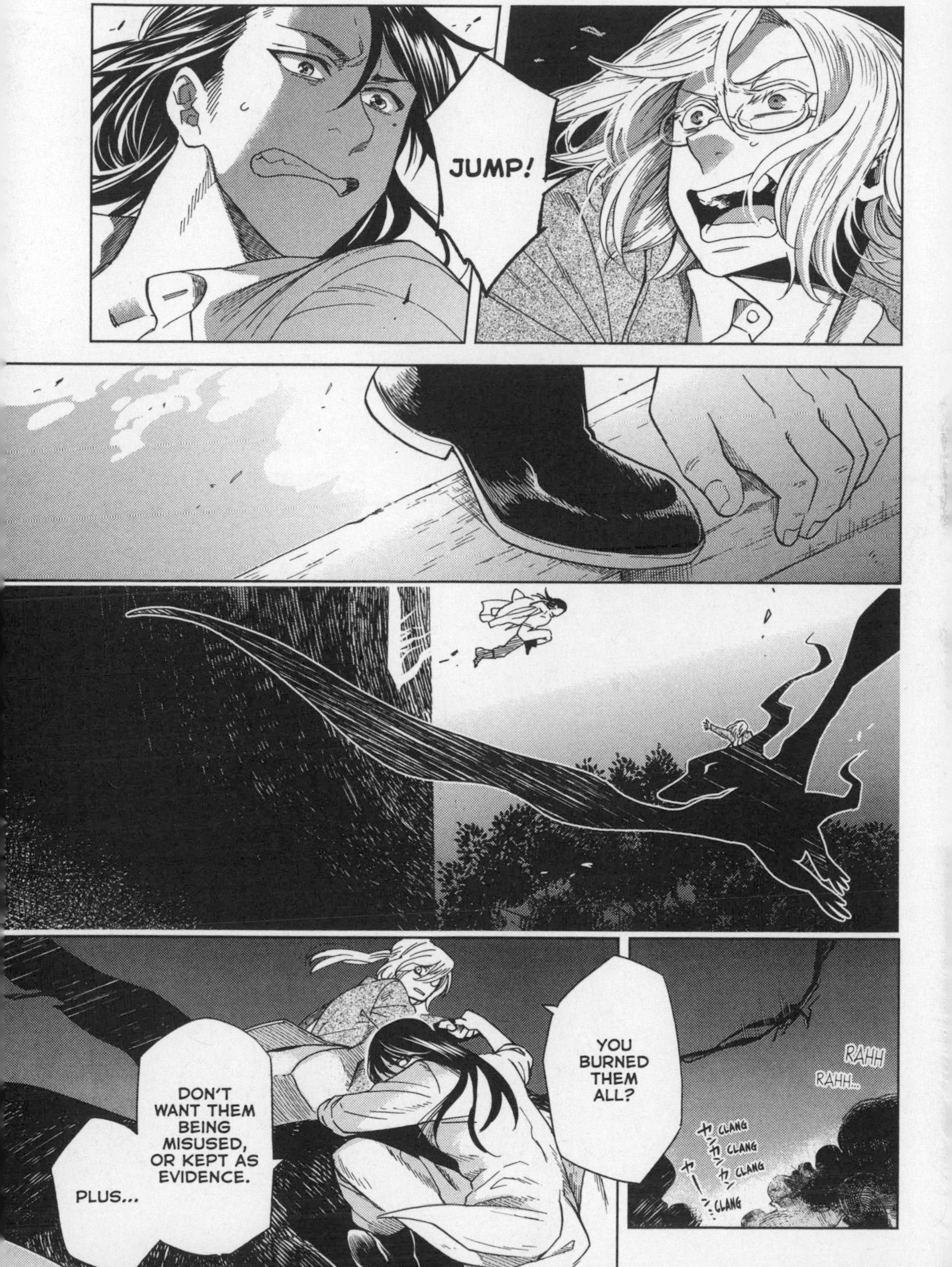
JUMP!
RAHH
RAHH...
CLANG
CLANG
CLANG
CLANG
YOU BURNED THEM ALL?
DON'T WANT THEM BEING MISUSED, OR KEPT AS EVIDENCE.
PLUS...

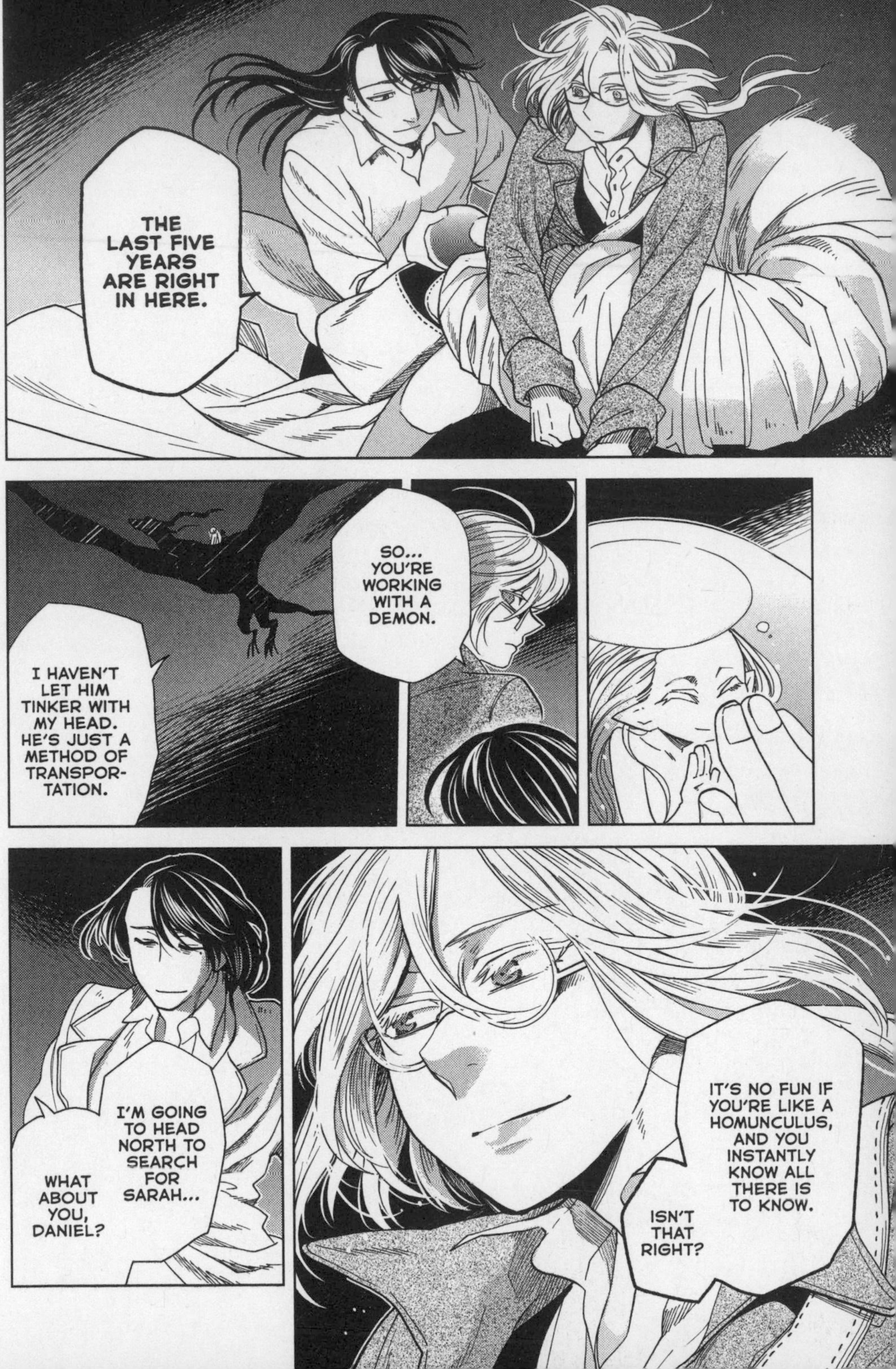
THE LAST FIVE YEARS ARE RIGHT IN HERE.
SO... YOU'RE WORKING WITH A DEMON.
I HAVEN'T LET HIM TINKER WITH MY HEAD. HE'S JUST A METHOD OF TRANSPORTATION.
IT'S NO FUN IF YOU'RE LIKE A HOMUNCULUS, AND YOU INSTANTLY KNOW ALL THERE IS TO KNOW.
ISN'T THAT RIGHT?
I'M GOING TO HEAD NORTH TO SEARCH FOR SARAH...
WHAT ABOUT YOU, DANIEL?

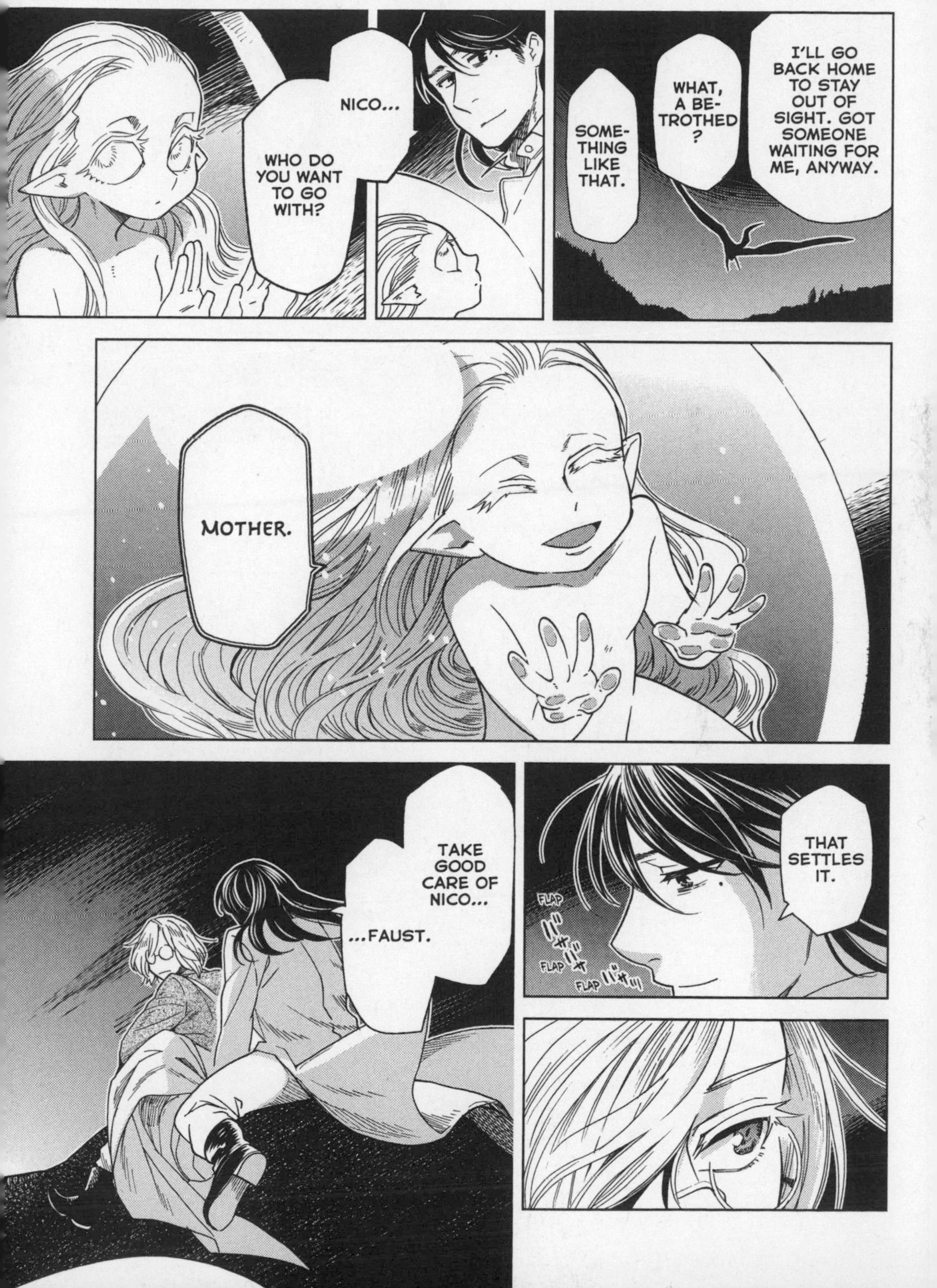
I'LL GO BACK HOME TO STAY OUT OF SIGHT. GOT SOMEONE WAITING FOR ME, ANYWAY.
WHAT, A BE-TROTHED?
SOME-THING LIKE THAT.
NICO...
WHO DO YOU WANT TO GO WITH?
MOTHER.
THAT SETTLES IT.
FLAP
FLAP
FLAP
TAKE GOOD CARE OF NICO...
...FAUST.

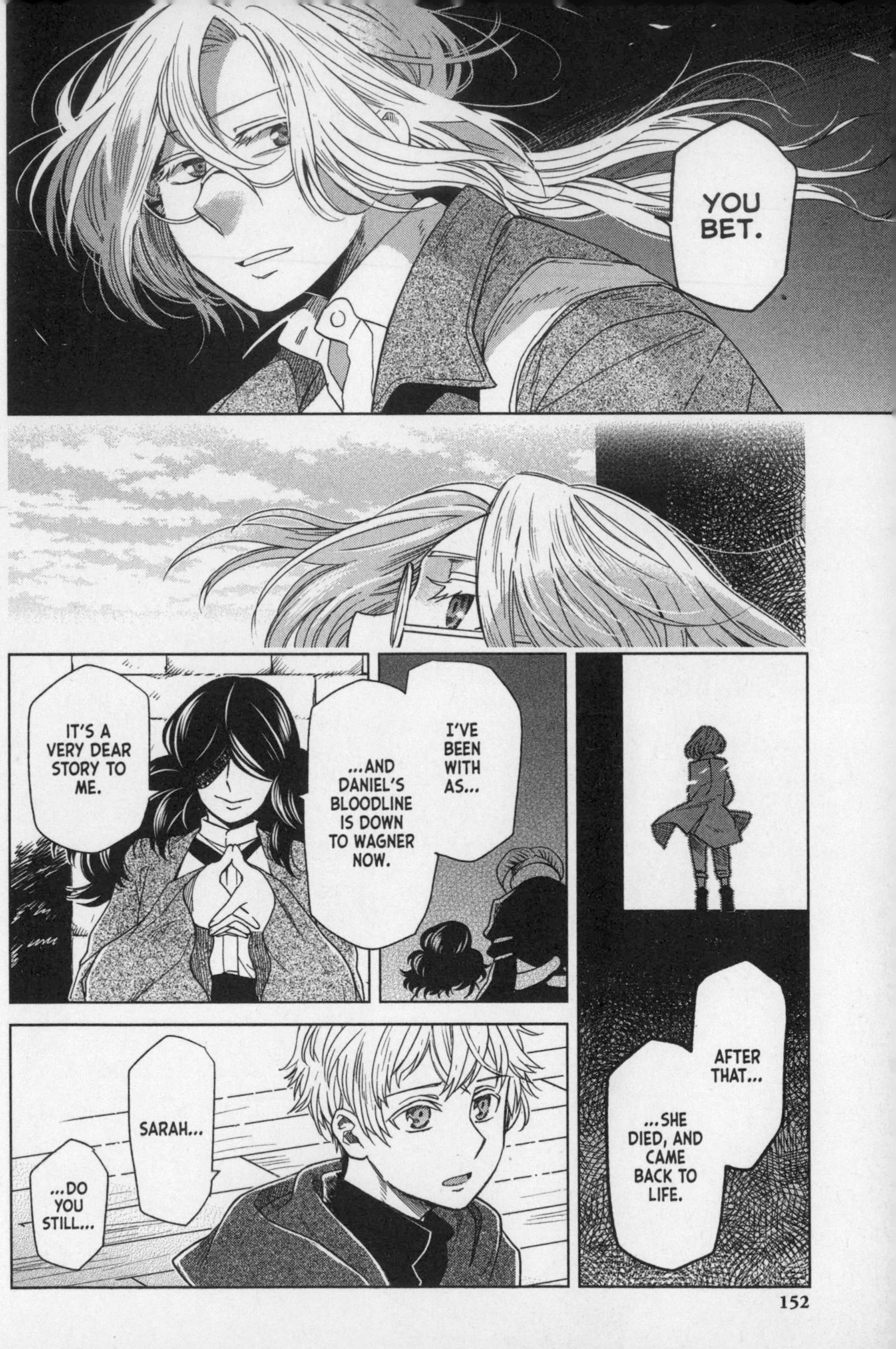
YOU BET.
AFTER THAT...
...SHE DIED, AND CAME BACK TO LIFE.
I'VE BEEN WITH AS...
...AND DANIEL'S BLOODLINE IS DOWN TO WAGNER NOW.
IT'S A VERY DEAR STORY TO ME.
SARAH...
...DO YOU STILL...

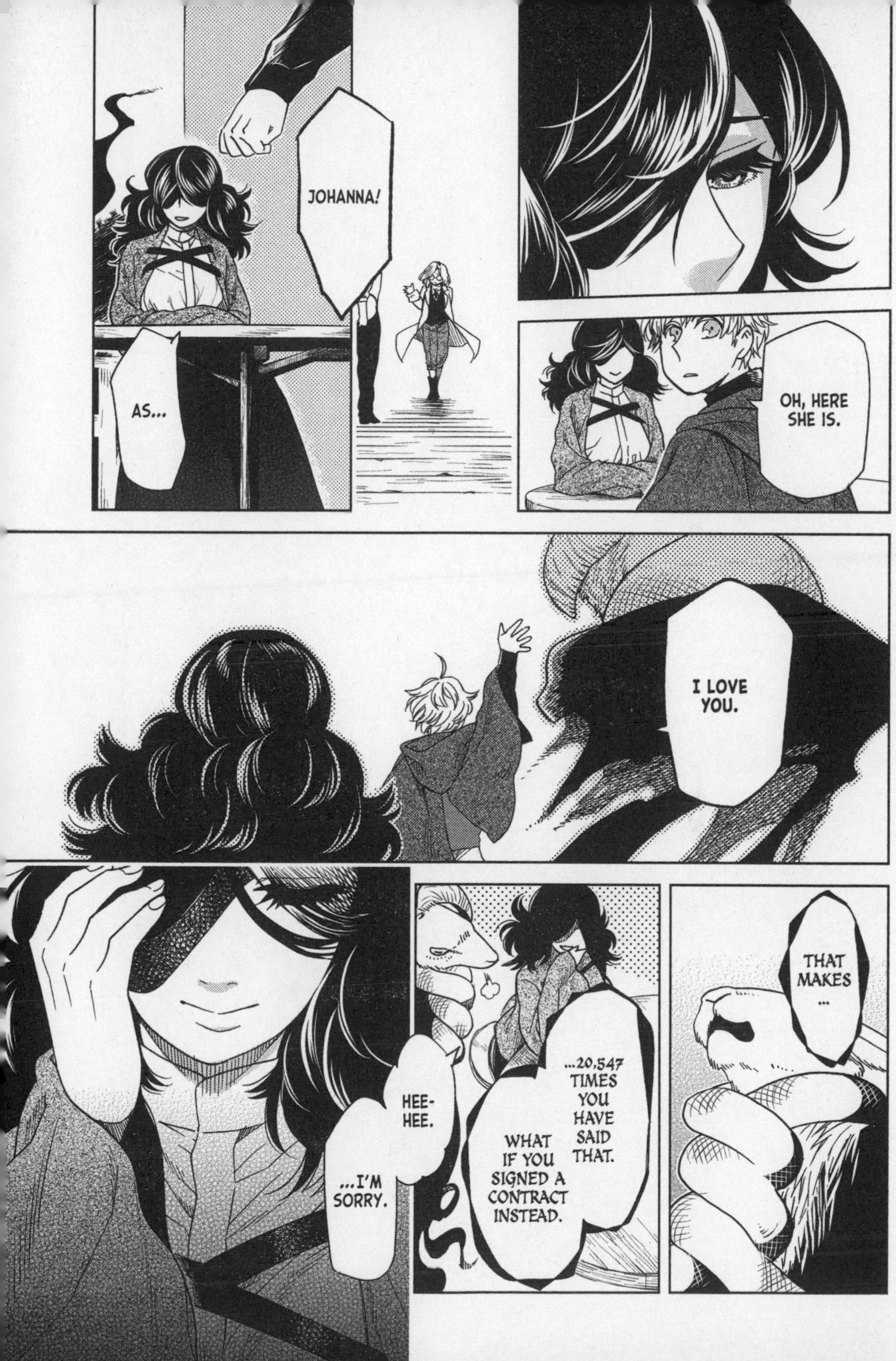
OH, HERE SHE IS.
JOHANNA!
AS...
I LOVE YOU.
THAT MAKES ...
...20,547 TIMES YOU HAVE SAID THAT.
WHAT IF YOU SIGNED A CONTRACT INSTEAD.
HEE-HEE.
...I'M SORRY.

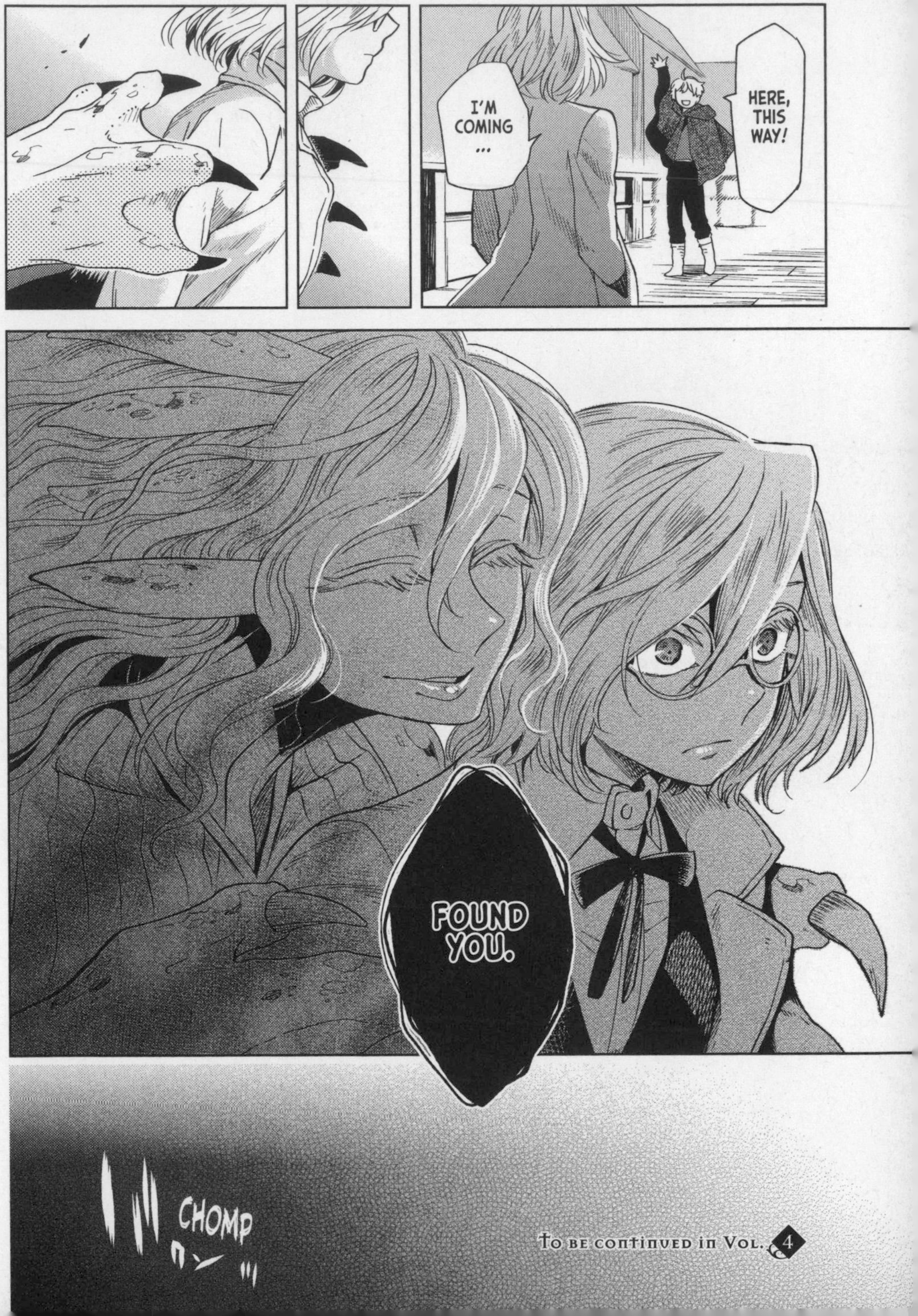
HERE, THIS WAY!
I'M COMING ...
FOUND YOU.
CHOMP

To be continued in Vol. 4

KORE
YAMAZAKI

I've made it to
Volume 3. Finally,
I had a chance
to visit Germany,
the basis for the
story's setting. I felt
as though I had
visions of Johanna
and company
striding through
the old medieval
city centers, amidst
the forthright and
picturesque fairy
tale atmosphere.

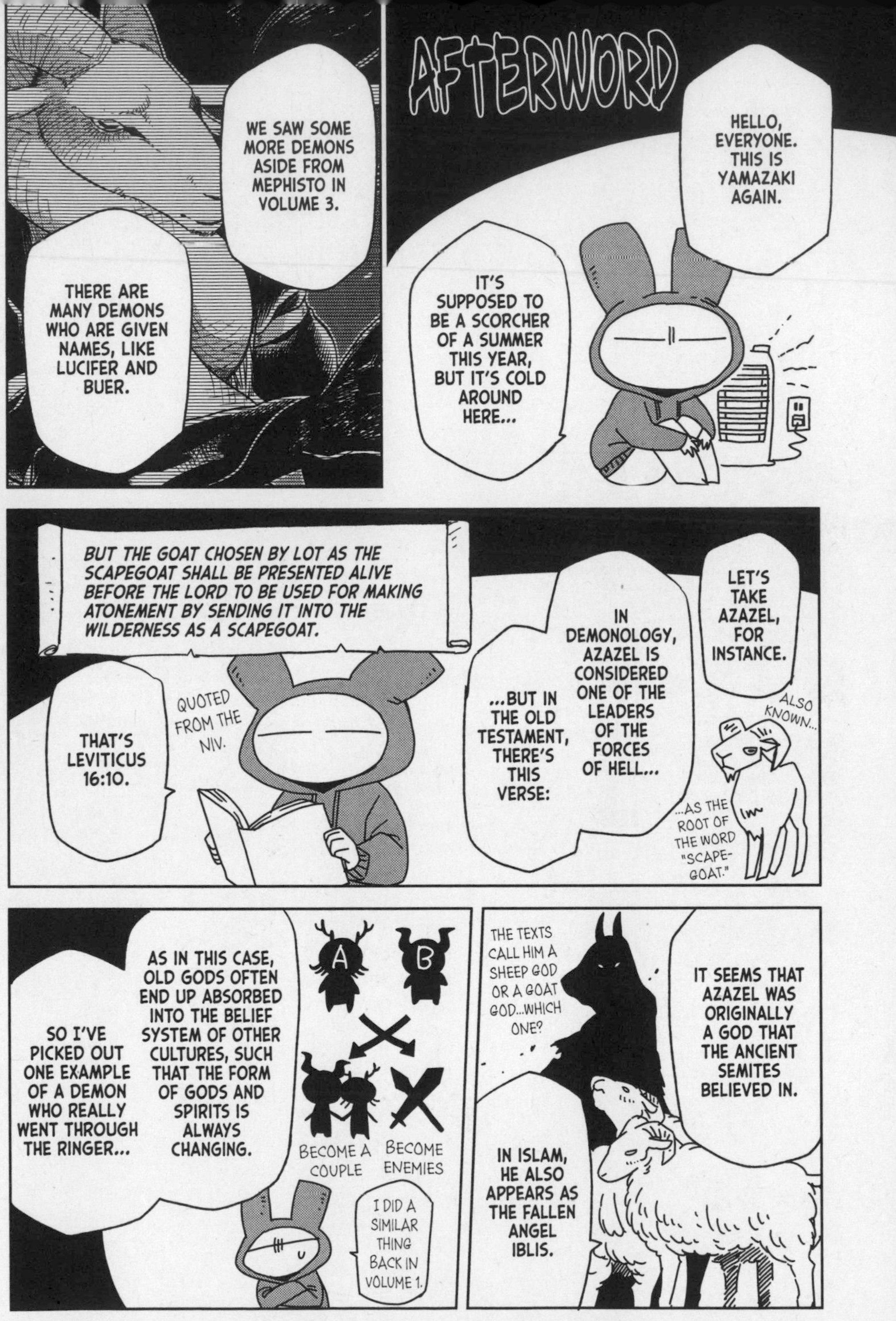
AFTERWORD
HELLO, EVERYONE. THIS IS YAMAZAKI AGAIN.
IT'S SUPPOSED TO BE A SCORCHER OF A SUMMER THIS YEAR, BUT IT'S COLD AROUND HERE...
WE SAW SOME MORE DEMONS ASIDE FROM MEPHISTO IN VOLUME 3.
THERE ARE MANY DEMONS WHO ARE GIVEN NAMES, LIKE LUCIFER AND BUER.
LET'S TAKE AZAZEL, FOR INSTANCE.
ALSO KNOWN...
...AS THE ROOT OF THE WORD "SCAPE-GOAT."
IN DEMONOLOGY, AZAZEL IS CONSIDERED ONE OF THE LEADERS OF THE FORCES OF HELL...
...BUT IN THE OLD TESTAMENT, THERE'S THIS VERSE:
BUT THE GOAT CHOSEN BY LOT AS THE SCAPEGOAT SHALL BE PRESENTED ALIVE BEFORE THE LORD TO BE USED FOR MAKING ATONEMENT BY SENDING IT INTO THE WILDERNESS AS A SCAPEGOAT.
QUOTED FROM THE NIV.
THAT'S LEVITICUS 16:10.
IT SEEMS THAT AZAZEL WAS ORIGINALLY A GOD THAT THE ANCIENT SEMITES BELIEVED IN.
THE TEXTS CALL HIM A SHEEP GOD OR A GOAT GOD...WHICH ONE?
IN ISLAM, HE ALSO APPEARS AS THE FALLEN ANGEL IBLIS.
AS IN THIS CASE, OLD GODS OFTEN END UP ABSORBED INTO THE BELIEF SYSTEM OF OTHER CULTURES, SUCH THAT THE FORM OF GODS AND SPIRITS IS ALWAYS CHANGING.
B
A
BECOME ENEMIES
BECOME A COUPLE
SO I'VE PICKED OUT ONE EXAMPLE OF A DEMON WHO REALLY WENT THROUGH THE RINGER...
I DID A SIMILAR THING BACK IN VOLUME 1.

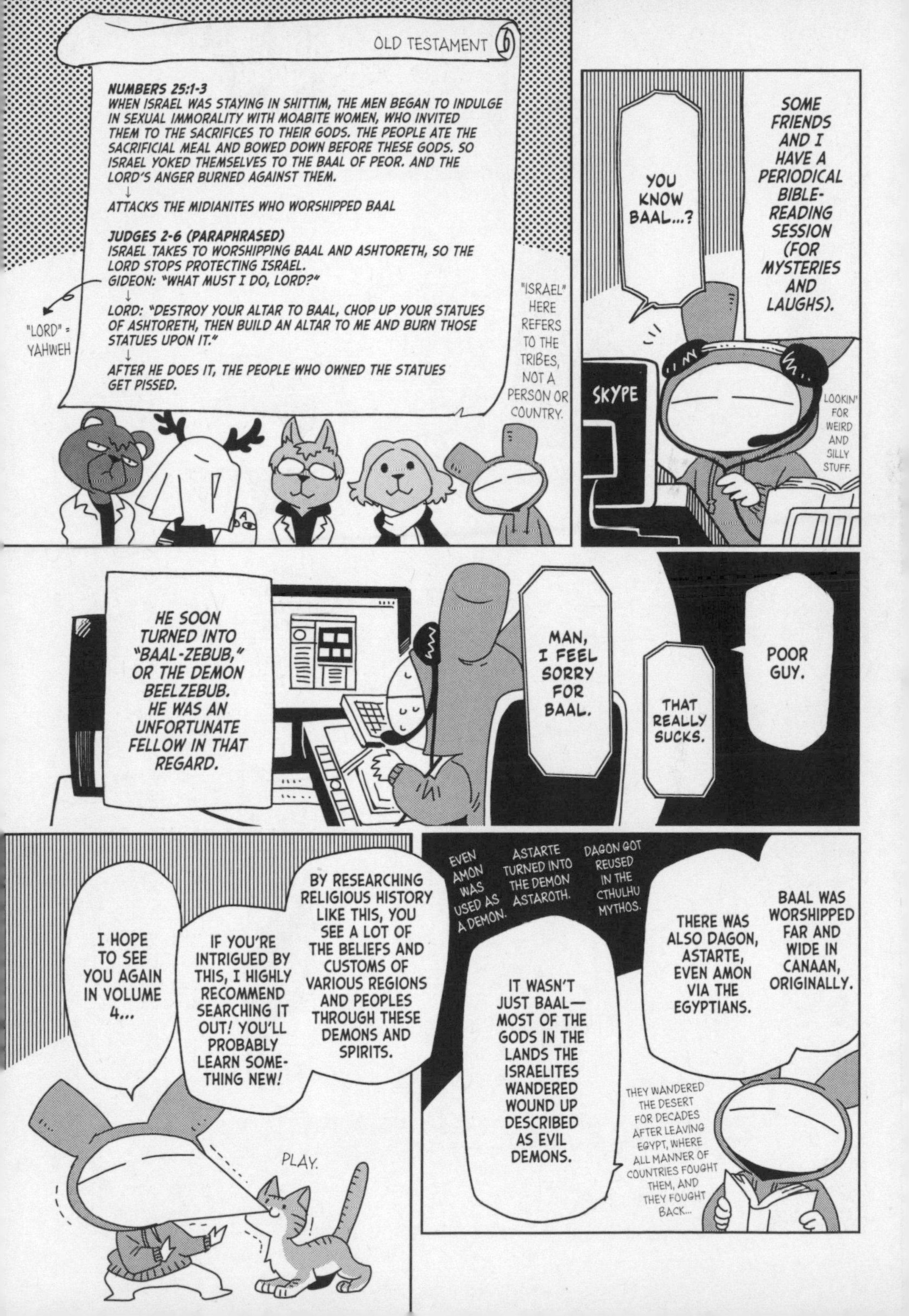

SOME FRIENDS AND I HAVE A PERIODICAL BIBLE-READING SESSION (FOR MYSTERIES AND LAUGHS).
YOU KNOW BAAL...?
SKYPE
LOOKIN' FOR WEIRD AND SILLY STUFF.
OLD TESTAMENT
NUMBERS 25:1-3
WHEN ISRAEL WAS STAYING IN SHITTIM, THE MEN BEGAN TO INDULGE IN SEXUAL IMMORALITY WITH MOABITE WOMEN, WHO INVITED THEM TO THE SACRIFICES TO THEIR GODS. THE PEOPLE ATE THE SACRIFICIAL MEAL AND BOWED DOWN BEFORE THESE GODS. SO ISRAEL YOKED THEMSELVES TO THE BAAL OF PEOR. AND THE LORD'S ANGER BURNED AGAINST THEM.
↓
ATTACKS THE MIDIANITES WHO WORSHIPPED BAAL
JUDGES 2-6 (PARAPHRASED)
ISRAEL TAKES TO WORSHIPPING BAAL AND ASHTORETH, SO THE LORD STOPS PROTECTING ISRAEL.
GIDEON: "WHAT MUST I DO, LORD?"
↓
LORD: "DESTROY YOUR ALTAR TO BAAL, CHOP UP YOUR STATUES OF ASHTORETH, THEN BUILD AN ALTAR TO ME AND BURN THOSE STATUES UPON IT."
↓
AFTER HE DOES IT, THE PEOPLE WHO OWNED THE STATUES GET PISSED.
"ISRAEL" HERE REFERS TO THE TRIBES, NOT A PERSON OR COUNTRY.
"LORD" = YAHWEH
POOR GUY.
THAT REALLY SUCKS.
MAN, I FEEL SORRY FOR BAAL.
HE SOON TURNED INTO "BAAL-ZEBUB," OR THE DEMON BEELZEBUB. HE WAS AN UNFORTUNATE FELLOW IN THAT REGARD.
BAAL WAS WORSHIPPED FAR AND WIDE IN CANAAN, ORIGINALLY.
THERE WAS ALSO DAGON, ASTARTE, EVEN AMON VIA THE EGYPTIANS.
DAGON GOT REUSED IN THE CTHULHU MYTHOS.
ASTARTE TURNED INTO THE DEMON ASTAROTH.
EVEN AMON WAS USED AS A DEMON.
IT WASN'T JUST BAAL—MOST OF THE GODS IN THE LANDS THE ISRAELITES WANDERED WOUND UP DESCRIBED AS EVIL DEMONS.
THEY WANDERED THE DESERT FOR DECADES AFTER LEAVING EGYPT, WHERE ALL MANNER OF COUNTRIES FOUGHT THEM, AND THEY FOUGHT BACK...
BY RESEARCHING RELIGIOUS HISTORY LIKE THIS, YOU SEE A LOT OF THE BELIEFS AND CUSTOMS OF VARIOUS REGIONS AND PEOPLES THROUGH THESE DEMONS AND SPIRITS.
IF YOU'RE INTRIGUED BY THIS, I HIGHLY RECOMMEND SEARCHING IT OUT! YOU'LL PROBABLY LEARN SOMETHING NEW!
I HOPE TO SEE YOU AGAIN IN VOLUME 4...
PLAY.

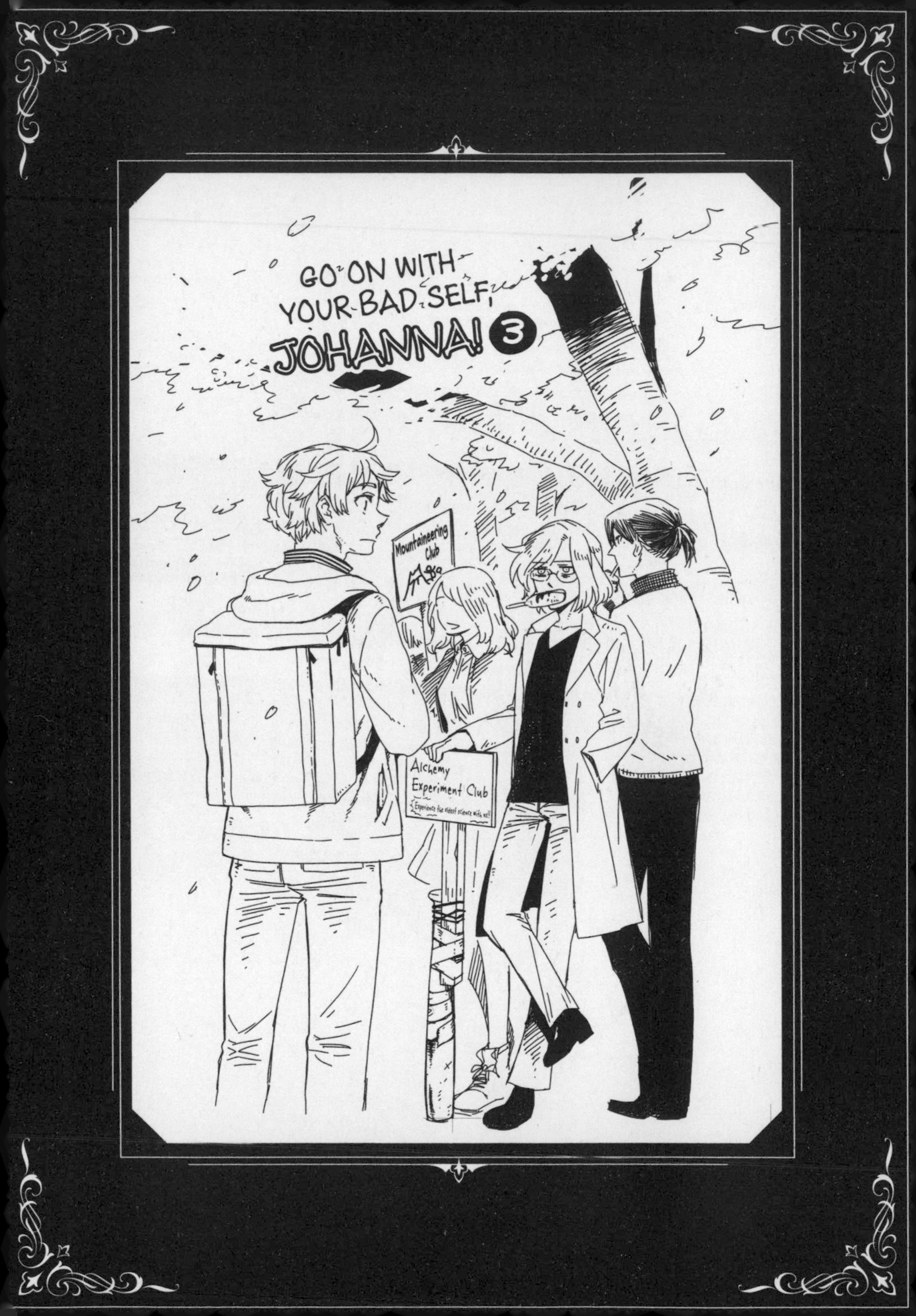
GO ON WITH YOUR BAD SELF, JOHANNA! 3
Mountaineering Club
Alchemy Experiment Club
Experience the oldest science with us!!

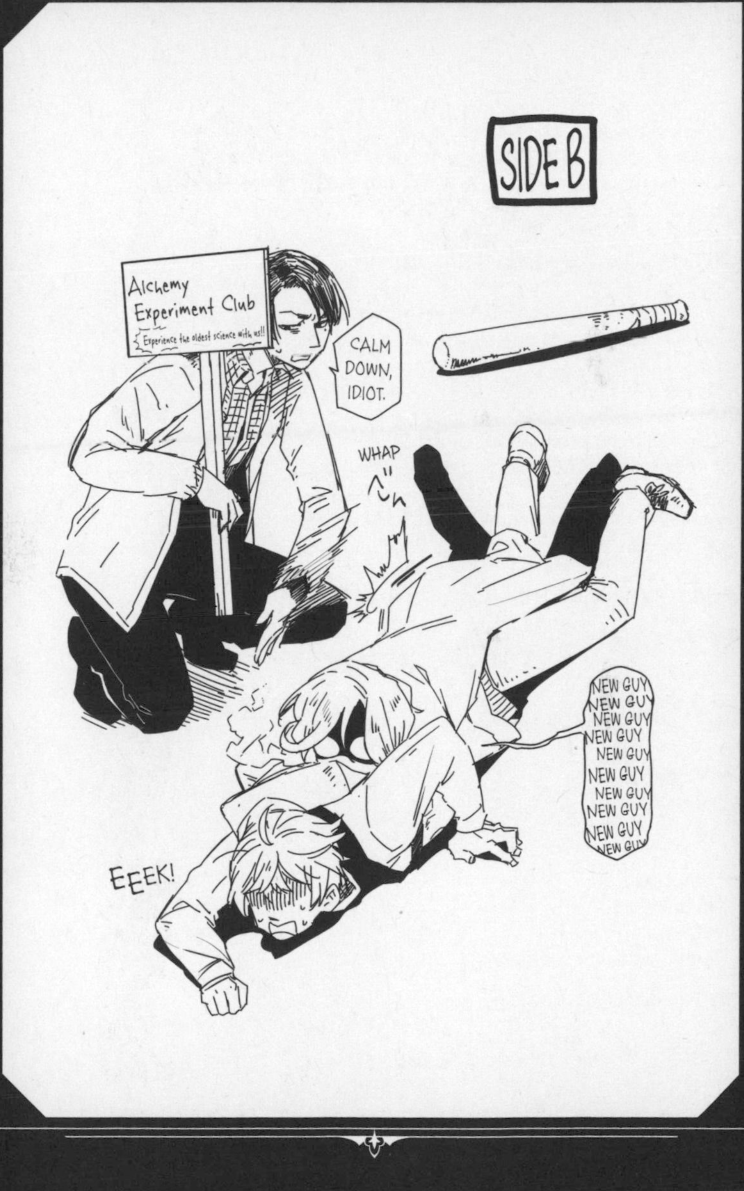
SIDE B
CALM DOWN, IDIOT.
Alchemy Experiment Club
Experience the oldest science with us!!
WHAP
べしん
NEW GUY NEW GUY NEW GUY NEW GUY NEW GUY NEW GUY NEW GUY NEW GUY NEW GUY NEW GUY
EEEK!

Lun
June/18

A Kodansha Comics Trade Paperback Original.

Frau Faust volume 3 copyright © 2016 Kore Yamazaki
English translation copyright © 2018 Kore Yamazaki

Published in the United States by Kodansha Comics,
an imprint of Kodansha USA Publishing, LLC, New York.

Publication rights for this English edition arranged through Kodansha Ltd.,
Tokyo.

First published in Japan in 2016 by Kodansha Ltd., Tokyo, as *Frau Faust*
volume 3.

ISBN 978-1-63236-549-1

Printed in the United States of America.

www.kodanshacomics.com

9 8 7 6 5 4 3 2 1

Translation: Stephen Paul
Lettering: Lys Blakeslee
Editing: Ajani Oloye
Kodansha Comics edition cover design: Phil Balsman